WHO'S MINDING THE CHILDREN?

THE HISTORY AND POLITICS
OF DAY CARE IN AMERICA

MARGARET O'BRIEN STEINFELS

SIMON AND SCHUSTER : NEW YORK

SBN 671-21597-3
LIBRARY OF CONGRESS CATALOG CARD NUMBER: 73-14093
DESIGNED BY IRVING PERKINS
MANUFACTURED IN THE UNITED STATES OF AMERICA
BY THE BOOK PRESS, BRATTLEBORO, VT.

2   3   4   5   6   7   8   9   10

DEDICATION

To those who cared for us as children, and to those children who ask our care today.

*To my parents
Mercedes and John O'Brien*

*To my parents-in-law
Margaret and Melville Steinfels*

*And to their grandchildren
Jeffrey, Kenneth and Shawn Doyle
Kimberley Handwerker
Nadu and Ushi Hussain
Gabrielle and John-Melville Steinfels
Jane Margaret Steinfels*

ACKNOWLEDGMENTS

A sizable portion of this book is the result of my visits to day care centers, where I had conversations with day care directors, teachers, and parents. Their generous offering of time, ideas, and opinions helped to make the descriptions in Chapters 4, 5, and 6 concrete and vivid.

Ed Marciniak provided me with several large folders of clippings, articles, pamphlets, and reports on day care which were highly useful while writing this book. For these, and for the assistance he gave me in meeting some day care directors, I am very grateful. Nancy Amidei, formerly of the Senate Subcommittee on Nutrition and Human Needs, provided me with a good deal of information as well as introductions to other Congressional staff people who were helpful and frank. James Steinfels, architect, visited several day care centers with me and discussed many of the architectural and space problems faced by day care centers. My friend Kay Voss helped with the bibliography and many other things. Alice Mayhew and Linda Healey of Simon and Schuster were incisive, tactful, and helpful. I must also thank Nancy Rambusch, Suzanna Doyle, Mary Eydt, and Sheila Rothman, who read the manuscript.

Peter Steinfels assisted in thousands of ways, big and small. The first chapter of this book was a joint effort which originally appeared in *Soundings* (Winter, 1972). Our discussions while writing that article helped focus my thinking about the whole project. Throughout he has encouraged, admonished, psychoanalyzed, spelled, and punctuated, and, at all the right moments, left me to stew in my own juices. I thank him.

Contents

1

Motives and Movements

CHAPTER 1

WHO WANTS DAY CARE AND WHY

Day care is an idea whose time has come. That does not necessarily mean it is a good idea, but simply that it is on the national agenda. It is on the national agenda because it is the common interest of a constellation of forces: government bureaucrats concerned with welfare reform, educators concerned with early child development, women concerned with "liberation." Some of these forces see day care as auguring major adjustments in American life, profound changes, for example, in the form of the family or the status of women. Others conceive of day care as a natural addition to present social institutions, an extention of the school system downward, or a substitution for the haphazard babysitting available to working mothers. But serious contemplation of the implications of day care remains strikingly slight, given the massive proportions of the programs many advocates propose.[1] The same person who one moment expresses the belief that "our schools are prisons" may, the next moment, endorse handing over infants to a large, school-like bureaucracy providing "twenty-four-hour day care."

It is, of course, a truism by now that reform measures often finish by defeating the reformers. David Rothman's *The Discovery of the Asylum,* which describes the utopian impulses animating the founding fathers of such institutions as asylums, workhouses, orphanages, and prisons, is only the most recent study to give pause to anyone contemplating a major "progressive" social innovation.² If one cannot assume that the future of day care lies along these lines, it is partially because some day care advocates are all too conscious of the dismal past, even if for many of them it only goes back as far as the Head Start legislation of the mid-sixties. Yet such a wide variety of groups and interests are presently pressing for the expansion of day care and child development services, for an equally wide variety of reasons, that it seems inevitable that someone be disappointed. Chicago's Crisis Committee for Day Care, for example, represents a broad range of organizations, from local day care centers to private welfare agencies to organizations of the three major religious faiths. The National Ad Hoc Coalition on Child Development manages to encompass both the Family Life Division of the U.S. Catholic Conference and Zero Population Growth.

All these groups seem to agree that services to young children, and day care in particular, need to be expanded. They provide, on both the local and national level, a large, effective, broad-ranging lobbying force, promoting legislation, funding, and administrative implementation. The vigorous lobbying effort is related to new perceptions about children, families, preschool education, women, and welfare—in effect related to what some see as a crisis in family life, child-rearing, and education; to what others see as a necessary adaptation of basic institutions such as the family and schools to a rapidly changing technological society; and to what still others see as a golden opportunity for introducing new values into American life.

No set of categories devised to characterize this multitude of motivations and hopes can be sewn together without some overlap here or some sawdust leaking at the seams there. Nevertheless, duly noting the danger of oversimplification, I would distinguish three attitudes toward the relationship between day care and the general movement of society.

1. Day care as patchwork. This outlook views day care services essentially as repairing breakdowns in present social institutions. It is a kind of first aid—for fatherless families, for children needing better care and extra educational assistance, for mothers prevented from providing full-time care for their children by economic or emotional difficulties. Day care helps to compensate for faults in family structure, educational resources, or the economic system.

Goals for day care are thus defined largely by the status quo in "mainstream" society. Day care should bring those disadvantaged in one way or another up to this standard, or keep them from falling below it if hardship strikes the home.

2. Day care as realization. This outlook fundamentally accepts the values and direction of the present society but feels these are far from realized in the status quo. By assuming duties of the home, day care would provide entry into advanced industrial society for a vast number of previously excluded women. Day care would offer to all children an early educational environment employing the best resources the society has developed, thus equipping the greatest possible number of them for successful entry into a rapidly changing society demanding refined skills. Day care would also buttress certain changes in family structure—its loosening, if not its disappearance altogether—already set in motion by the mobility, individualization, and egalitarianism of modern industrialism. Women and children would be freed from the patriarchal nuclear household. Society would accept new responsibilities for the care and development of children.

3. Day care as utopia. This outlook views day care as a means of renewing society in a way radically discontinuous with the present. The possibility of changing society by infusing new values into the young has always been part of the utopian inheritance. So, too, has been the potential of women as a reforming force not yet fully integrated into a society largely formed by men. Day care would not maintain the status quo or even extend the logic of the society to its full realization, but would in some significant ways attempt to block the present direction of society and start it off in a new one.

Perhaps this triad of views should be considered points on a spectrum rather than sharply distinct alternatives. On the one hand, the further realization of advanced industrial society, through the entrance of more women into the labor force and the early education of greater numbers of children, might be considered a form of "patchwork" on a large scale, even though the patches would be coming to equal or surpass the original garment. On the other hand, the drive toward full realization of the society's logic, whether conceived of simply in terms of fulfilling the "American Dream" or more strictly in terms of extending the technical rationality of industrialism into areas which have eluded it, suggests a kind of utopian effort (some might consider it a negative utopia); it becomes hard to draw a line between those reforms of the family, for example, which promise the "same" society to the nth degree and those which promise something not only new but basically different. Finally, this triad does not imply some kind of normative hierarchy. Within each category will be found those whose attitudes toward day care is more or less well thought out, or more or less self-serving.

The patchwork view, to begin, has dominated the rationale for day care since the establishment of the first "day nurseries" a century ago. In fact, that view was reinforced after World War I by the influx of professional social workers into what had been the domain, and a rather flourishing one, too, of amateur "day nursery ladies." Where these amateurs had been unimaginative enough to treat day care as a relatively straightforward response to economic hardship, the professionals regarded the application for day care as an indication of "maladjustment" and the family's need for extensive casework. It was repeatedly asserted that day care, like patchwork, was only a temporary expedient, and piously hoped that it would be rendered unnecessary by improved family or social conditions.[3]

If the renewed interest in day care hardly suggests a phenomenon about to disappear, neither does it suggest that the patchwork view has any fewer adherents. They might be divided, however, by what it is they primarily hope to patch: the tax rolls, touched and in some cases strained by never-popular welfare costs; the economic duress of poor families, especially the female-headed families who constitute such an imposing percentage of the welfare population; or the emotional and intellectual deprivation of children from such homes.

Day care, it should be understood, has been and continues to be closely connected with welfare. At the local level, the intake procedures and the financing of day care centers have been intertwined with the work of the welfare department. Welfare departments are always under pressure to put recipients to work. In some cases day care has provided a means of pressuring welfare mothers to take jobs, although the scarcity of day care space has meant that, in fact, there may have been many more welfare mothers desiring to work but unable to do so because day care was not available than welfare mothers forced to work because it was. At least to the present.

But the expansion of day care services has been spurred by federally assisted work-training programs for welfare mothers as well as by a growing public realization that welfare rolls are not filled with "able-bodied men." Day care has become an essential ingredient of welfare reform plans. Whether it will help combine the needs and desires of welfare mothers concerning work and child care so that they truly can better themselves economically, or whether it will be aimed primarily at cutting welfare costs, providing only minimal care so as to assuage consciences uneasy about pressuring mothers of young children to take jobs, is one of the essential questions of the day care debate.

Three efforts at day care legislation which preoccupied the 91st and 92nd Congresses (1969–1971) exemplify the great differences that can exist within the patchwork category.

1. The Nixon Administration's welfare reform bill (the Family Assistance Plan) depended upon greatly expanded day care facilities within a few years' time. Mothers of school-aged children could be obliged to use these facilities and take available jobs or else lose all welfare assistance—an aspect of the Nixon reform measure which disturbed observers familiar with the abuse of work requirements at the local level. Their concern was justified by federal approval of pilot projects in California, Illinois, and New York that would force welfare mothers, even of preschool children, either to take jobs or to care for the children of other welfare mothers who were working—a measure, said the critics, raising serious problems of family rights as well as of the quality of care these children might be receiving.

2. Senator Russell Long, chairman of the Senate Finance Committee, also introduced a bill (Child Care Services Act, S. 2003) that would have created a national Day Care Corporation to lend money to local groups who wished to provide day care.[4] His bill stood little chance of passage, but since he was chairman of the Senate Finance Committee, other day care bills passed through his hands for funding. If his own bill was any indication, he seemed to favor strong work requirements in exchange for day care funding, little community control over day care centers, and a minimum of federal expenditure, without which there could be no quality day care. While Long's bill had the attractive feature of raising the income level for sliding scale fees and broadening the income tax deduction

for child care,* the day care center would have been largely funded by parent-paid fees, almost certainly resulting in custodial centers with minimum standards for staff ratio and programming.

3. The Comprehensive Child Development Act (Title V of the Economic Opportunity Amendments of 1971) emerged from a House-Senate Conference which reconciled bills introduced by Senator Walter Mondale and Representative John Brademas and passed by the Senate and House respectively. The measure, approved by Congress and then vetoed by President Nixon, was meant to fulfill the stated aims of the Administration's welfare reform program (the Family Assistance Program) by freeing women on relief as well as assisting the "working poor" to move into the economic mainstream. But the bill went beyond work-oriented economic patchwork to offer another justification and organizing concept for day care, namely child development. The first hope was to break the "poverty cycle": if children were given good medical care, sound nutrition, and a stimulating environment in their earliest, most impressionable years, then perhaps widespread retardation, medical problems, and school failure might not handicap the children presently condemned to becoming second- and third-generation welfare recipients.[5]

The intent of the Comprehensive Child Development Act of 1971 was, in fact, a radical departure from previous government attitudes toward early childhood services. The legislation still provided free or subsidized services, largely to disadvantaged families (including the "working poor"), but the bill's language and provisions were concerned with nothing less than providing "every child with a fair and full opportunity to reach his full potential. . . ."[6] "The bill is as American as apple pie," declared Senator Alan Cranston during Senate debate, comparing the measure with the American tradition of public education. Day care, in this case, becomes not merely a means of repairing anomalies but a next step in the evolution of society.

---

* A proposal actually put into effect by the Tax Reform Bill of 1971, which allows working mothers to deduct the cost of child care: two hundred dollars per month for one child, three hundred dollars for two children, and four hundred dollars for three or more children. Limitations on the amount of the deduction are imposed on families whose adjusted gross income exceeds eighteen thousand dollars.

The fact that Title V represented a new departure was firmly admitted, even exaggerated, in the President's veto message, which cited it as grounds for rejection of the measure. "For the Federal Government to plunge headlong financially into supporting child development would commit the vast moral authority of the National Government to the side of communal approaches to child-rearing over against the family-centered approach."[7] By declaring that the need for the comprehensive program had not been demonstrated, that it duplicated in part his own welfare reform effort, that it was too expensive, that its decentralized local control features left no role for the state governments, and that it might "diminish both parental authority and parental involvement with children," the President signaled his own more strictly patchwork view of day care as an unfortunate but necessary deviation from American norms, a minimal effort associated with the poor and public welfare.

Allied to the Mondale-Brademas approach to child care, and similarly straddling the patchwork and realization notions, is the work of numerous educators and psychologists in child development.

The notions of early child development have been part of educational baggage for well over a century (Froebel, Montessori) if not longer (Rousseau, Pestalozzi, and Mill). Froebel and Montessori even enjoyed a short-lived popularity in the United States before World War I, but it is only since World War II that such thinking has had a large-scale impact here. The works of Swiss psychologist Jean Piaget, and of the American psychologists Jerome Bruner and J. McViker Hunt, have had a tremendous influence in pointing out the early and rapid cognitive development of children long before the age of five or six, when they traditionally begin school. From its first day an infant begins to learn, to construct theories, to have expectations about other people's behavior, and by the age of two has, as Noam Chomsky showed, reinvented the basic grammatical and syntactical rules of his language. This scientific work is the basis for many of the changing attitudes toward children, child-rearing, and preschool education.[8]

For a variety of historical and social reasons it has been difficult to put these theories to work. Thinking about the infant and small child has been governed until recently by Freudian analysts and dominated by the work of such people as Anna Freud and John Bowlby, whose emphasis on the affective relationship between mother and child has supported the prevalent American prejudice against the mothers of young children leaving their care to mother substitutes or day care centers and nursery schools.[9] About the best one was able to do by way of providing for child development in any formal way was to send a child to a nursery school from the age of three, and at that only for a half-day. This was a course open almost exclusively to those who could pay stiff tuition fees and therefore almost universally closed to the poor.[10]

Until the early sixties, when the Montessori method was reintroduced into the United States and some of Piaget's theories began to be circulated, even these nursery schools could be considered little more than playschools. Whatever day care centers existed operated in much the same way in terms of educational offerings. This all changed radically in the sixties. The beginning of Project Head Start in 1965 more than any other single factor helped to publicize and popularize the importance of child development theories and the importance of early childhood learning.

In addressing its program primarily to what were described as "culturally disadvantaged" children, Head Start inspired a number of programs and techniques especially addressed to the needs of children from deprived environments. From this perspective Head Start has been largely directed to patchwork efforts—to giving children a "head start" in their primary school years, compensation for the apparent inability of public schools to teach, educate, or understand the non-Anglo or non-middle-class child. For the same reasons preschool education has come to seem an attractive addition to day care. The hope that potential school nonachievers, with the proper intellectual, emotional, and social stimulation, will improve their chances in school is a politically attractive counterbalance to the considerable cost of adding effective education programs to day care centers.

It is hard to dispute the aims of the patchwork approach to day care. But it is less difficult to wonder whether these aims will be accomplished and to point out the ways in which different patchwork approaches work against one another. To begin with, day care is expensive. The cost per child of full day care in a center was estimated at $1,245 a year in 1967 for *minimum* care—that which was "essential to maintaining the health and safety of the child, but with relatively little attention to his developmental needs." A "desirable" program replete with individual developmental activities was estimated at $2,320 per child. In fact, the present makeshift care arranged by working mothers or welfare mothers in work-training programs averages less than $500 a year in cost, when it is done for remuneration at all.[11]

Those who imagine day care as a cheap instrument for getting women off welfare rolls are apt to be disappointed—or they tend to support extremely minimal care, bringing unconscionable pressures on mothers to surrender child-rearing to institutions they distrust. Such minimal care, of course, runs directly against the intentions of those who see day care as providing a healthy and educational environment presently not available in poor homes. These intentions imply a considerable expenditure. Nor are funds the only question mark.

Jerome Bruner, director of Harvard's Center for Cognitive Studies, has recently taken a cautious position regarding the present state of developmental studies and their potential for day care programming. He made special note of the problems that white, middle-class social scientists have in seeing their theories as culture-bound and therefore subject to some of the criticism that blacks, Chicanos, and Puerto Ricans have made about Head Start and other compensatory education programs.[12] In testimony before the Mondale Committee, Evelyn Moore, director of the Black Child Development Institute, took a strong critical stance against the research provisions of the Comprehensive Child Development Act on the grounds that past efforts have had little program effect and that these efforts inevitably—by language, project design, and limits of white, middle-class perceptions—end in denigrating the black child.[13] Indeed, scientific respect for cultural pluralism may be hard to attain in developing educational programs for day care. In the same volume in which Jerome Bruner takes a critical look at early childhood studies, Jerome Kagan, his colleague at Harvard, began an article on "Cognitive Development and Programs for Day Care" with the following observation:

> Most Americans believe that the young child should: 1) feel loved and valued by the adults who care for him, develop trust

in, and affection and respect for those adults, so that in the future the child will 2) develop an autonomous identity and believe that he can determine his own actions and decide what he alone should believe, 3) be free of fear and anxiety and be able to enjoy life, 4) develop his intellectual capacities to the fullest and perform with competence on those problems society presents to him.[14]

At first glance such a supposed consensus may seem unexceptionable, although even a casual observer might note a certain middle-class-professional tone to the language (which could simply be accepted as Kagan's way of putting what others might express differently). The fact is that even on such generalities as these, the problem is greater than one of tone. Even if many Americans would agree in theory that their children should develop an "autonomous identity" (it sounds up-to-date, after all), in practice they have something else in mind. And other Americans would not even grant the point in theory. For them children should *not* believe they can determine their own actions or individually decide what to believe. Nor is developing "intellectual capacities to the fullest" necessarily such a clearly held ideal in situations where other capacities—social, athletic, etcetera—may compete for attention. Any reader of Herbert Gans' *Urban Villagers* knows that many Italians, to name one relatively intact ethnic group, think there are community values more important than "autonomous identity." These are not quibbles, for people operating programs can sadly learn that "autonomous identity" translates very differently from culture to culture and class to class.[15]

Nor is the absence of commonly agreed-upon child-rearing values the last difficulty facing day care programmers. Trained personnel for day care programs are also in short supply. The day care provisions foreseen under the 1967 Work Incentive Program foundered on this very point. "Directors and head teachers are so scarce that problems of financing and licensing would seem small next to lack of staff," read one report on the program.[16]

The basic problem faced by the patchwork approach is that in our society quality services, whether in medicine, transportation, or schooling, are more likely to be available to the middle class than the poor, even when subsidized. The Mondale-Brademas legislation, like the Family Assistance Plan, attempted to obtain wider support for better services by including the working poor along with the welfare poor in its consideration, and indeed the Mondale bill received enthusiastic backing from the AFL-CIO. The patchwork view of day care today differs from its earlier version, which asserted that the ideal was always the mother in the home. The new version springs, partially, from a great suspicion that the lower-class family is a defective socializing agent for children. But the fallout from changing attitudes toward work, home, and day care, the expansion of *quality* services as well as the change in ideology, may yet, as in so many other cases, limit the poor to the "trickle-down" from the more affluent.

While Head Start has been directed toward patchwork efforts, its underlying impetus, and that of most early learning centers, is clearly concerned with the goals of realization, of pushing present tendencies along their logical course, toward equal opportunity for all members of American society to make it through the educational system—a process which has become the single most important standard for judging whether people are employable, and thus prepared to fit into a rapidly evolving technological society. Maya Pines, in *Revolution in Learning*, realistically assesses the expectations of most preschool educators when she writes:

> The pioneers of early learning want to give every child a chance to develop his capacities to the fullest. Their techniques will increase man's variety, not reduce it. If they succeed, middle-class children will no longer be held back to some comfortable average —and poor children will no longer be crushed before they can learn to learn. Both will be allowed to find their own intellectual identities. Both still come closer to reaching their potential. This should make each human life more interesting, more productive, and more rewarding.[17]

The tendency of some legislators and educators to treat day care as a normal, not merely remedial, advance in American society, as a natural realization of the society's direction, also gets support from working women, some industrial and franchise day care services, and an important segment of the Women's Liberation movement. At one end of the spectrum marked by this category, working women —some 4.5 million of them have children under six—simply seek a satisfactory solution for a problem which less and less can be handled by family and friends and more and more is viewed as a normal part of economic life. At the other end, futurists imagine our "super-industrialism" logically issuing not only in day care but in "professional parenthood":

> Raising children, after all, requires skills that are by no means universal. We don't let "just anyone" perform brain surgery. . . . Yet we allow virtually anyone . . . to try his or her hand at raising young human beings. . . . the greatest single preserve of the amateur.
>
> As the present system cracks and the super-industrial revolution rolls over us . . . we can expect vociferous demands for an end to parental dilettantism. . . . professional parenthood is certain to be proposed, if only because it fits so perfectly with the society's overall push toward specialization. . . . Even now millions of parents, given the opportunity, would happily relinquish their parental responsibilities—and not necessarily through irresponsibility or lack of love. Harried, frenzied, up against the wall, they have come to see themselves as inadequate to the tasks. Given affluence and the existence of specially equipped and licensed professional parents, many of today's parents would not only gladly surrender their children to them, but would look upon it as an act of love, rather than rejection.[18]

Among the more workaday efforts to adjust the demands of child care to the demands of full employment for women are industrial and franchise day care centers. A few manufacturing and service organizations with a high percentage of women employees have expressed interest in or actually established day care centers. Such centers, it is argued, will help provide a stable work force, reduce tardiness and absenteeism, and increase the level of production by insuring working mothers "peace of mind." So far, however, interest—on the part of workers, unions, and the companies themselves—has far outrun action. Many companies are hesitant to expand fringe benefits in the direction of day care. The New York Bell Telephone Company, despite union pressure, has expressed great reluctance to initiate day care for its employees, although it has a 70 percent staff turnover every year. They cite as reasons cost, lack of adequate space, and the fact that mothers would have to travel during the rush hour with small children. On the other hand, Illinois Bell Telephone has taken a step in assisting its employees by setting up a day care staff that helps employees find day care homes in their own neighborhoods. The company, aside from staff expenses, gives no financial aid toward day care.[19] Other industries—KLH in Cambridge, Avco in Boston, and Tioga Sportswear in Fall River, Massachusetts—have all opened centers to provide day care for their employees and, in the case of KLH, to community residents as well. If these pioneering companies succeed in proving that, indeed, day care will cut employee turnover, tardiness, and absenteeism, and increase production, then it could become as commonplace for a factory to have a day care center as a cafeteria.

A related development is franchise day care, sometimes referred to as "Kentucky Fried Children." Franchise centers, which must be able to make a profit, are a riskier operation than industrial centers, and many observers feel that the future of such operations will depend on welfare reform and the availability of government funds. On the other hand, industrial and franchise day care may end by addressing different population groups, although the result will be the same: easier entry of women into the labor market. Industrial centers will largely serve a population of semi-skilled and skilled "blue-collar" women—telephone operators, factory operators, hospital staff, clerks, etcetera. Franchise centers are more likely to serve a population of "white-collar" women—teachers, executives, professionals. They could therefore charge sufficiently high fees, probably stressing in return the "latest" in early learning techniques for an appreciative middle- and upper-middle-class clientele.

Low-income working women and welfare mothers tend to see quality day care as supportive of their family situation, a means of keeping the family intact and functioning while a mother either becomes a primary or absolutely necessary secondary breadwinner. The feminist movement does not challenge such an outlook, and most feminist literature tries to keep the interests of low-income and welfare women in mind; but feminists' hopes for day care certainly go beyond the income question. For them, day care offers a means of encouraging basic social changes, changes with which low-income and poor women are not necessarily in agreement.

Women's liberation is, of course, a diverse movement, embodying many common concerns and including many groups, but the National Organization for Women (NOW) probably represents a broader consensus than any other group. Like other women's liberation groups, it has emerged from the general American Left; hence its demands are stated as sharp criticisms of the nation's status quo. Nonetheless, NOW's aims appear more directed at *opening up* the present economic structures to women than at challenging these structures. While NOW has learned from the tactics of black militancy by analogy to the racial situation, its philosophical attitude toward American society is still more integrationist than separatist or revolutionary. Its thinking tends in the direction of encouraging women to adopt the qualifications and orientation of the male-dominated work ethic. Its three major demands (abortion on demand, free twenty-four-hour-day care, equal pay for equal work) are directly related to freeing women from their sex-role occupations and allowing them to participate equally with men in the labor market. It is interesting to note that two of the three demands are concerned with motherhood and only one with the situation at the workplace. Day care is a crucial ingredient in a view of women's liberation that focuses on "integrating" present economic structures. It does not simply propose that women should have equal child-rearing responsibilities with men (which could be accomplished a number of other ways, e.g., shorter work week), but proposes that women should have no greater child-rearing responsibilities than do men *in our present society*. Day care, in effect, would fulfill the functions women presently fill.[20]

Other feminists, such as Eva Figes and Shulamith Firestone, are more radical in their predictions that present pressures on the family are, and should be, only preliminaries to its total withering away, or at least its transformation into an entirely egalitarian and nonpermanent form of companionship.

Shulamith Firestone, in *The Dialectic of Sex*, has pushed the logic of anatomy-ought-not-to-be-destiny to an extreme conclusion. She describes the ultimate revolution as one in which the feminist and cybernetic revolutions will have joined to create a new paradise on earth which would include: "1. The freeing of women from the tyranny of their biology by any means available [including artificial reproduction] and the diffusion of the childbearing and child-rearing to the society as a whole, to men and other children as well as women; 2. the economic independence and self-determination of all [including children]; and 3. the total integration of women and children into the larger society." In the society that she foresees there would be no necessary sex or economic roles for individuals and thus the family would become superfluous—children would belong to everyone and be cared for by everyone. Interestingly enough, in the short term Firestone sees day care centers as they are now constituted as a means of taking pressure off women and thereby undermining their revolutionary consciousness. As she says, "Daycare centers buy women off."[21]

Eva Figes, in *Patriarchal Attitudes*, is equally forthright in her prediction that, one way or the other, marriage will disappear: "Either one goes on liberalizing the divorce laws, until marriage stands exposed as a hollow sham . . . or one takes a shortcut and abolishes marriage altogether. . . . Women must be treated as total human beings in their own right. . . . Children must be treated as primarily the property of the state. . . . This means fairly substantial child allowances for all children, and sufficient state and/or industrial nurseries for children."[22]

Firestone's and Figes' positions would certainly be labeled "utopian" by most of the public, if harsher language were not employed. Firestone without question, and possibly Figes, and surely many other feminists consider such proposals "radical" and "utopian" themselves. But it is just as reasonable to consider them under the "day care as realization" heading: they regard day care as part of a process in which the autonomy and freedom of action of the individual, woman or child, is the overriding goal. Their views seem to be further extensions of an affluent, technologically advanced, production-oriented society which puts relatively little value on contemplation, permanency, tradition, and community.

Some radical feminists, opposed to the family as they may be, nonetheless recognize that its passing would not guarantee a society different from the one they contest. Linda Gordon, a Marxist feminist, points out that, "If it were clever enough . . . the system could survive the destruction of the family."

> The system gave us the vote and equal rights, and it still exploits us all, woman and man. The system could give us equal wages, equal education, and could probably provide day care centers and jobs for us all. . . .
>
> In contemporary society men and women could be equal—equally harnessed to the demands of consumption, technology and imperialism. . . . Child care could be given over to large nurseries and schools (probably still run by women), as well adapted

as families to the task of brainwashing children. . . . Women could win the freedom to produce children only at will, with partners (or injections) of their choice, and with state-provided facilities for their care, without making themselves whole human beings.[23]

"Some of these nightmares may not be so fantastic," writes Gordon. In certain strata of society the breakdown of the family is well under way. This development is "objectively revolutionary" but not, the author adds, "entirely desirable . . . nor do we think its outcome predetermined."[24]

It would be unfair, however, to suggest that women's liberation, in looking upon day care as an instrument for modifying the whole family structure, is concerned solely with achieving economic freedom for mothers. According to feminists, the nuclear family is not a good place for women to spend their lives or for children to grow up in: the nuclear family, one might say, is not healthy for children or other living things. Thus, in concluding that "quality child care programs are good for children," NOW argues that

> Young children need peer relationships, additional adult models, enriched educational programs, particularly true because half of the intellectual development of a child is achieved by age 4. . . . A child socialized by one whose human role is limited, essentially, to motherhood may be proportionately deprived of varied learning experiences. In a circular fashion, the development of children has been intimately influenced by the development of women.[25]

Although the rest of the NOW statement reads like that of any parent group demanding the "best for our children," it does introduce a certain utopian element in its suggestion that a generation of children reared outside the grasp of oppressed women would be significantly enriched in learning and experience. Generally, emphasis on the "children's liberation" aspect of day care marks the utopian approach to the issue. Collective child-rearing has been a common feature of utopian schemes throughout history; in the American context, it has been seen as one way to mitigate traits thought undesirable in the American character: competitiveness, selfishness, violence, intolerance, acquisitiveness. Such views are current today in the American commune movement, but not limited to it. One day care licensing official remarked, in an interview, that he saw day care as a means of creating a cooperative, nonauthoritarian society. Children would be changed by their day care experience, learn to share, to be tolerant . . . and in changing children one would change the society regardless of its political or economic structure.

Other voices of the utopian school are less sanguine about this greening of the children, and more conscious of the need to put a special stamp on day care lest it become just another prop of unredeemed society. The Radical Education Project distributes a pamphlet attacking government and industrial day care as a means of tracking women into low-paying jobs. "If the need for child care is isolated from other needs, women will be caught in limited reforms that will only add public to private exploitation." While maintaining women in "exploitative jobs, the day care centers will also train children to be docile, obedient workers that the system needs."[26] Another Women's Liberation document, making a similar case, provides an excellent statement of the utopian attitude. "We think it is a mistake to view day care solely as an issue of women's liberation. We would like to assert that day care centers in which children are raised in groups by men and women could be as important for the liberation of children as [they] would be for the liberation of women. Group child care has a radical potential through its impact on young children."[27]

Historically, the paper argues, day care has been a function of the need for women in the labor force; if it has emerged slowly in the United States, that is due to the belief that young children and mothers belong at home. The Women's Liberation movement is rejecting this ideology. However, "the movement's present demand parallels the historical attitudes toward day care in its non-child-centered approach." The paper accuses the "majority of existing U.S. day care centers" of being "glorified babysitting services," teaching children passivity, programming them through routine, and instructing them in an "invisible curriculum" of attitudes toward work, race, sex roles, competition, and cooperation.

Day care poses the problem of sharply conflicting value systems, and radicals, the paper states, should limit their demands to "space and money" while running their own centers themselves. The precise ways in which the radical center would be different are illustrated with examples concerning sex roles—the treatment of the "housekeeping corner," the presence of men teachers, etcetera—and the paper concludes: "Although women will benefit from a good day care program, in the final analysis their liberation depends on a total transformation of society. However, the radical restructuring of one institution (child care) can help to transform the society, for the way that children develop is a part of that transformation."[28]

The Russian, Chinese, and Israeli child care systems have naturally been of special interest to those who see day care as a means of instilling radically new values. The *kibbutzim* and Children's Collectives are seen as evidence not only that group rearing of children and multiple mothering are not psychologically harmful but also that group child care could be a positive and relatively fast means of introducing and reinforcing social change at the same time as providing socialization and intellectual stimulation.

Urie Bronfenbrenner, a student of Russian child care practices, has supported day care as a means for freeing women—presumably not just disadvantaged women—from the isolation and "drudgery" of the nuclear family system. In that regard, Bronfenbrenner does not differ much from the day-care-as-realization approach; however, he makes much of the importance of parent participation in day care—male as well as female—and elsewhere Bronfenbrenner has elaborated a new approach toward child-rearing in the United States which reveals sharp differences in emphasis with the Women's Liberation spokeswomen primarily concerned with granting mothers economic independence. Bronfenbrenner protests the segregation of children from adult activities and the "real world." He would restructure community, school, and work life to break down the barriers between play, education, productive work, and between the assigned roles of men and women, and children, employed adults and the aged. Bronfenbrenner is clearly proposing the family and child-rearing as the fulcrum for shifting American values and institutions in a utopian direction.[29]

Bronfenbrenner's proposals do not depend strictly on his study of Soviet child-rearing. But the relevance of the Russian and Israeli examples is a problem in any case. The primary feature of their child-care systems, after all, is that they are only part of a larger radical, conscious, and planned system for social change within the whole society. They exist in a national and ideological context quite different from anything in the United States.

In general, the utopian approach to day care is thus far stronger in intention than in program. Government and industrial cooptation is feared; the desire to create a different sort of child is announced, but insofar as the method to this end is described, it seems like rather minor variations on the techniques of other day care programs. (This is not true of Bronfenbrenner, of course, whose innovations are less within the day care center itself than in the patterns of employment, school, and local community, which he would restyle in order to integrate children with other age groups and with adult activities.) Even the utopian goals are stated rather vaguely. Bettye Caldwell, whose work in Syracuse has convinced her of the vast possibilities of early learning in infant day care centers, has criticized all approaches in this regard.

> With our tradition of valuing rugged individualism, we have been reluctant to say much about the kinds of children we want. Do we want obedient children? Happy children? Adaptive children? Children who remain faithful to the values of their families? Militant children? Bright children? Group-oriented children? Woodstock and Maypole youth or Peace Corps youth? Eventual adults who can slip from one type to another? . . .
>
> At this moment in history, when we are on the threshold of embarking on a nationwide program of social intervention offered through comprehensive child care, we let ourselves prattle about such things as cost per child, physical facilities, or even community control. And when we begin to think big about what kinds of children we want to have in the next generation, about which human characteristics will stand them in good stead in a world changing so rapidly, we fall back on generalities such as care and protection.[30]

Perhaps what Bettye Caldwell considers a failure of nerve is an understandable modesty before the somewhat awesome task she proposes: thinking "big about what kinds of children we want to have in the next generation." But it is interesting that not even among those who oppose the present direction of society is much such "thinking big" done.

Will day care services be expanded? If nothing else, the broad range of forces desiring day care and the great need of many women for day care practically guarantees growth of some sort. But the combination of forces and the immense need may produce unexpected results. Two examples will suffice.

1. A conflict exists between the patchwork outlook, which foresees a large but still limited constituency for day care, and the realization outlook, which foresees day care (and the working mother) as part of the normal pattern of American family life. The former may determine the funding of day care while the latter, increasingly accepted, may determine the demand. The consequence of a demand that far outstrips the supply will be custodial care or educational care that could easily duplicate the mistakes of the urban school systems.

2. Another possibility is that the realization and utopian views may be less influential in accomplishing their own aims than in unwittingly reinforcing the ability of some patchworkers to force welfare mothers to leave their children in day care and take jobs against their will. Ironically, the "mother at home" stereotype which women's liberation understandably criticizes has also been an uncertain but nonetheless real protection for welfare mothers against the dictates of local authorities. And if the support given day care by women's liberation, both in its realization and utopian branches, may prove all too congruent with the aims of the penny-pinching version of patchwork, on the issue of the family it is theoretically at odds with the more generous version of patchwork day care. The latter envisions day care as part of a welfare reform program with the ultimate end of strengthening the family unit. Women's liberation, on the other hand, has envisioned day care as part of the process of loosening or even dissolving the family unit. Patchwork theorists see day care as a step toward enabling families, especially female-headed ones, finally to take responsibility themselves for their children's upkeep rather than have it be a poorly borne state burden. Many realization and utopian supporters of day care, however, see it at least partially as a transferral of responsibility for children to the state.

One can imagine other conflicts and convergences among those presently debating the future of day care—and one ought to. Those who believe in the great potential of day care would be wise to indulge in a little futurism, speculating on the books to be written twenty years hence chronicling the disappointments and controversies surrounding the national day care system. Those who believe that day care is dangerous and unnecessary would be equally wise to imagine a future in which children's needs continue to be minimized and ignored.

No effort to imagine the future, however, can succeed unless it is based on a sense of the past. The questions which seem so new to us today have often been posed in different forms, throughout the history of day care in America.

CHAPTER 2

A HISTORY OF DAY CARE:

FROM THE BEGINNING

TO WORLD WAR II

The history of day care is yet to be written. The fact that hundreds of graduate students have not yet produced the corresponding number of monographs on day care and child care, as they have, for example, on the great debate between Andrew Jackson and Nicholas Biddle over the creation of a National Bank, or the burning issue of whether Teddy Roosevelt deserved to lose the nomination of his party in 1912, is a sign both of the nascent state of American social history and the low esteem in which day care, child welfare services, and changes in child-rearing attitudes are held, not only by historians but by the public as well. Even a full-fledged history of day care will probably fail to counteract the tendency to treat day care as though it were the discovery of yesterday's newspaper.

Day care not only has a history that goes back over a century, but even enjoyed a modest Golden Age. In 1910, for example, New York City had eighty-five nurseries serving more than five thousand children daily, at an annual expenditure of $358,897.[1] Nationwide there were four hundred and fifty centers known to the Association of Day Nurseries. In many of these day nurseries, as they were then called, a wide range of services were available to a working mother and her children. The centers were, then as now, the focus of a vigorous argument. Was day care good or bad for children, for their mother, for family life? Did it encourage or discourage parental responsibility and family stability? Did the centers adequately meet the child's nutritional, medical, physical, emotional, and educational needs?

Today the exploding demand for day care has given the impression that a brand-new need and a striking solution have appeared on the scene. It would be foolish to deny that there is nothing new in the present debate. On the other hand, we can learn from past efforts to answer the recurring questions about day care. We can recognize, moreover, that certain factors in the day care equation—the close connection between day care and social welfare services, to name only the most obvious—are the direct inheritance of this past experience.

Shadowy past and indecisive present are united in one fact: the vast need for day care has never been adequately met. Underlying the persistent unwillingness to recognize that need and the continuing reluctance to spend the money for good day care is a profound ambivalence surrounding the proposition that the child-rearing task of parents can be shared with others.

Although the day nursery did not become popular in America until the last decades of the nineteenth century, there were many halting attempts to use the "day nursery idea" for the betterment of American children long before then. Many of these efforts drew upon the widespread and successful attempts to provide care for the children of working mothers in France and England from the first decades of the century. Robert Owen, the British philanthropist and social reformer, had been particularly influential in establishing English infant schools for the education of preschool children from the age of two.[2] In 1816, in "An Address to the Inhabitants of New Lanark," one of his Scottish villages, Owen defined the scope of his infant schools:

> For this purpose the Institution has been devised to afford the means of receiving your children at an early age, as soon almost as they can walk. By this means many of you, mothers of families, will be enabled to earn a better maintenance or support for your children; you will have less care and anxiety about them; while the children will be prevented from acquiring any bad habits, and gradually prepared to learn the best.[3]

When Owen established his utopian community in New Harmony, Indiana, in 1825, it was only natural that he included in its structure a nursery school for young children.[4]

There are other early examples of preschool education in America, examples that combine what we now carefully distinguish as nursery schools, kindergartens, and day care centers, each of which eventually acquired a separate history and line of development during the nineteenth century. We have, for instance, the constitution of the Boston Infant School, dating from 1828. The trustees justified their intent to open what might have been the first day care center in America by pointing out that "such a school would be of eminent service, both to parents and children. By relieving mothers of a part of their domestic cares, it would enable them to seek employment." At the same time the children "would be removed from the unhappy association of want and vice, and be placed under better influences. . . ."[5] Children were to be accepted between the ages of 18 months and 4 years. All students had to "be presented each day at school clean, washed, and dressed in whole and clean clothes." The school was to be open from 6 A.M. to 7 P.M. in the summer, and from 8 A.M. to 5 P.M. in the winter. The weekly charge was set at six cents per family, and lunch was to be provided by the parents. Mr. Amos B. Alcott was the proposed superintendent of the Infant School.

In 1854 New York Hospital established its Nursery for the Children of Poor Women, which provided care for the children of wet nurses (children who often died for lack of sufficient milk) and for infants of working parents. Hospital sponsorship made this nursery effort, unlike the Boston Infant School, a strictly hygienic enterprise. Every twelve children were in the care of a nurse whose first duty was keep her charges neat and clean. Rule Number One for the children, ranging in age from 6 weeks to 6 years, was to be perfectly clean when presented for admission. Even so, they were to be bathed and then dressed in hospital clothes when they arrived in the morning.[6]

At approximately the same period, the kindergarten movement was being introduced into the United States. The German emigrés of 1848 brought their native institution with them and gave it its now universal name of "kindergarten." But it was Elizabeth Peabody, a member of Emerson's transcendentalist circle (and the sister-in-law of Horace Mann, the educational reformer), who opened the first kindergarten for English-speaking children in Boston in 1860. She trained the next generation of kindergarten teachers, and one of her disciples opened the first public kindergarten in St. Louis in 1873.[7]

Between the kindergarten and day nursery movements, there was, however, a basic difference. The former was concerned primarily with education for young children, the latter primarily with the physical care of young children whose mothers worked. While many of the day nurseries established in the next decades were to include an educative element in their services, they drew their ideas and inspiration not from the kindergarten movement nor Owen's English infant schools but from the French model. In 1863, one of the innumerable Misses Biddles opened a day nursery for the children of Philadelphia modeled on the Paris *crèche*, which henceforth became the model for the American day nursery.

The popularity and rapid growth of the day nursery in the United States during the 1880's and 1890's was the result of two evolving factors. The social dislocations caused on the one hand by the rapid industrialization and urbanization of the country, and on the other by a massive influx of immigrants, brought about a wholesale breakdown in the normal socialization processes of the family, particularly child-rearing. How to meet these unprecedented problems? At approximately this same time, and largely as a response to the challenge of Americanizing and urbanizing the immigrant, there was a shift in attitudes toward the poor and the causes of poverty. As well, the enormous numbers involved compelled many people to look upon the needs of the poor with greater sympathy and to meet those needs with greater imagination and flexibility than they had in the past.

Industrialization, urbanization, and immigration created a node of social problems that, among other circumstances, resulted in the disruption of what most Americans considered normal family life. The whole gamut of poverty and vice which nineteenth-century Americans saw displayed in their cities was, at first, only infrequently and vaguely connected to the broad-ranging economic and social changes that were transforming American society. Given to an individualistic interpretation of evil, most Americans had little reason to look beyond immediate situations—broken families, abandoned children, deserted mothers, drunken fathers, delinquent adolescents, prostitution—to find there sufficient explanations for both poverty and vice. If the cause was not sin, then certainly it was shiftlessness, improvidence, or laziness.[8]

Philip Bagenal, an English visitor to America in 1882, described the domestic life of the slums with these words:

> Everywhere the moral atmosphere is one of degradation and human demoralization. Gross sensuality prevails. The sense of shame, if ever known, in [sic] early stifled. Domestic morals are too often abandoned and simple manners are things of the past. There is no family life possible in such surroundings; no noble traditions can descend from father to son. The fireside is hired by the week, the intimate is a hireling, and his family are most probably chained as hirelings also in some great neighboring factory mill.[9]

Of particular concern to many charity workers was the fact that such conditions were producing children who had no brighter future than that of their own parents, if indeed their future were not more bleak. In fact, Charles Loring Brace, a New York philanthropist and social worker, in his book *The Dangerous Classes of New York*, referred not to the immigrants themselves but to their children as the "dangerous class."

> The young ruffians of New York are the products of accident, ignorance, and vice. Among a million people, such as compose the population of this city and its suburbs, there will always be a great number of misfortunes; fathers die, and leave their children unprovided for; parents drink, and abuse their little ones, and they float away on the currents of the street; step-mothers or step-fathers drive out, by neglect and ill-treatment, their sons from home. Thousands are the children of poor foreigners, who have permitted them to grow up without school, education or religion. All the neglect and bad education and evil example of a poor class tend to form others, who as they mature swell the ranks of ruffians and criminals. So, at length, a great multitude of ignorant, untrained, passionate, irreligious boys and young men are formed, who become the "dangerous class" of our city.[10]

That phenomenon we call "the generation gap" was a widespread and serious problem at the end of the nineteenth century, related as it was to the serious dislocation of immigrant families and the breakdown of their child-rearing capabilities in a society that was socializing their children into a new culture. The Americanization of the immigrant child was a difficult but necessary task in the eyes of reformers like Charles Brace. It was, they believed, probably the most important philanthropic effort to which they could address themselves.

The immigrant family, however, carried a somewhat different burden. For them the problem was not only one of acculturation, but more basically of survival—finding work and keeping it. Often enough the mother of the family was required to join in this labor. Whether because of early death, desertion, or low wages of the father, many mothers had to work to support their families. While agricultural and domestic tasks might be readily combined, the work to be found in urban industrial areas did not fit their customary domestic responsibilities; rather, their work took them away from home and children. Since the larger society regarded the mother's domestic duties as primary, the working mother found herself in a dilemma. How could a child be raised properly if its mother was not there to do it? How could the child survive if its mother did not bring home the bacon? How could a home be considered normal without a mother presiding over it? How could there even be a home without the mother working to pay for it?

It was no easy task to devise solutions to this unprecedented breakdown in family life and child-rearing. The method of choice in dealing with such social problems as poverty, insanity, dependency, and deviancy had been, since the Jacksonian era, incarceration in the almshouse, the orphanage, the workhouse, the penitentiary, the asylum, or the reformatory. By the time of the Civil War it was clear that these institutions were less and less capable of meeting their stated purpose: to provide an orderly and well-regulated environment geared to the redevelopment of a disciplined and trained individual who would leave the institution prepared to assume his proper place in society. It was thus doubtful whether institutionalization, even if sufficient space and facilities were available, could offer any solution to the child-rearing problem.[11]

Furthermore many philanthropists and charity workers came to view the institutionalization of children as an evil to be avoided, even if the alternative for young children, the day nursery, was not altogether to their liking either. Beginning in the 1870's and 1880's, reformers such as Charles Brace and groups such as the Children's Aid Society and the National Conference of Charities and Correction attempted to devise a series of child-saving schemes that would preserve the child from an institutional upbringing. Sending orphaned children out West to live with farm families was one, ultimately unpopular, proposal for child-saving; another, to board children out in homes providing foster care. In later decades the whole juvenile court system with its complement of family judges and probation officers was instituted to provide sympathetic supervision of juvenile delinquents. The motivating sentiment behind these schemes was both to provide families or family-like settings for children without parents and to offer supervisory assistance to families that did not control their children.[12]

With the example of the French *crèche* before them, and the often tragic evidence that many young children, even babies, were left alone while their mothers worked, a number of enthusiastic and philanthropically inclined women came to see the day nursery as an obvious solution to one aspect of the crisis in child-rearing. One of these, Josephine Shaw Lowell, president of the New York Charity Organization Society, urged the National Federation of Day Nurseries in 1900 to increase the number of day nurseries as one means of avoiding the over-institutionalization of children. She acknowledged that there might be a decrease in the sense of parental responsibility if day nurseries were widely available, but measured against the tragic separation of families and the expense to the taxpayer of orphanages, day nurseries were both "more humane and less expensive."[13] To the same group in 1905 the Reverend Harris E. Adriance pointed out "the institutional child, is not a normal child"; therefore, he went on to argue, the day nursery is a necessity for mothers who work, or who have been widowed and abandoned.[14]

Dr. Edward T. Devine, secretary of the New York Charity Organization Society, seconded the words of Reverend Adriance in acknowledging that the day nursery kept institutionalization of children to a minimum. He added, of course, the admonition always addressed to day nurseries, first by charity workers and later by social workers: The day nursery was only one arm of philanthropic work, and to be truly effective it must cooperate with other kinds of philanthropic services.[15] In other words, no day care without social welfare services.

As the institutionalization of neglected and orphaned children came to be regarded then as abnormal, the ideal of philanthropic work became the preservation of the family or the creation of family-like alternatives. The day nurseries fit perfectly into this view of things; the time was right for their large-scale development, which occurred between the 1870's and the First World War, not for the purpose of destroying the family but preserving it.

During the 1870's and 1880's the idea of the day nursery captured the imagination of well-meaning, upper-class women, women who might well have thrilled to the words of one of their number, Mrs. Ellis Meredith: "The new truth, electrifying, glorifying American womanhood today, is the discovery that the State is but the larger family, the nation the old homestead, and that in this national home there is a room and a corner and a duty for 'mother.' "[16] Motherhood had become popular as the rationale for the entrance of women into public life, and what was more redolent of motherhood than the day nursery. It was, in fact, motherhood writ large. The day nursery women were usually married, the wives of wealthy men, with the leisure time to attend board meetings, to supervise the matron and staff of the day nursery, to plan fund-raising events like balls, fairs, and concerts, and to cajole their peers into donating food, bedding, and toys. At a time when the upper and upper-middle classes were the chief dispensers of charity, and before the days of broad-ranging public welfare, when charity organizations were run by men, it seemed only natural that these women, mothers themselves, felt some special calling to deal with the children of the poor.

Such women expressed great concern for the plight of small, dirty, ill-behaved, lower-class children who were left alone daily, often tied to the bedpost or to the casual oversight of neighbors or older siblings, while their mothers went off to the factory or domestic work. The day nursery ladies are easily enough criticized for their *noblesse oblige*, their condescension, the foisting of their own values on the poor. "Although . . . bored at home and unhappy with their lack of participation in the 'real world,' they vigorously defended the virtue of traditional family life and emphasized the dependence of the social order on the proper socialization of children."[17] Due consideration being taken of these shortcomings, it is nonetheless remarkable that, given their limited class interests and narrow experience, these women managed to create the American day nursery. In retrospect their creation seems flexible, practical, and, above all, genuinely responsive to the needs of working mothers.

From the widespread establishment of day nurseries in the 1880's down to World War I, a variety of services and organizations were offered to preschool children and their families under the one roof of the day nursery. The nurseries, usually converted houses or brownstones, were open six days a week, twelve hours a day. A great age span could be found in most nurseries: infants and children from the ages of 2 weeks to 6 years—the addition of after-school programs brought that range to the elderly level of 8 and 9. Some day nurseries provided emergency night care when a mother was ill; others allowed a child to be dropped off for a few hours; some hired a visiting nurse to assist mothers when children were ill; others held classes for mothers in sewing, cooking, English, and child care. There was, to be sure, much lacking in these nurseries; nonetheless, the board of managers and matrons did not define their tasks narrowly. Given their sense of what the deserving poor needed, if perhaps did not want, the day nursery sponsors and staff offered a broad range of services.

The Helen Day Nursery in Chicago, a self-styled "progressive day nursery," may have been somewhat atypical in its variety of services. Upon its opening in 1905 it cared for a daily average of twenty-four children; one half of these remained for the full day. Of the remaining twelve, some came to the day nursery after a half-day at kindergarten; others were left at the nursery for only a few hours by their mothers. A special night shelter was offered for emergencies. The directors felt that their efforts should reach not only the small child but the whole family, father, older children, Aunt Betsy, and Grandma.

Conscious of the work patterns in the neighborhood, the nursery realized that the average mother in the district did not actually work regularly or full-time but, rather, received "some charitable relief which she supplements by her own small earnings. She peddles, or she scrubs and washes and does the occasional job which presents itself. . . . Her working hours are spasmodic so that she can have her children with her a good portion of the time." There-fore the Helen Day Nursery offered part-time day care and even what 1973 utopians call drop-in service. The nursery considered itself "a place where children who need shelter and protection by day or night may be cared for during the mother's working hours; a place which shall provide temporary refuge in emergency; and an industrial, educational, and social center for mothers from which shall emanate standards of respectable living."[18]

Concern for the mother was typical of most day nurseries. Unless widowed, she was often considered the victim of an irresponsible husband. The day nursery proposed to help her in three ways: child care, employment, and training. First and most important, it took care of her children. Second, many day nurseries offered an employ-ment service or "employment book," in which were entered the names of the mothers who were searching for domestic work. The Leila Day Nursery had what it called an "intelligence department," which provided work for widows and the wives of drunkards. A call or letter to the day nursery could supply a middle- or upper-class family with a laundress or domestic. Having found that some mothers were inadequately prepared to perform these household tasks, some day nurseries even devised systems to train them for domestic employment.

This training usually consisted of the mother doing laundry or housekeeping in the nursery, under the supervision of the matron, or else one of the women who made up the board of managers oversaw such training in her own home. Along with the number of children cared for, day nurseries often pointed proudly to the number of days of work it had found for the mothers.

It is not difficult, however, to imagine the abuses that went along with this system. Since most day nurseries were intended to care for the children of working mothers, a nonworking mother might be quickly and forcibly supplied with a job. And it is not inconceivable that a mother with a child in the day nursery and herself employed by the nursery might not find herself as much an ill-used victim as she had been before the day nursery had discovered her—although she would now have the distinction of being among the "working poor."

Finally, most day nurseries organized "mothers' clubs," which usually met weekly or bi-weekly in the evenings. The purposes of these groups varied and were often vaguely stated in the annual reports. Most were probably brief social gatherings in which the mothers might be lectured on hygiene or child care and given tea and cookies. At New York's Wayside Day Nursery, a patroness of the nursery met with the mothers weekly. She "reads to them, counsels and comforts them, while they sew on garments which can afterwards be bought by them at cost of the material."[19] The Wayside Day Nursery was also one of the few that held parents' meetings, in order that the fathers might visit the day nursery. Considered a source of many of the mother's and child's difficulties, the father seems not to have been a familiar or welcome figure in most day nurseries.

Many day nurseries also responded to the plight of the older child—free and unsupervised between the hour he left school and the hour his mother arrived home from work. It was frustrating for many nursery workers to see one of their recent graduates of 6 or 7 condemned to the street life from which they had saved him as a young child. As a result day nurseries often provided after-school care, some even supplying a noon meal for public school children. Knitting and sewing classes were often available for the girls. The St. Agnes Day Nursery and Kindergarten provided after-school care for their own graduates, and in the kitchen garden carried on "the Kindergarten principle of learning through play by teaching the children right methods of washing, cleaning, bed making, and other household duties, which may be practical in their own homes."[20]

The variety of services offered in the day nursery should not over-shadow the fact the care of preschool children was very much the center of day nursery work; but the existence of such services does underline the day nursery ideal, that the preservation and restoration of the total family was its ultimate goal.

The day nurseries considered themselves a substitute for home and mother; in some cases, a substitute better than home and mother. The Armitage Day Nursery in New York City reflected this view on the home life of their children. "It has been said that the most important period in the foundation of character is from two to eight years of age. If this is true, what are the possibilities and responsibilities of the day nursery and kindergarten? Who has not felt disheartened when visiting among the poor, at the incapability of the mothers to make and keep a home in the truest sense? And who has not noted in men seeking employment in time of business depression the lack of adaptability to the needs of the hour? It is to lay the foundation for these elements, so essential to successful manhood and womanhood, that we are striving in our work. . . ."[21] One day nursery worker's declaration, "Slum babies would all be better off in nurseries," summed up in a radical way an undercurrent of feeling that many of her fellow-workers probably shared, but did not so baldly or openly make known.[22]

On a day-to-day level, the day nursery's primary concern was physical care of the children—feeding, bathing, and keeping them safe from the evils and danger of street and tenement. But most day nurseries expressed an equally strong concern for the moral care and proper upbringing of the child. The Virginia Nursery asked in 1896, "Can we put a little happiness into the lives of these children and give them some ideas of cleanliness, obedience, unselfishness, truthfulness?" The aim of the Riverside Day Nursery was not only "to provide a shelter for the children of mothers dependent upon their own exertions for their daily bread, [but] also to rear useful citizens among the class represented by the children whom we reach." St. Agnes Day Nursery and Kindergarten fostered habits of cleanliness and order as well as obedience and industry.[23]

In discussing the administration of the day nursery, Marjorie Hall, secretary of the New York Day Nursery Association, justified the day nursery by the need to create good citizens. "The lower the home, the greater the need of the child. It is some day to be an American citizen, and to this end it ought to be given the trend toward personal cleanliness and order."[24] The moral order of the day nursery was well grounded in a secure foundation of soapsuds. Cleanliness was next to godliness and American citizenship.

The affairs of the nursery were under the immediate supervision of a matron who, unless she had an army of servants to assist her, was largely responsible for a considerable amount of laundry, cooking, housecleaning, and child-rearing. In many cases she might indeed be thought of as the harassed and overworked mother of a large family. It is undoubtedly an index of the board of managers' dependence on hard-working, reliable, and enduring matrons that the annual report always makes a point of praising the fine work of the matron. "Miss Mile . . . is heartily interested in her work and proved herself very capable in the management of her household." In 1903, Miss Elliot of the Lisa Day Nursery was "our most efficient of matrons"; in 1904, "our most conscientious matron."[25] And well they might have praised the matron, for it is apparent that a number of day nurseries in their early years had *only* a matron. Whether she had help depended very much on the size and finances of the day nursery.

The Wayside Day Nursery in 1884 had a matron and two assistants who were 14 years of age. The three performed all the work of the nursery, including "washing and breadmaking, except during the summer months." Their day began at 6 A.M. when they lit the fires and ended at 9 P.M. when they banked them; from 7 A.M. to 7 P.M. they cared for about sixty children. St. Agnes had a matron and servant for fourteen children on an average day. Their duty was to prepare and give the children proper meals, and "to take general charge of them." On the other hand, the Sunnyside Day Nursery, which in 1884 had one room, decided to limit its enrollment to thirty children, since the matron was assisted only by a kindergarten teacher for two hours every afternoon.[26] As the day nurseries expanded, they began to add personnel: a full-time "kindergartener," cooks, laundresses, assistant matrons, and nurses. Theoretically all members of the board of managers had to serve their turns as "visitors" to the day nursery; some obviously did no more than inspect the premises; others assisted the matron in caring for the children.

There is no reliable guide as to the number of children per each adult. But the ratio was undoubtedly high in most day nurseries and, as a result, the nursery depended on a set routine in order to get through the day's work. The children usually arrived between 7 A.M. and 9 A.M.; the better day nurseries prided themselves on the fact that each child was bathed and given a set of nursery clothes upon arrival. The child's own clothes were aired and disinfected in a special room. This bathing and changing routine became a sort of hygienic ideal, but many day nurseries were hard put to supply space for a bathing room and enough personnel to do the bathing. For a while debate raged as to whether the proper duty of the day nursery was to bathe the child or to demand that the mother do so.

The first rule of the day nursery was, typically, that each child be brought *clean*, but its very statement and restatement over the years suggests that it was more honored in the breach than the observance. Annual reports commonly mention that the mothers often brought the infant or child in his nightclothes, or that children had not been undressed since the day before. Having worked ten to twelve hours herself, a mother might have little time or energy to spend the evening fetching water, often up three or four flights, heating it, and bathing her child. With a combination of resignation and recognition of the facts, most day nurseries assumed the responsibility of bathing the children. After they were bathed, all children, whether in their own or nursery clothes, were given an ubiquitous gingham smock, which they wore the rest of the day.

If there were any infants in the day nursery, they were put back to bed and the older children sent to play, in "the sunny front parlor." Dinner was eaten at noon; the children returned to play afterwards; supper was served about 5 or 6 P.M.; and the day ended with children gradually being picked up. It is difficult to get a picture of what happened to the children during their ten to twelve hours in the nursery. Many nurseries in the 1890's began to hire kindergarteners to help the matron supervise the children, who then could attend kindergarten for two hours in the morning or two in the afternoon. Or if the day nursery could not itself staff and supply the kindergarten, there was often a public or private one open to day nursery children. At the Leila Day Nursery, the Free Kindergarten Association of New Haven took the older children from 9 A.M. to noon every day.[27]

But it is equally difficult to discover exactly what kind of kindergarten activities were offered day nursery children. The Sunnyside Day Nursery, which first met in one room of the Wilson Mission on New York's Lower East Side, brought a kindergartener in to assist the matron for two hours each afternoon. This "gives the children a sense of order and discipline." In 1895 the same day nursery published in its annual report a picture of the kindergarten, which along with the day nursery had moved to larger quarters. The room is bare except for a large library table around which are sitting some dozen children, all with books open, all with eyes glued to the pages, and all under the watchful eye of two women—presumably the kindergarten teacher and the matron. Photographic conventions might have required the room be swept clean of all objects; and the primitive camera techniques certainly required the children to remain still. But all told, the scene is, indeed, one of order and discipline. Another photo, this time of the "playroom," is equally ordered and disciplined; the children, all gathered in a corner, are in a large circle playing a game; no toys, no books, no equipment in sight.[28]

The Little Sisters' Infant School in San Francisco, which combined an orphanage and day nursery, had a specific set of tasks to set before the kindergarten children. The teacher's report from 1884 says that she had between forty and forty-five scholars ranging in age from 3 to 6. She "taught the scholars during the past year all the several gifts and occupations of Froebel, namely: weaving, sewing cards, stick, tablet and ring laying, drawing, paper folding, peas work, block building, paper-cutting, pricking, embossing, lessons in color and form, reading, spelling, writing, gymnastic games, songs, and reading stories once a week to the scholars."[29]

Froebel's pedagogical techniques are often enough mentioned in day nursery reports, but the presence of specific teaching philosophy and methods was probably more an exception than the rule in the typical day nursery.

Ethel Beer, who first went to the Brightside Nursery on New York's Lower East Side in 1915 and remained active in its organization for almost 40 years, paints, in retrospect, a somewhat dreary picture of the day nursery.

> My first impression of Brightside Day Nursery was anything but favorable. The building was gloomy. The walls of the rooms were a nondescript shade, best described as institutional gray. The woodwork was dead white, showing every smudge of small fingers. A glass memorial window in the Nursery department effectively kept out the light, and row after row of ugly iron cribs with plaques advertising their donors left little space to play on this floor or the one above used by the younger preschool group. Older preschool children did not even have cots for their rest period. Instead, they napped sitting up, their arms cushioning their heads on the tables in front of them. Both boys and girls wore checked gingham pinafores over their own clothes, which were not always clean. Meals were served in shifts in the dining room, one group waiting in line for another to finish.

Zealous to relieve the plight of working mothers, it was often overcrowded. Regimentation was the rule rather than the exception. At the most, the older preschool group had a few hours of kindergarten, and the younger children had no education at all. The toys, frequently the discards of more fortunate boys and girls, were in the cupboards as much as in the children's hands. On the whole, the personnel was untrained and some were mentally dull. The diet was sadly lacking in vitamins. Orange juice and cod-liver oil were considered too extravagant to provide. Even milk was a scarce commodity, and the majority of children drank cocoa diluted with water.[30]

Whatever the pioneers of day care accomplished, the good, bad, or merely passable was done in the face of considerable antagonism from many solid citizens. A number of arguments were mounted against the day nursery idea. When several women began to organize the Leila Day Nursery in 1885, New Haven townsmen argued against the innovation on the grounds that two orphan asylums and a county children's home were sufficient to meet the child care needs of the community. There seemed to be little recognition on their part that the day nursery was the answer to a new child care need, that of the mother who wanted to keep her children but had, at the same time, to work to support them. The day care groups' motto boiled down to "helping those who help themselves," giving the mothers a chance to work while their children were cared for in the day nursery.[31]

Even so, a variety of often contradictory arguments were mounted against the day nursery: it loosened family ties; it lessened the mother's sense of responsibility and made her lazy by caring for her children for her; it minimized the father's sense of responsibility for being the sole breadwinner; it encouraged the mother to work; it depressed male wages; etcetera. In addition to these charges, professional philanthropists distrusted the allegedly soft-hearted women who made up the day nursery boards; they were accused of being insufficiently suspicious of the mothers whose children were admitted to the day nursery. Edward Devine put it as politely as anyone in his *Principles of Relief:*

> It has already become reasonably clear that indiscriminate aid in the form of care for children in day nurseries is nearly as objectionable as any other indiscriminate relief. To enable the mother

to work when the father is lazy or shiftless or incompetent is sometimes to incur direct responsibility for perpetuating bad family conditions. . . . Such are the economic and social problems which are beginning to complicate the day nursery, as indeed, they affect all charitable work. They are not incapable of solution. Here, as in other forms of child-saving work a snare lies before those who hope "to save the child," disregarding the other members of the family. The family must be considered as a whole. Neither the child nor the adult can be dealt with separately. The managers of the day nursery who are actuated by a desire to be of real service to the families whose children are received must in each instance face the question as to whether the family is a proper one to receive this particular form of assistance—whether the result in this particular instance is likely on the whole to be beneficial. . . .[32]

Devine, as we have seen, was among those encouraging the work of the day nursery as an alternative to sending children to institutions. On the other hand, simply caring for young children was not a sufficient justification for day nursery work. Like other forms of relief, the day nursery was thought of as a temporary expedient; ideally, it would eventually go out of business, when mothers were restored to their proper places in their homes. Meantime the nurseries should be operated so as to hasten, not delay, that day. They should screen applicants to make sure that day nursery services were not in fact simply encouraging the mother to work for luxuries.

In response to these criticisms the day nursery movement evolved an elaborate justification for their work; written examples frequently appeared in the foremost social work journal of the day.[33] First, the day nursery movement accepted the notion that the day nursery was a form of charity. It followed from this that a mother who applied to the day nursery had to have some sort of problem, which the day nursery had the obligation to verify and help remedy. Second, to counter the charge of aiding and abetting the breakdown of the family, the day nursery adopted as its first principle, "the preservation and maintenance of the home." This it claimed to accomplish by allowing the mother to keep her children near her, a better solution, it was widely agreed, than institutionalization. Third, the children were considered to be better off in the day nursery than in their own tenement apartment, even with their mothers present. The special care and treatment the children received in the day nursery was an object lesson in child-rearing for the mother herself; and the child, observing and benefiting from the day nursery's example of nutrition, hygiene, and good behavior, became a sort of junior teacher in his own home. Finally, the movement argued that the early and positive influence of the day nursery rendered a child far less likely to become a relief problem himself.

This was the official stance of the day nursery movement, though not necessarily the attitude of individual day nurseries. Some day nurseries sent "friendly visitors" to investigate applicants to the day nursery; others did not. Some day nurseries organized mothers and older siblings for social or learning activities, in other words, tried to be of assistance to the whole family; others did not. It is fairly clear from day nursery annual reports and the polite but continuing criticism voiced by charity workers that the day nurseries considered their primary task the care of young children, regardless of the supposed risk of encouraging the "undeserving poor," and so were less than terribly scrupulous in their investigative work. Nor did they take a therapeutic attitude toward the children's families. They obviously helped where and when they could, but for the most part mothers were left to resolve their problems—economic and personal—in their own way.

Even the official attitude, as expressed in the bulletins and conferences of the National Federation of Day Nurseries, founded in 1898, and of local day nursery associations in New York and Cleveland, was at some variance with the stern philanthropic mind. Charity organizations saw the day nursery as a temporary expedient which, with improving economic and social conditions, would naturally be phased out of existence. In a plea for widows' pensions, Dr. Lee K. Frankel told the 1905 conference of the National Federation that, "The Day Nursery is only a make-shift. The great issue is the family, and the proper place for development is the home. Any system that permits the breaking up of home surroundings must be make-shift."[34]

But the local and national federations were not so apt to think of their work as a makeshift. Mrs. Arthur M. Dodge, founder and president of the National Federation of Day Nurseries, while supporting the proposal for widows' pensions, also knew that not all women with children in the day nursery were widows, and that long after the widows' pension came into existence the day nursery would remain necessary.[35] In a survey conducted by ten of its member nurseries in 1913, the Association of Day Nurseries in New York found that only 17 percent of their participating mothers were widows; of the rest, 20 percent had been deserted, 27 percent had sick husbands, 17 percent had husbands whose income was insufficient, 13 percent had husbands who worked only part-time, 6 percent had unemployed husbands.[36] These figures bespoke a variety of conditions not to be readily ameliorated, beyond which, of course, there was the movement's claim that day nurseries offered *positive* advantages that many poor homes simply could not provide.

The day nursery movement tended to go its own way in practice and sometimes even in preachment. But the justifications and rationalizations it acceded to the philanthropists would have a telling effect on its development after World War I.

Every description that remains of these early day nurseries suggests to the modern eye a child care service more custodial than educational or developmental. In fact, most of these early day nurseries would appear less than adequate given what we now know about health, nutrition, and child development. Yet despite their limited knowledge and even more limited resources, the day nurseries and especially the day nursery associations made a constant effort to improve the quality of child care services. From a rather superficial moralism in the early 1890's, they began in the years before World War I to examine seriously the components of quality care and made substantive efforts to improve child care provided in the day nursery.

In her opening remarks to the Day Nursery Conference in 1892, Mrs. Gasper Griswold, in a Gilded Age analogy, compared the day nursery to a corporation. "Mothers go out to their work and the Every Day Framing and Disciplinary Company, (Limited.) look after their children. The capital stock of this company is patience, unselfishness and intelligent devotion. Its dividends are dear faces, good manners, tidy habits, stronger bodies and better morals."[37]

By 1912, the Day Nursery Association of New York had a more precise notion of how the "Every Day Framing and Disciplinary Company" ought to go about its tasks. The test of success for the day nursery was no longer numbers: neither the "number of children cared for" nor "the families kept together, but . . . the quality of work that is done." The test of quality was to be gauged by the physical, medical and educational services that the day nursery could provide its children.

> As there can be no earnest effort without progress, almost every nursery has made some advances in methods and standards. There is more particular attention given the individual child all along the line, physical, medical and educational. The progressive nursery pays special attention to the varieties of food that will most effectually nourish every part of the child's body, provides better facilities for open-air exercise, gives more thorough medical and surgical care, more thought to the backward child.
>
> It is no longer a question, "Shall we have a kindergarten?" but where can we find the teacher best fitted to train the senses, to help the child express itself through practical activities carried on as far as possible in the open air.[38]

As an indicator of increased safety and health measures, the report noted that many nurseries were having fire alarms installed in their buildings, and that the New York City Board of Health was taking an intelligent interest in supervising the day nurseries. Some nurseries, in an attempt at self-examination, were trying to maintain contact with "graduates" of their nurseries in order to evaluate the long-term consequences of their work. A Social Service Exchange had been set up to coordinate the "investigative" aspect of the day nursery. To their credit, these attempts at regulation and self-regulation did not narrow the broad outlook of the day nurseries, as witnessed in an interesting exchange between Dr. Max G. Schlapp, head of the Clearing House for Mentally Defective Individuals at Post-Graduate Hospital, and the indomitable Mrs. Arthur Dodge. Dr. Schlapp urged the day nurseries to remove from their premises idiots, feeble-minded children, or children not developing correctly. In a counterargument that underlined the continuing inclusiveness rather than the exclusiveness of the day nursery, Mrs. Dodge pointed with pride to the day nurseries that had shown that apparently feeble-minded children responded to special attention, their condition often showing marked improvement after admission to the day nursery.

From 1912 until the war years, the Day Nursery Association of New York printed in its annual report a series of articles designed to improve the quality of child care and the intelligence with which day nursery staffs approached their children. There were articles on nutrition, the training of nursemaids, emergency night shelters, the value of Montessori in the day nursery, the performance of adenoid and tonsil operations in the day nursery, the importance of regular medical examinations, fireproofing and fire escapes, and the importance of using the Bureau of Social Investigation. In 1917 the Association summarized these years of urgings by publishing a simple list of standards for the day nursery.

1. Hygenic plumbing;
2. Walls, ceiling, floors, must be finished so as to be washable;
3. Examination of child by physician before entrance;
4. Examination of children once a month, stripped if possible;
5. Investigation of cases before entrance;
6. Thorough investigation of cases where exceptional;
7. All children should be given two meals a day;
8. All children should wear nursery aprons, and infants be dressed in nursery clothes where possible;
9. Dietary recommended by Federation should be used;
10. Separate towels, spoons, etc. for each child obligatory;
11. Only eight infants or sixteen runabouts [toddlers] should be under the care of one attendant. A kindergarten teacher should have an assistant for more than thirty children;
12. Simple record for each child must be kept. Annual report should be printed following suggestions of Federation.[39]

Since membership in the Day Nursery Association was, of course, voluntary, the pressure for compliance depended on educational efforts rather than punitive measures; only one day nursery was ever dropped from the Association rolls for noncompliance.[40] It is fairly clear that the Association, at least in New York, did not so much represent its member nurseries as act as a conduit for professional ideas about day care. One feels, in reading these old reports, a gap between advice and practice. The Day Nursery Association could only advise; the day nurseries themselves remained the responsibility of their boards of managers, whose compliance or noncompliance depended on their own ideas about good child care and on their willingness and ability to meet the greater financial burdens that higher standards involved.

The National Federation of Day Nurseries followed a similar line in its conference reports and (monthly) bulletins. There was the same emphasis on health and hygiene, with a secondary stress on education. The health duties of the day nursery were not limited simply to watching out for runny noses and contagious diseases. "As the nursery has agreed to assume the care of the child, it is the duty of the director to see that all remedial defects such as diseased tonsils, bad teeth, faulty posture, and malnutritions are corrected." In keeping with its comprehensive health ideas, the Federation printed articles underlining the importance of dental examinations, vaccinations, sun lamps, sun baths, window glass that let in ultra-violet rays; they published a series of exercises for flat feet, poor posture, constipation, and knocked-knees.[41]

The bulletin also carried notices of new and unusual day nursery centers, like the one near a veterans' hospital in Minnesota, established to encourage women to visit their husbands more frequently,[42] or the one opened by the Kellogg Company in Battle Creek, Michigan; it operated on two shifts, from 7 A.M. to 3 P.M. and from 3 P.M. to 11 P.M.[43] There were also frequent notes on the Montessori method, then being introduced into various nursery centers.[44]

While the bulletins were of a house organ nature, the conference reports often treated more general issues, such as the widows' pension, municipal funding, or the day nursery's relation to family and community, and to charity and welfare. Important discussions went on about the relation of the day nursery to the family and community. Of particular importance was a discussion that began to appear in the bulletins about 1910, a discussion that plagues us still: infant day care.

From the beginning day nurseries had taken infants as young as 2 weeks without question or second thoughts; they, who were totally helpless, needed care even more than older children. Some day nursery workers even argued that for nutrition and discipline the day nursery was superior to the indulgent or neglectful tenement home in the care of infants.[45] In the quest for quality the question of maintaining infant care in the day nursery came by way of a perennial debate in America: bottle versus breast. The use of the bottle was the only practical way of feeding infants in the day nursery, but it came to be seen as an inferior form of feeding by many who thought the day nursery should not take infants. Dr. Carolyn Hedger, in addressing the 1912 conference, pointed out the superior immunological and psychological benefits available to a baby when nursed by its own mother. Not only did the bottle not substitute for the breast, but the practice of many overworked day nursery staffs of propping a bottle on a pillow rather than feeding their charges by hand also impaired, Dr. Hedger believed, the emotional development of the infant. "It takes mother-love, mother arms, mother breast and considerable common sense to grow a human properly for the first nine months, and no institution, no matter how scientific, how philanthropic, can replace these things." If the day nursery absolutely had to take infants, she advised a wet nurse rather than bottles.

Henceforth one of the regular rallying points for quality care was the exclusion of infants from the day nursery. Before the days of maternity leaves this could create an intolerable financial situation for a mother, and some day nurseries attempted to provide financial support for at least two months after childbirth, a measure seen as beneficial both to the health of the mother as well as the infant.[46]

Nonetheless most day nurseries continued to take infants and the National Federation of Day Nurseries recognized this was so in advising a ratio of one nurse for every eight babies. The effort to remove the infant from the day nursery was always tempered by the same reality that had necessitated infant care in the first place: without the day nursery babies would be left alone, or to the indifferent care of a neighbor or sibling. The effort at excluding infants was, however, the opening wedge in the attempt to raise the minimum age of the day nursery, which in our own day usually falls between two and one-half and three years of age.

These efforts at self-regulation may not have resulted in what we think of today as "quality day care," but they did provide a minimum standard against which the day nursery could measure itself; they also resulted in increased interest by civil authorities, at least in the physical conditions of the buildings in which day nurseries were housed. As early as 1910, the New York City Board of Health and the Fire Department took an interest in the health and safety measures practiced by the city's nurseries; California had a state law governing day nurseries in 1917; and in 1918 the Cleveland Day Nursery Association was instrumental in creating a city ordinance regulating day nurseries.[47]

Through the war years and beyond there continued a fitful effort at formulating some kind of public policy toward day care as well as an effort at self-regulation. For those day nurseries that met the standards of the local day nursery associations, one can assume that most provided adequate health services, proper nutrition, and a safe building. Most of them probably offered, in addition, a modest educational program based on the traditional kindergarten or the newer ideas of Maria Montessori. Those day nurseries that did not belong to the associations were reputed to be miserable, unsanitary hovels where children were virtually imprisoned during the day, but there is little way of knowing their true condition. Aside from the annual reports, what is known about all of these early day nurseries was written by professionals who took an interest in the day nursery in the 1920's, and who perceived that before their own blessed arrival on the scene day nurseries were at best a custodial service, at worst, dens for the neglect and abuse of children.

Throughout the 1920's and 1930's the day nursery attracted professional workers, especially teachers and social workers whose goals for the day nursery brought it more clearly into line with the social welfare goals that the day nursery ladies had resisted in earlier years. The long-term effect of professionalization was to change the task of the day nursery as well as its attitudes toward the families and children it served. As the components of quality nursery care— health, nutrition, mental hygiene, education, and social services— came to dominate the thinking of day nursery boards, day nursery associations, and city and state regulatory agencies, it was inevitable that the professional who performed those services too began to take a serious look at the day nursery.

The nursery school teachers, as distinct from the kindergarteners and the social workers, were the first professional workers to move into day care on a full-time basis. Their skills and influence undoubtedly raised the quality of child care; unfortunately, their transcending professional outlook redefined the task of the day nursery.

The kindergarten had been a distinct and welcome presence in the day nursery from the 1890's. Specific methods and theories were never fully spelled out in the annual reports, partly because they were so well known. Singing, drawing, sewing, story reading, and supervised play are frequently described as activities for those children, ranging in age from toddlers to 5-year-olds, who attended the kindergarten. Teachers trained in the Froebel or Montessori methods had a specific set of tasks and procedures which were introduced on the basis of a child's age and capacities; photographs of Montessori classrooms in day nurseries in the years immediately before and after World War I portray a preschool scene not too different from what one might see in a contemporary scene. The introduction in the 1920's of the nursery school teacher altered the educative aspect of the day nursery and reoriented the services the day nursery could offer a working mother.

One observer of this movement of the nursery school teachers into the day nursery found this process a mixed blessing.

> We in the Day-Nursery world rejoiced as one by one attendants were replaced by these trained teachers. However, various other problems cropped up immediately. At first the teachers would not stay all day. Only after years of struggle did they consent to remain seven or eight hours, working in shifts to cover the whole schedule . . . The pick of the graduates was not always available because the Day Nursery paid comparatively little for more time.
>
> Undoubtedly the Nursery School did a great deal to wean the Day Nursery from custodial care, but this does not make the Day Nursery a Nursery School. The educational department is only part of the Day-Nursery program and must be balanced by the special needs of this particular group of children.[48]

The nursery school teachers replaced not only the kindergartener but the nursery attendants as well; their emphasis on the educative aspect of the day nursery to the exclusion of the affective and physical needs of the children meant that infants and younger children did not thrive in the care of nursery school teachers. Nursery school teachers had no theory or methods for dealing with these younger children, hence their presence raised the minimum age at which the day nursery could hope to deal effectively with children. When the nursery attendants left, the infant was barred from the day nursery; ultimately the toddler, too, was restricted.

The exclusion of the two-year-olds after the babies' departments were closed is easy to understand. Up to that time they could remain with the babies until they learned the elements of physical care, particularly toilet control, from the infant nurses. Once the nurses vanished from the Day Nursery, the Nursery-School teachers were faced with these tasks, which they often were not equipped to handle skillfully. . . . Hence the two-year-olds did not always prosper in the Day Nursery and as a consequence were not considered eligible any more.[49]

Despite the obvious benefits of hiring professionally trained teachers to work in the day nursery, there were these unintended consequences. The early day nursery had defined its task broadly—to care for the children of working mothers, often including after-school care for school-aged children. From the 1920's on, the presence of infants and younger children came to be considered inappropriate. This happened not because the need for such care had passed but because the new personnel of the day nursery were not prepared to care for them. A similar restriction and limitation of the day nursery took place as social workers came to exercise considerable influence over the admissions policies of the day nursery.

From its earliest days the day nursery was part of the child-saving movement and enjoyed extensive support, moral if not financial, from a variety of charitable and philanthropic organizations. Support, however, did not mean control; the decentralized state of charity and welfare efforts allowed groups like the day nursery a large degree of self-definition, autonomy, and freedom. The professionalization of social work and social workers in the 1920's led to a thorough rethinking of all aspects of charitable work, including the day nursery.

The result was that the day nursery came under close scrutiny by a group whose philosophy and predispositions were unsympathetic to the notion that a mother should work and that a child should be cared for outside his home in a group setting. This attitude differed from that of the early charity workers who, though they disapproved of working mothers and the group care of children, recognized that necessity dictated that many mothers must work. For them the day nursery was a superior alternative to total institutionalization of the child. The view of the professional social worker came to dominate thinking in the day care field at the same time as it projected an image to the public of the day nursery as a custodial and undesirable service for women and families who were not normal.

The prototype of the social worker, the "friendly visitor" or "home visitor," was a rarity in most day nurseries. When day nurseries had such a person, her primary task was to ascertain if the family really needed day care. Did the mother really have to work? Had the father actually deserted the family? Was he totally incapacitated? Very often this work was done by a member of the board of managers, or the matron herself; those nurseries who hired visiting nurses often had her look in on new families. The investigation was construed by these women as part of a larger educational task: to help or advise the mother in her home; to talk to her about nutritious foods; to show her how to bathe her children; etcetera. Now, of course, many day nurseries had neither the time, inclination, nor personnel to investigate their applicants; this was one of their chief points of contention with the charity organizations, who felt that the day nursery was often indiscriminate in helping families. Day nurseries, the charity organizations believed, might actually be pauperizing a family or loosening family bonds or, even worse, giving something away for nothing.

Recognizing this lackadaisical attitude on the part of individual day nurseries, a few local associations hired independent investigators, who were available for visiting the families of all member nurseries. The Cleveland Day Nursery and Free Kindergarten Association traced a direct line from their first home visitors to a behavior clinic which opened in 1926 and a social service department which opened in 1934. From the "friendly visitor" to the social service department, from investigation of new families to family casework, was not a large step to take. From finding a family in need to doing something for them was a logical and humanitarian step—a step many day nurseries took before the notion of family casework appeared on the scene.

After World War I, however, the day nursery came under regular and rigorous scrutiny concerning its proper role and function within the larger social welfare picture. The first question asked in this broad-ranging analysis was: What standards of admission should the day nursery adopt? The answer depended, of course, on prior assumptions about what the day nursery was. If the day nursery was primarily a service for working mothers, then the standards of admission were clear: the day nursery accepted children whose mothers worked. If, on the other hand, the day nursery was a social welfare agency, then the standards of admission were somewhat more complicated.

In 1919, for the first time, the day nursery became a regular topic of discussion for the National Conference of Social Work. Grace Caldwell of the New England Center of Day Nurseries addressed the conference on "Standards of Admission to Day Nurseries," in terms that have characterized day care's public image down to a very few years ago. Expressions such as "problem families," "maladjustment," "temporary expedients," "correct social diagnosis," "social evil and the larger picture" dominated her discussion of the day nursery and the families who used them. Miss Caldwell began her speech with a tripartite definition of the place of the day nursery. The day nursery, first of all, deals with a family problem.

> That we spend the greater part of our funds for the care of children does not alter the fact that the reason we do so is because of some maladjustment in the families of which they are members, and it is to get at the cause of this maladjustment and to build up normal family conditions that our nursery care works towards. . . . This brings us to our second factor, the recognition of nursery care as a temporary expedient. If we see our job in the large, our objective will be to get Johnny back into a normal home as soon as constructive work will allow. As a part of thorough work, we will make Johnny a healthy, happy, clean-minded boy while we have him, but our real problem is helping eliminate the trouble which made Johnny's care necessary. And a third factor which must influence us in shaping our policy is the economic dangers of an extension of our work in the form of industrial nurseries or in localities where large foreign groups and low wages for men exist, together.[50]

Among the notable elements in Miss Caldwell's view of the relationship between day nursery and family is the notion that the day nursery serves families living in a pathological situation, a position drastically different from the earlier formulation, which saw the day nursery as a service to families living in poverty conditions who were attempting to improve their lives by having the mother work. Insofar as poverty came to be defined as pathological, perhaps she is only describing an old situation with a new term. But, in fact, poverty in the minds of the first day nursery workers (as distinct from the professional philanthropists who harassed them) was perceived to be the results of conditions external to the family—industrialization, urbanization, and immigration—but having a strong effect on the family. The sense in which Miss Caldwell elaborates "maladjustment" suggests conditions internal to the family. The great number of applicants, she finds, "have only a bitter knowledge of trouble, but *no intelligent conception of the real problems involved,* seeing only the acute situation which can be relieved by the temporary care of a child."[51] In the "new" day nursery the family becomes a passive receptor of services—not services the family necessarily requested, since they may be turned down for child care, but services which "scientific" social work indicates are necessary. The old-fashioned day nursery, which was merely being helpful, was obviously looked upon with disfavor. "I am sure there can be only one nursery like that reported to me a few months ago, a nursery which prided itself on never refusing an applicant who came to it for help, feeling sure that no one would ever come who was not in need and that nursery help must be the remedy because they asked for it!"[52]

Such high-mindedness as Miss Caldwell evidences could only result in day nurseries becoming a highly selective and restrictive service granted by benevolent social workers to suppliant families. Thus day care centers should exist only so long as social workers found them necessary and only in those places where social workers found them useful and only for people whom social workers found sufficiently troubled. The day nursery was consequently only a temporary expedient until family life could be reconstructed and the mother restored to her rightful place at home. The day nursery should not be established in areas where poverty or low wages characterized the economic situation of the population. In other words, in areas where they were most needed. The day nursery movement had always expressed concern with the possibility that working women depressed the male wage level, making it difficult for men to earn a family wage. Nonetheless they still made efforts to locate day nurseries where they were most needed, in low-income, tenement areas where working mothers most usually lived.

Miss Caldwell's speech in 1919 marked the beginning of a long process of change in the day nursery, from a useful, broadly defined, simple child-helping service to a marginal and limited agent of social welfare. And except for a brief interlude during World War II, the expansion and contraction of day care services occurred without particular reference to the needs of working mothers.

The new thinking about day care, because it was carried on among professionals either in journals or at annual conferences, dominated the conversation, so to speak, and by virtue of that domination succeeded in classifying day care as a welfare service. Such ideals as Miss Caldwell and others proposed were, of course, a long time in seeping down to day nursery practices, often because there were so few trained professionals to carry out the work. Day nurseries managed then to secure a somewhat tawdry public reputation from the social work view without particularly benefiting on an individual level from the social work services that theoretically went along with a social welfare service. By definition it became more and more exceptional for a working mother to place her child in group care, since by doing so she found herself labeled a "problem" mother with a maladjusted family.

In defining the day nursery as a form of family and child welfare, social workers succeeded in communicating to applicants that day care was not a service for the normal. To the credit of many applicants this attempted flim-flam was not so easily carried out, as witnessed by the complaints of many social workers who went to work in the day nursery.

The Leila Day Nursery, whose origins we looked at earlier, hired their own social worker in the mid-thirties, and began to formulate new policies of selection. The social worker, who found her work difficult, expressed some consternation at the attitude of neighborhood families who used the nursery.

> In most of the families [she complained], the parents' attitude is that the Nursery is a community resource, such as the public school, and it is, therefore, for them to use as they wish. Families find it difficult to see the need of discussing financial, social and personal factors affecting their lives, as in their minds these facts are not related to nursery care.[53]

Her counterpart at the Troy Day Home in Troy, New York, one of the oldest day nurseries in the country, faced similar parental resistance to new definitions. Her own view was that parental use of the day nursery ought not to be so casual or open as it had been, since "the day nursery is no longer a parking place for working mothers."[54] To enforce this policy she made home visits to the day nursery families, and she, along with the matron, decided who was to be accepted or rejected for admission. It remained for her to convince parents that continued enrollment of a child in the day nursery ought to be a matter of joint discussion and not a matter for parents alone to decide.[55]

Ethel Beer, in her memoir of the day nursery, argues that it was a mistake to allow family casework into the day nursery, and calls attention to the struggle that often went on between parent and social worker over the question of admitting a child to the local day nursery.

> Starting with intake—that is, admission to the Day Nursery—the whole approach is different than in family casework, when assistance is requested. Most mothers who ask for help from a Day Nursery simply want to place their children, and do not wish advice. . . . Often these mothers resent being told what to do, no matter how kindly the intentions. Leaving the office after an intake interview with the Day-Nursery caseworker, Mrs. Santo sputtered: "I guess I know my own business best. She can refuse my baby if she wants to. But telling me to stay at home is too much!"[56]

In telling mothers to stay at home social workers were probably reflecting the sentiments of the larger society. While social welfare views did give a peculiar twist to the definition of day care from the 1920's onward, it was a definition that public opinion easily accepted. First, the reform spirit of the progressive period was dealt a fatal blow by the war, and the day nursery, as other innovative ideas, suffered a decline in interest and popularity. Second, wide-scale immigration stopped in 1921 with the passage of legislation restricting immigrants. The quota system that evolved into the Johnson-Reed Act of 1924 effectively cut off the movement of people to the United States whose children, to a considerable extent, had formed the day nursery population.[57] This was not immediately reflected in a wholesale decline of day nursery enrollment,

although a 1924 report on the New York day nurseries suggests that
the waiting lists had declined and many day nurseries no longer
operated at their former capacities.[58] Third, the collapse of militant
feminism after the passage of the Nineteenth Amendment giving
women the right to vote probably removed the counterbalance to
the widespread opinion that the mother's place was in the home.
And the passage of widows' pensions in many states allowed a large
group of mothers to stay home and raise their children in genteel
poverty. Fourth, after a mild business recession the decade took on
that spirit of affluence and economic expansion which helped give
rise to the image of the Roaring Twenties. This did not actually get
rid of slums or poverty, but in flush times there seemed to be less
reason to notice that not everyone's street was paved with gold. If
men were working they could support their families, and that made
the day nursery seem less of a necessity.

The day nurseries themselves suffered from a falling off in the
philanthropic sentiment of the upper class who, for the most part,
had supported them. Only in Cleveland were day nursery funds
given through the Community Chest; elsewhere there was little or
no public funding of the day nursery. It remained the duty of day
nursery boards to secure the funds, only part of which continued to
be raised by parent payments. With rising costs and rising standards,
and, perhaps, declining gratification, fund-raising became more and
more of an onerous task. The dwindling number of day nurseries
was widely decimated by the Depression.

The opinions of social workers, the changes in public attitudes,
and the decline in day nursery enrollment notwithstanding, there
remained a great need for day nurseries during the twenties.
Mothers continued to work, especially mothers who were least able
to pay for home care. While immigration from abroad had dwin-
dled, internal migration from rural to urban areas and from the
South to the North had grown rapidly, creating the same kind of
urban dislocation that had characterized the earlier immigration.

The migration of rural southern blacks to the large cities of the
North—Chicago, New York, Detroit, and Cleveland—was made up
of families as desperately in need of day care as the Irish, Germans,
Jews, Poles, and Italians had been before them. The NFDN Bulletin
often made appeals for the expansion or extension of day nurseries

to care for "colored" children. While some day nurseries had taken all children regardless of race,* no one in the 1920's sprang to meet their special need. The Kips Bay Day Nursery on New York's East Side found itself in 1928 in the midst of a growing commercial district with few mothers in need of day care. The board of managers, in searching for a new location, turned down a request by a worker from the Association for Improving the Condition of the Poor to locate in Harlem, a largely black district, or in the Bronx, with a growing Jewish population.[59]

The growing number of middle-class women who pursued careers had their needs met primarily through the booming nursery schools or home care. And they were, of course, very reluctant to place their children in day nurseries, whose public image of pathological and abnormal families made such a move extremely difficult.

By the end of the decade, then, the day nursery had become an underfinanced, often understaffed, marginal child care service for those families who had no choice but to suffer under the onerous designation "pathological." By 1931, the National Federation of Day Nurseries had completely succumbed to the social welfare service mentality, and in one of its last bulletins, before it ceased publication in 1931, they printed several articles which granted that, indeed, the day nursery child represented a social problem, and that the day nursery ought to be the last choice in the care of children, after that of the mother staying home, of relatives caring for the child, or the child being placed in foster-home day care, i.e., the day care of children with individual women in their own homes. The Philadelphia day nurseries, the mother of them all, had in fact completely given up the group care of children. They had banded together to organize and supervise a system of foster-home day care.

This picture reversed itself rapidly and drastically after the election of Roosevelt and the advent of the Federal Economic Recovery Act and Works Projects Administration—legislation designed to mitigate the worst effects of the Depression. Beginning in 1933, federal funds became available for the expansion of day care—not primarily in order to care for children, but to supply jobs for

* A policy verified by group photographs published from time to time in the annual reports.

unemployed teachers, nurses, nutritionists, clerical workers, cooks, and janitors. By 1937, the programs had set up nineteen hundred nurseries caring for about forty thousand children, and were notable in two respects. For the first time public funds, both federal and state, became available for day care; and the WPA nurseries, as they came to be called, were "identified primarily as an educational service and [were] usually located in school buildings."[60] After the demise of the WPA programs the day nursery again declined in numbers only to be resurrected by World War II.[61]

The massive mobilization of men, women, and materials after America's entrance into the war made it a patriotic necessity for women to go to work, including the mothers of young children. Under the impact of the war fervor, all previous prejudices, arguments, and opinions about the danger of working mothers and day care of children quickly disappeared, except among social workers and child welfare agencies.

It became clear early in the war that labor-starved war industries could never attract young mothers and keep their absenteeism to a minimum if some large-scale effort was not made to care for their children. To meet the need for all varieties of social services growing out of the dislocations caused by the war, Congress passed, in 1941, the Community Facilities Act (or Lanham Act) to meet on a fifty-fifty basis the social service needs of war-impacted areas. In 1942, the Lanham Act was interpreted as being applicable to day care, and in October of that year the first grants were made to operate day care centers, more than eleven hundred of them former WPA nurseries.[62]

By 1945 and the end of the war, nearly fifty million dollars had been spent for day care—three million for construction and almost forty-three for operating expenses. In July, 1945, more than a million and a half children were in day care.[63] In some areas, not considered war-impacted, state governments supplied day care funds. In New York State it amounted to seven hundred thousand dollars; in Washington State, five hundred thousand dollars. Many industries, too, funded and ran day care centers; the most notable among them was organized and maintained by the Kaiser shipbuilding yards on the West Coast.[64]

Lanham funds were administered through the Federal Works Agency, whose primary motivation was not to provide day care but to encourage women to work in defense plants. In order to facilitate the rapid expansion of day care programs, the agency channeled funds for day care through local school systems, largely bypassing the child and social welfare agencies who considered day nurseries their special province. The FWA theory was that school systems were most likely "to have the space available for facilities and an administrative staff familiar with the techniques required for handling children in groups."[65] Despite pleas by social workers to make casework and family day care eligible for the funds, the agency ruled that these were not considered public works and were, therefore, ineligible for funding.[66] The drawback to the fact that the agency had been concerned primarily with supplying labor for war industries was that no standards had been set for day care services, and the care provided was wholly supervised by local groups who had agreed to sponsor the centers. The quality of care, therefore, varied considerably. After the war, it was this factor that led social welfare forces to look upon the wartime day care centers as a disaster quickly done away with and, hopefully, never to be repeated.[67]

CHAPTER 3

A HISTORY OF DAY CARE:
FROM WORLD WAR II TO 1970

Although a massive government effort had gone into providing day care during World War II, it was not generally thought worth preserving. It had been an expedient. The end of the war, the return of the troops, the changeover from a wartime to a peacetime economy, the apparent return to normalcy, made day care, like rationing, seem an unhappy necessity during the emergency, and to be done away with happily after the Armistice.

The closing of twenty-eight hundred centers left over a million and a half children without day care services. Congressmen, government officials, local sponsors, social workers, and teachers, of course, believed that the need was over. Working women would return to their rightful places at home; children would be properly cared for by their mothers; fathers would once again take their places as the breadwinners and heads of the family. Yet labor force statistics show that many women did not give up their jobs after the war, and that many more continued to enter the labor market. Whatever the opinion and attitude of policymakers, legislators, social welfare professionals, and, to a great extent, the public itself, there was a continuing need after World War II for the day care of young children. But a combination of ideological, economic, and psychological reasons precluded serious consideration of the needs of working mothers and young children for day care services.

On February 28, 1946, Lanham funds were withdrawn and the federal government ended its brief but important support of child care services. Several states and localities, especially in those areas that had established centers before the war, continued to operate them on a limited basis. The states of California, Washington, and Massachusetts, and the cities of Washington, D.C., Hartford, Detroit, New York, and Philadelphia provided public support for some twelve thousand preschool children, down drastically from the national figure of one and a half million during the war.[1]

Despite the limited number of public day care places available, in 1950 one and two-thirds million women who had children under six were working, and their numbers increased.[2] Between April, 1948, and March, 1966, the labor force participation rate of married women with husbands present and with children under six increased from 10.8 percent to 24.2 percent. Put another way, nearly 25 percent of the married women who lived with their husbands and had children under six worked or searched for work in 1966.[3] Naturally, this figure would be considerably higher if it included the number of working mothers with children under six who were single, divorced, or not living with their husbands.

From 1940, when one in eight mothers worked, to the end of the sixties when almost two in five worked, there has been a steady increase in their numbers. In summing up the changes that have taken place in the number of working mothers, Eli Ginzburg has noted that not only are more mothers working but that the mothers of young children showed, in particular, "the most rapid increase in labor force participation . . . ; this group showed a gain in labor market participation of over sixty percent during the past decade, with the result that now almost one-third of such mothers work."[4]

In the face of such meager resources for child care, why did so many women confound everyone's expectations at the end of the war that they would return to their homes, and instead stay at their jobs? There are, of course, many sociological and psychological reasons at hand to explain the working-mother phenomenon, but the most obvious explanation is economic—women worked because they had to. The deaths and family disruption caused by the war are one explanation; many women were left as widows or wives of incapacitated husbands. By 1956, the combined numbers of women with children under six who were widowed, divorced, deserted, or not living with their husbands had reached one million. Almost one-half of these women worked even though their children were of preschool age. Furthermore, for many families the way out of poverty into the middle-class required two wage earners, usually mother and father. Although there is no statistical breakdown according to the ages of children, we do know that in 1956, 70 percent of those families with incomes in the middle-class range of seven to fifteen thousand dollars a year had two wage earners. In a sense two American dreams were at odds with one another—a mother at home, but in a middle-class home; for many, a middle-class home required a mother at work. Not only were individual and family economic needs met by the working mother, so were the requirements of the national economy.[5]

Expectations that women would return to the domestic scene after the war were supported by the widespread belief that a depression would probably follow the decline in war-related industrial work. Rather than a depression, the decade following the war was one of unprecedented prosperity combined with a rather severe labor shortage—the result of low birth rates during the Depression. Hence not only did many women wish to continue working but there was a genuine need for them to do so.[6]

The ideal of the mother in the home allowed everyone to overlook, however, the absence of so many other women from their homes; not only did the ideal obscure the absence of the working mother but frequently it cast an aura of the pathological or negligent on her. Not surprisingly, then, the needs of these mothers for child care (all-day care for their preschoolers and after-school care for their school-aged children) was not looked upon with the same emergency quality as the war-work needs had been. Every survey conducted on the question of who cares for the children of working mothers has found that most working mothers had to organize their own child care, consequently the vast majority of children were and are cared for at home by a relative or neighbor, and only a small percentage are in day care centers.[7] Whatever the benefits or drawbacks of particular kinds of child care, these arrangements were not for the most part what many many mothers considered an ideal or even a desirable situation. Until quite recently the larger society had almost no consciousness of the problems of working mothers and their needs for good child care. It was, as Maya Pines wrote, "the problem nobody wants to face."[8] And it was a problem nobody wanted to face because the working mother was a problem, in 1945 as in 1920, that nobody thought should exist.

As we have seen, the inter-war years, 1920 to 1940, had been an era when day care services were curtailed and limited because of their definition as a child welfare service. This view reasserted itself after the war and dominated thinking about day care in the following decades.[9]

In 1960, the Child Welfare League of America defined day care as a way ". . . to protect children by providing part-time care, supervision and guidance when their families are unable to meet their needs without some assistance from the community . . ." And the Children's Bureau in 1963 found that

> The child who needs day care has a family problem which makes it impossible for his parents to fulfill their parental responsibilities without supplementary help. . . .
>   Day care makes it possible for many parents to keep their children with them in their own homes and to retain their legal and financial responsibility. Therefore, day care is a way of strengthening family life, preventing neglect of some children, and reducing risk of separation from their families for others.[10]

As a service for the pathological or socially deviant, no one could advocate the expansion of day care services except under the most extreme conditions, such as the war. Mothers who did send their children to day care centers had also to accept the onerous definition of not being fit. In short, no one, those who needed it and those who controlled it, had a good word for day care.

Yet the day care needs of working mothers had to be met in some way. A survey by the Bureau of the Census and the Children's Bureau in 1958 showed that 80 percent of children under twelve whose mothers worked full-time were cared for in their own homes, and of these, 8 percent cared for themselves; 20 percent of the children were cared for outside their homes—18 percent by a relative or neighbor and 2 percent in a day care center or nursery school.[11] Another survey of selected communities in 1962 showed the same configuration of arrangements for child care, with 73 percent cared for at home by a father, grandmother, siblings, friend, or neighbor; about 11 percent of the children were cared for outside their own homes, in the home of a relative or neighbor; in 7 percent of the cases the child took care of himself; in 3 percent the mother cared for the child while working; and in 3 percent, the child was in group care.[12]

At the same time, where publicly funded, nonprofit day care continued to exist, considerable efforts were made to raise the standards under which it operated. The ironic outcome of the situation was that fewer and fewer children found places in the better centers closely regulated by governmental agencies or child welfare agencies. This left more and more children to be cared for in commercial, run-for-profit centers where there was often no outside supervision or regulation, while even more children were kept at home in arrangements that mothers often found unsatisfactory. But neither were these mothers certain that they would find group care satisfactory if it were available to them.[13] A new definition of day care was needed to rid it of the pathological connotations with which it had become associated.

But even if child welfare professionals had seen day care as a legitimate need of the working mother, without regard to her mental or emotional state, it is doubtful that they would have been very successful at marshaling a change in public opinion, or, even more important, gathering the political support necessary for government subsidy. For, finally, the child welfare view on children, mothers, and families was supported by prevailing social mores and the opinions of most social and behavioral scientists. The social mythology of motherhood and the research involved in isolating the phenomenon of maternal deprivation were mutually supportive—the best place for mother and child was together at home.

The "feminine mystique" had passed into the language as a byword for the notion that a woman's place was in the home. However accurately descriptive or pervasive the "problem without a name," culminating in the feminine mystique of the fifties and early sixties, its influence was so widespread as to keep from public consciousness the fact that one-third of all American women were employed outside their homes. The fact that the feminine mystique, with its strong elements of escapism and consumerism, was a phenomenon confined to the middle- and upper-middle-class, who established norms, made it even easier for the country as a whole to ignore the needs of the many mothers who did work.

That the working mother was considered abnormal, as Betty Friedan pointed out, was the result of a combination of Freudianism, functional sociology, and the death of militant feminism.[14] These combined to define the normal woman as one who found her life and fulfillment complete within the home and family circle. Freud's American popularizers chose to emphasize his culturally narrow and time-bound description of the women of his time as universally true and applicable. Hence women ought to be most happy, most satisfied in living their lives through males, be it husbands, fathers, sons, or brothers.[15] Women who worked and had careers of their own suffered from a "masculinity complex."

Functional sociology enshrined this analytic view in a structure replete with nuclear family and "woman's place." "By giving an absolute meaning and a sanctimonious value to the generic term 'woman's role,' functionalism put American women into a kind of deep freeze—like Sleeping Beauties, waiting for a Prince Charming to waken them, while all around the magic circle the world moved on."[16]

Finally the feminist movement, which had won whatever political and legal rights women enjoyed, had disappeared from the scene, making it difficult for women to organize around a more positive program for winning equal rights in other areas—employment, education, and salaries. Whatever the limitations or exaggerations to be found in the notion of the feminine mystique, it accurately described the life experience of many college-educated, middle-class women. And that was probably the chief social problem resulting from the syndrome of the feminine mystique: the designation applied to women who from an economic point of view probably had little need to work but who, in staying home and defining the normative activity of woman as mother and housewife, masked the needs of many other women who had to work and whose need for alternative sources of child care, though considerable, went unmet.

The view that mothers, particularly those of young children, ought to stay home was given further support by a number of researchers who began to identify and define a phenomenon they called maternal deprivation. Maternal deprivation referred to the early and prolonged separation of mother and infant which often resulted in the death of the child and, if not death, then a strong pattern of retardation characterized by the failure of these infants and young children to form strong emotional bonds and to show normal rates of social and cognitive development. The most famous of these studies, John Bowlby's *Maternal Care and Mental Health*, first published in 1951,[17] focused on infants and children who were living or had lived in total institutions entailing a prolonged and/or permanent separation from their mothers.

Bowlby defined the problem in this way:

> What is believed to be essential for mental health is that the infant and young child should experience a warm, intimate, and continuous relationship with his mother (or permanent mother-substitute) in which both find satisfaction and enjoyment. Given this relationship, the emotions of anxiety and guilt, which in excess characterize mental ill-health, will develop in a moderate and organized way. When this happens, the child's characteristic and contradictory demands, on the one hand for unlimited love from his parents and on the other for revenge upon them when he feels that they do not love him enough, will likewise remain of moderate strength and become amenable to the control of his gradually developing personality. It is this complex, rich, and rewarding relationship with the mother in the early years, varied in countless ways by relations with the father and with siblings, that child psychiatrists and many others now believe to underlie the development of character and of mental health.
>
> A state of affairs in which the child does not have this relationship is termed "maternal deprivation."[18]

Further research has refined and elaborated upon Bowlby's thesis since 1951, noting certain distinctions between separation and deprivation, probing the differences between temporary and permanent separation, and underlining the importance of a mother-substitute when separation and/or deprivation do occur. His work has undoubtedly brought beneficial effects to child welfare policies concerning the negative effects of institutionalizing children in hospitals or orphanages and the positive effects of early adoption or placement in foster homes.

Yet at the time his theories were first propounded, they fit in very well with the feminine mystique and served to reinforce the importance the mystique placed on the mother remaining at home with her children. Bowlby's Freudian emphasis on the unique quality of early childhood experiences meshed neatly with the Freudian emphasis, at least in America, on women finding their satisfaction and life role through their husbands and children. Furthermore, the "separation" aspect of the whole theory buttressed the prevailing views of child welfare agencies that their most important task was to maintain the mother-child relationship intact and uninterrupted.

From 1945 to the early sixties, day care was a marginal child welfare service which did not begin to meet the needs of children or the needs of working mothers. Its expansion, or even serious consideration of its improvement, was barred by significant public attitudes concerning family life and by professional child welfare attitudes concerning the motherly role and the needs of young children for close maternal supervision and attention. This state of restriction and the volume of unmet needs could not remain hidden forever.

And during the sixties attitudes began to change among many sectors of the population, including child welfare professionals, educators, psychologists, government officials, welfare workers, social workers, working mothers, and feminists. While a more favorable attitude toward day care emerged among these groups, so did conflict about the goals and purposes of day care. And although many of the effects of day care on infants and children are yet unknown, more overriding concerns have held these unknowns in temporary abeyance.

There is no single event which initiated these changes in outlook, but a variety of ideas and movements converged, breaking down the mental and political blocks to a realistic appraisal of the facts: no matter what one's ideas about the proper relationship between mother and children, and the proper place of women, people needed day care that could, when properly organized, provide a healthy and stimulating experience for children.

First of all, the indissoluble bonds linking mother and child have been shown through pilot projects in infant care not to be so fragile. While differences of opinion remain as to all the possible consequences of "multiple mothering," this research suggests that the maternal deprivation syndrome does not have to be a necessary consequence of mother-infant separation. Second, there has been a growing awareness that women form an important and necessary part of the labor force. The Women's Liberation movement has argued successfully that women need not apologize for their work; they have the right to equal access, promotion and pay. Third, continuing research on child development has strongly indicated that a child's preschool years are crucially important for his emotional, cognitive, and social development. These years are the foundation for a normal childhood and development into a reasonably happy and well-functioning adult. Finally, beginning in the middle sixties, there was a growing desire on the part of many government officials, policy-makers, and legislators to control the rising costs of welfare by having women on welfare go to work. This decision led to extensive government subsidy of day care services for those women who went to work and had children below school age.

To begin, let us look at the changing opinion of the government and child welfare establishments concerned with day care.

One of the more important signals of a new attitude was a special issue of *Child Welfare*, the journal of the Child Welfare League of America, in March, 1965, dealing with day care. Among the articles were two that addressed themselves in a critical manner to the prevailing attitude about maternal deprivation and separation, and infant day care.[19] Another sign of changing opinion was the interest that the Women's Bureau of the Labor Department and the Children's Bureau of Health, Education and Welfare took in expanding day care resources—an interest exhibited by the calling of a National Conference on Day Care Services in May, 1965, and a Consultation on Working Women and Day Care Needs in 1967.[20] And beginning in 1962, with the Public Welfare Amendments, Congress, too, in a desultory and halting fashion, appropriated day care funds on a limited basis; though not greatly expanding existing resources, this action did supply money for upgrading centers that already existed.

In his article in *Child Welfare*, "Day Care: A Reassessment," Milton Willner took child welfare professionals to task for missing the subtleties and new research being done on the maternal deprivation problem. He reminded them:

> The original studies were concerned with the phenomenon of maternal deprivation—not of separation. These studies were made in impersonal institutions where no mother substitute was pro-

vided. . . . Because these studies were made in institutions and not in the home of the children, however, the changes resulting from deprivation were also considered to be brought about by separation. In effect, separation was equated with maternal deprivation.[21]

The applicability then of the maternal deprivation research was, in Willner's view, only marginal to the question of day care services. While children might be separated from their mothers, they were not, in good day care, deprived of good mothering; in fact, day care could be considered a unique service with positive values: "day care can offer something valuable to children *because* they are separated from their parents."

Too often children were not only separated from their mothers but deprived as well of decent alternative arrangements. Hence the rationale by which child welfare professionals minimized the importance of day care and used it only for limited purposes had exactly the opposite of its intended effect. Willner pointed out,

> The field, despite its manifest interest in the welfare of children and its deep knowledge of the importance of family life and close family relationships, deliberately creates a situation in which working mothers are forced to place thousands and thousands of children in unsupervised arrangements.[22]

Through their lack of support for day care for working mothers and their reluctance to support expanded day care services, child welfare professionals were driving mothers to some of the worst kinds of child care arrangements; their policies did not prevent mother-child separation and the arrangements the mothers had to make were usually worse and more "deprived" than the care a child could receive in a good center or a properly supervised day care home.

Another article in the same issue took up the totally taboo subject of day care for infants and very young children. Bettye Caldwell and Julius B. Richmond described an experimental project, just then beginning, that would test the effect of day care on young children from 6 to 36 months. Although recognizing that many states prohibited day care for children under 3, they cited as a rationale for their break with this prohibition against day care for infants several strong arguments:

1. The increase in privately initiated substitute child care arrangements; 2. Increased number of studies failing to show deleterious consequences of short-term intermittent maternal separation; and 3. The influence of the first three years of life on subsequent cognitive, social, and emotional functioning.[23]

The paper went on to describe a new program being set up at the State University of New York in Syracuse, whose purpose was

the development of a day care program for children three years of age and under to foster their subsequent educability. In order to accomplish this aim, an attempt will be made to program an environment which will foster healthy social and emotional development as well as provide stimulation for cognitive growth during a developmental period that is critical for its priming. The program is based on the proposition that, while environmental supplements for deprived children may be beneficial at any age, sensitivity to enrichment declines with age. Thus the program is geared to the very young and is designed to provide whatever environmental supplements are needed to decrease the subsequent visibility of underprivileged children—to forestall the verbal and motivational deficit which can be observed on the first day of formal schooling and which all too frequently remains like a symbolic scarlet letter about their necks until the frequently premature termination of their school careers.[24]

The project seemed to hold a traditional view of day care in that it was directed toward a population of high-risk children—those who in the child welfare context were considered potentially problem children from problem families—and yet in many ways it marked a radical break with that view. The project proposed that very young children could benefit from an environment especially prepared to meet their developmental needs and, beyond that, that their educability, even at a very young age, was of concern to a day care center.

The Syracuse infant center was funded by a grant from the Children's Bureau, which reflected an interest on the part of the government, at least, in investigating whether day care could be an adequate substitute or supplement to mother and home. But if the Children's Bureau was primarily interested in developing a model for optimal conditions in day care, other government departments, particularly the Labor Department, were looking to day care as a means for enabling and encouraging welfare mothers to seek training and jobs.

In May, 1965, the Children's Bureau held a National Conference on Day Care Services in which a variety of speakers from labor, business, and educational organizations took a positive look at what day care might do for children. Perhaps the most important aspect of the conference was the address by Mary Dublin Keyserling, the director of the Women's Bureau, on "The Nation's Working Mothers and the Need for Day Care," in which she called for day care for every child who needs it. Although the speech linked this need to the inadequacy of most child care arrangements, it avoided the pathological definition usually attached to the use of day care, finding that not only the individual child and mother but society in general suffered the consequences of the minimal services then available.

> Society, no less than the individual, pays a terrible price for the lifetime blight which follows all too often from inadequate child care. And because we believe so strongly that a fair start in life is the birthright of every American, we are resolved to face up more realistically than ever before to the hard and inescapable fact that, as a nation, we are not fulfilling this essential promise of our democracy for all too many of our nation's children.[25]

Throughout the speeches from notables such as Hubert Humphrey, then Vice-President, Francis Keppel, Commissioner of Education, and Julius B. Richmond, program director of Project Head Start, there ran a common theme, which looked upon the working mother not as an abnormality but as a fact of economic life; her needs and her children's needs had to be met through some expanded system of day care. Not only was day care not seen as a service for the pathological but many even argued that it could become the first educational resource to meet the challenge which the country seemed to embrace in 1965—making education a source for equal opportunity.[26]

Two years later, the Children's Bureau and Women's Bureau jointly sponsored "A Consultation on Working Women and Day Care Needs," in which the needs of working mothers for good day care were once again underlined. In fact, the consultation elicited something of a public confession for past dereliction on the part of the Children's Bureau. In her remarks, Katherine Oettinger, then chief of the Bureau, said,

> For too long, we and the child care specialists held the view that mothers of children under 3 should not work; that if they did work, it was a deprivation to the child because of the separation of mother and child at a critical life stage. The Children's Bureau must share part of the blame for the failure to look at reality in today's day care picture, when thousands of infants and young children are being placed in haphazard situations because their mothers are working.[27]

A comprehensive survey published the following year, "Child Care Arrangements of Working Mothers in the United States," provided an exclamation point to the new view obtaining among government bureaucrats concerning day care: Day care for the children of working mothers was woefully inadequate.[28]

But changes in policy at the top level did not necessarily produce results at operating levels. In addition, the proliferation of other government programs for children, such as Head Start and the Office of Child Development, while focusing attention on a variety of needs, did not serve to bring about a uniform and consistent government policy concerning day care.[29] Differences in viewpoint between the Department of Labor and the Department of Health, Education and Welfare, regarding the use of day care as a means of enhancing the employability of welfare mothers or instead as a child-centered, educationally oriented service, were also reflected among most Congressmen, who in the next several years debated the merits and drawbacks of various systems and kinds of day care.[30]

In spite of this considerable amount of philosophical and policy confusion within the government and Congress concerning day care, Congress did, in 1967, amend the Social Security Act to provide funds for day care. Federal funds granted to states on a three-to-one matching basis under Title IV-A and IV-B became the primary source for day care funds. In fiscal year 1971 they were estimated to amount to $301 million dollars, with states and local governments contributing about $145 million.[31] These funds were intended primarily to meet the needs of mothers receiving Aid for Dependent Children, past or potential welfare families, or women in work-training programs; they were open-ended and did not require further Congressional appropriation; and they were limited only by the ability of state and local governments or private sources like United Fund to meet 25 percent of the funding. The revenue-sharing act of 1972 carried with it an amendment limiting the amount of Title IV-A and IV-B funds any one state could receive. This ceiling on funds hit particularly hard in states like California and New York with large day care systems and whose budgets far exceeded the new limitations. In theory, revenue-sharing funds could be used, if the states so decided, to make up the gap in funding, although day care now had to compete for these funds with a wide range of other services, such as police and fire protection.

The changes we have traced in government and child welfare attitudes toward day care did not occur in a vacuum. At the same time larger questions were being posed about the best means for implementing social change, ensuring equal opportunities, and encouraging population limitation. The sixties were years of rapid change, and some of these broader movements only touched upon the day care movement indirectly. Among these, the use of education to promote racial equality and integration, and the discovery of effective contraceptive techniques that allowed many families to space and limit their children, helped to change attitudes and perceptions about the good life for children and mothers. For many people who had to deal with the consequences of these changes in the formulation of social policies, day care came to be one of a number of respectable alternatives to the exclusive and isolated rearing of children in their own homes. Among the more direct influences on the growing consciousness of day care needs and possibilities were new theories about the education of young children, the establishment of Head Start centers, the growth of nursery schools, and the Women's Liberation movement.

The education of young children is a phenomenon certain to have an explosive impact on the future of American society. Yet traveling as it does in the guise of childlike interests and concerns, it manages to dissimulate its considerable import. Even so, it has attracted a considerable amount of attention, even notoriety, because of Head Start, the striking growth of nursery schools, and a wealth of new information on how children learn.

The renewed interest in the education of young children is part of the criticism and reform of American education that began when the first Sputnik was launched in 1957. The fear of "falling behind" the Russians created a new atmosphere which welcomed and embraced new educational methods, philosophies, and insights. It would have been, indeed, surprising if this revolution in education had not begun to stir those concerned with young children. In particular, concern about the "culturally disadvantaged," or the slow learner, or whatever euphemism is used to describe the child who does not "fit" in school, has sparked research and teaching efforts that have benefited a wide range of children, including the very brightest ones. And it is no exaggeration to say that the whole attitude toward day care has been revolutionized by the fact that the years from infancy to five are now known to be crucially important in a child's cognitive development, as well as its emotional and social development.

Today, this understanding about children seems commonplace; one may trace the interest in young children back over several centuries to educators and philosophers such as Comenius, Locke, Rousseau, Itard, Pestalozzi, Froebel, and Montessori, but the focus on early cognitive development in the past decade has raised our level of consciousness about the capacities, the intelligence, and the potential of young children.

Of all the findings of early-learning specialists, perhaps the most important for the purposes of preschool education were: 1) the intelligence level is not fixed at birth; and 2) a child's development is not predetermined. In a brilliant exposition of "The Psychological Basis for Using Pre-School Enrichment as an Antidote for Cultural Deprivation," J. McVicker Hunt looks back over half a century of child study and research and examines the effects that the opposite of those two propositions has had.[32] If the intelligence and developmental level is predetermined and fixed, then the quality of a child's environment, or intervention in the case of a retarded or slow child, is of little use in mediating the quality of his inherited potential. If, however, a child's environment does have an effect on the development of cognitive, emotional, and social patterns, then one may reasonably argue that intelligence and development are considerably more flexible than many psychologists and educators previously thought.

Prior to the work of John Bowlby, which showed the deleterious effects on intelligence and development of mother-infant separation, there were several interesting but highly criticized studies of orphaned children which showed that the level of a child's IQ was correlated with the quality of his environment, particularly the attention it received from a mother-substitute. The most famous of these was a study undertaken by Harold Skeels in 1938 in which a group of orphaned babies were placed in the care of institutionalized feeble-minded adolescent girls.[33] Compared to a group of peers who remained in the unstimulating environment of the orphanage, those children who were cared for and loved by the asylum inmates developed normally. The work of Skeels, Dennis, and, finally, of Bowlby convincingly showed that gross deprivation did indeed affect the intelligence and developmental level of children. In an unreceptive and unstimulating environment no child would follow a normal pattern of development or reach a predetermined level of intelligence. In his argument, then, Hunt managed to show the similarities between what Bowlby had described as infant deprivation and the cultural deprivation of children who though not separated from their mothers did not show normal patterns of development. Hunt went on to suggest then that it should be possible to correct these deficiencies by providing cognitive stimulation in an educational setting like a day care center or nursery school.

In terms of the nascent preschool movement, Hunt's argument effectively broke the connection between maternal separation and consequent deprivation. It was now possible for educators and psychologists to argue that temporary daily separation from an unstimulating environment and inadequate parents rather than traumatizing children might actually benefit them. These perceptions opened a floodgate of research experiments, and early educational projects like Head Start. Even though these endeavors were at first addressed to the needs of the culturally deprived and the poor, it did not take long for them to be extended to all children, regardless of their state of culture privilege or deprivation. In this as in many other areas of innovation, the poor acted as guinea pigs for a fortunately successful program.

We shall look now briefly at some of the more general programs that the findings of Hunt, Bruner, and Piaget inspired, noting how they too influenced a variety of opinions about day care.

Head Start, although it ultimately evolved into a full-day, year-round program, began as a summer program specifically geared to offering children a preschool experience. Its primary focus was the children of the poor, and it has always been considered one of the more successful programs in the War on Poverty. Its merits and demerits have been argued over extensively, particularly the long-term educational benefits to children who participated in Head Start activities. It is probably an argument that will never be settled. What is more certain is that Head Start rekindled government interest in financing preschool education; it directly connected child care with educational rather than custodial activities; it popularized the notion that early childhood education was appropriate for all children; and it helped turn the climate of opinion about proper care for young children.

The need for a "head start" was based on the premise that given a pre-kindergarten or pre-first grade experience in a school setting, children from "culturally deprived" homes could break the syndrome of school failure and future poverty. As we now know the problem was vastly more complicated, involving the cultural narrowness of many schools and teachers just as much as the cultural deprivation of the students. Furthermore, child development research, as it began to uncover the patterns of cognitive, emotional, and social development, pointed to the fact that by the time many children—at the age of 4 or 5—reached Head Start programs, most of their potential had been dissipated in unstimulating home environments. The effect of Head Start was indeed to help some children make a better adjustment to school, but for others it pointed up the need for even earlier and more prolonged educational experiences. Thus Head Start served to minimize the fears about mother-child separation, while maximizing the realization that equal educational opportunity might depend on extensive preschooling.

Although many Head Start centers were criticized for being

nothing more than babysitting, or for having inappropriate educational activities for young children, their ultimate contribution to day care was to underline the need for education in programs for young children. The more traditional medical, nutritional, and social development programs in many day care centers were seen then to be somewhat inadequate, and simple custodial day care was seen to be totally useless in terms of child development. Head Start helped to raise standards and expectations not only among professionals, teachers, social workers, etcetera, but also among parents of participating children.

There was, paralleling this movement for preschool education of lower-income children, a growth in the number of what had been traditionally called nursery schools, but which were turning in fact into preschools, catering to the children of the middle class. In 1965 there were approximately 890,000 3- and 4-year-olds enrolled in preschools; in 1970 the figures increased to 1,150,000 children.[34] While nursery schools had been immensely popular in the twenties, and were often connected with university research and teacher-training programs, they had declined in influence and importance, as we have seen, for the same reasons that day care services had declined in the inter-war years.

Furthermore, the Freudian emphasis on psychosexual development as the chief concern of the early childhood years had eclipsed the equally important cognitive development of young children. Where nursery schools continued to exist, their emphasis was almost exclusively on social and emotional development. Bettye Caldwell, in recalling the atmosphere at that time in early childhood education, has written, "It is not unfair to imply that during the late 1950's and early 1960's a sure path to ostracism . . . was to emphasize attendance at nursery school as an influence on intellectual development. . . ."[35] This attitude changed markedly during the course of the sixties; private preschools were, as much as Head Start, the beneficiaries of new theories about child development, and the success of Head Start fed the great interest middle-class parents had for providing for their children's future educational accomplishments.

As the movement for early childhood education has given day care a previously unknown respectability, justification, and purpose, the Women's Liberation movement has put day care on the political map. What was once a marginal social service of interest to no one but social workers has become a key item in the Movement's program for complete social and economic equality. As we have seen, there is considerable variation in the kinds of day care and the conditions under which differing groups within the women's movement will support day care; these differences should not overshadow the fact that the women's movement has succeeded in changing the opinion of many middle-class women about the rights and supports a working mother should have in order to be a successful mother and worker.

Women's Liberation is largely a middle-class movement, whose aspirations for working women tend to be career-oriented rather than job-oriented. The problems faced by a mother pursuing a career are not exactly the same as those faced by a mother holding a job, but in many ways their child care needs have gone equally unmet.[36] The middle-class family and middle-class mother have set the norm for "family" behavior; as long as these women remained home to care for their children, particularly preschool children, the question of day care for the children of working mothers posed no particular question to the body politic. But as more middle-class women have finished college and gone on to graduate or professional schools, their career aspirations and the nation's womanpower needs have highlighted the total inadequacy of child care in this country.[37] It is true that educated middle-class women have always worked, but more and more they seem willing to abandon their former pattern of waiting until their youngest child reaches school age, or tailoring their work hours to their children's school hours. Women who aspire to be taken seriously in the professions now recognize that a five- to ten-year hiatus dedicated exclusively to child-rearing is often fatal for a career in medicine, law, teaching, or business. They also recognize that the usual alternative of housekeeper or babysitter does not meet their standards for adequate child-rearing. The Women's Liberation movement has helped to fuse their needs with those of mothers who have always worked.

Among feminists the lack of adequate alternative child-rearing systems has been considered one of the surest barriers to women pursuing training for professional careers, and, if they have the training, of pursuing those careers. Among the demands around which the women's movement originally gathered, day care, free and universally available, was seen as a key element in allowing women to pursue careers on an equal basis with men. The women's movement served to unite the long-standing needs of working mothers who, in the late forties, the fifties, and sixties worked because of economic need, with the more recent movement of middle- and upper-class women away from total involvement in child-rearing and toward the pursuit of employment and careers for reasons of self-fulfillment. In essence, then, day care for both groups of women represents the means for their dedication to work and career being taken seriously.

It remains to be seen whether this coalition will maintain itself when the economic and social policy conflicts inherent in the demands for free and universally available day care for all working mothers become apparent. For the moment it is clear that the women's movement has been crucial in changing attitudes about day care and laying to rest the orthodoxy of a mother beside every potty.

At the beginning of the seventies a rather formidable coalition of groups was prepared to do battle for the expansion of day care services. A variety of Congressional hearings and a plethora of bills designed to bring more money and higher quality into day care centers were a response to this pressure.

Before looking at the political legislation and debate which grew out of these new attitudes toward women, children, and day care, we ought to look in a concrete fashion at how day care works, what day care looks like, and what it means for the people who use it.

11

Day Care Observed

Despite a good deal of discussion about the pros and cons of day care, about its past and future, on its problems and possibilities, very few people have ever visited a day care center or looked at a family day care home. It is undoubtedly a sign of day care's rising status that politicians are as likely now to be photographed for campaign purposes visiting a day care center as leaning over a baby carriage to plant a kiss on some innocent forehead—and yet the image of those photographs, of several teachers (usually women) doing something with lots of children confirms the vague idea that most people have about day care. I intend, in the following three chapters, to supply the materials that will give the reader a better idea of what day care looks like and how it operates. Hopefully these descriptions will suggest that day care is a good deal more complicated and precise an operation than we would guess from grainy newspaper photographs.

There is not a wealth of written descriptive materials about day care; there is some. The Abt Associates' in-depth study of thirteen centers, Mary Dublin Keyserling's survey of hundreds of centers and homes in *Windows on Day Care*, and Elizabeth Prescott's description of typical California centers in *The Politics of Day Care* are useful sources against which I checked and tested my own observations. While gathering material for this book I visited about thirty-five centers and ten to fifteen family day care homes in different parts of the country. In most cases I went as a journalist writing about day care centers; in some cases I casually "dropped in" and introduced myself as a parent and potential user of the center; in another case I accompanied a licensing official on his rounds. These visits were informative and useful, and form the core of my observations and descriptions in the following chapters.

Although I am not a professional educator or child psychologist, I had read a good deal and visited enough schools for young children to have a strong sense of what to look for in these visits: most importantly, what adults and children did together, and then, what kinds of activities, equipment, planning, and attitudes characterized the center or family day care home. Since my intent has been to describe what is, rather than what ought to be, I have tried to avoid labeling and judging with a predetermined set of criteria. At the same time, where I felt it was helpful to inject an opinion or note a contradiction or controversy, I have done so.

Day care services can be categorized in a number of ways: by the services they offer (custodial, educational, developmental); by how they are financed (parent fees, on a sliding scale with government and private funds supplementing parent fees, unions, industries, or voluntary groups); by what age groups they serve (infants, preschoolers, school-aged); by their location (home or center); by the population they serve (black, white, Hispanic/poor or middle-income). Since no one category is all-inclusive, I have used the broadest categories first, hence my first division into for-profit and not-for-profit day care centers. Under each of these broader categories there are divisions into special kinds of day care, such as the franchised center, the union-sponsored center, family day care, and infant day care, among others. As one might expect with any service like day care that has been erratically financed and poorly supported, a great variety of quality exists, ranging from excellent to inadequate. I have tried to describe this variety in some detail to let the reader see the rather intricate working of many factors that makes day care the complicated and mixed-bag of reality that it is.

CHAPTER 4

HOW DAY CARE WORKS: SPACE,

STAFFING, PROGRAMMING,

ADMINISTRATION, LICENSING,

UNIONIZATION, AND CONTROL

According to most licensing codes, an effective day care center must meet the physical needs of children for adequate space, outdoor activities, and good food; the psychological needs of children for affection, acceptance, and consistent adult behavior; the intellectual needs of children for stimulating and absorbing play, for activities that enlarge their imaginations and activate their curiosity. All of this will depend on having an administrative structure and, in particular, a director who can maintain the balance among all these elements by training, observing, evaluating, and supporting the staff, and by understanding and meeting parental desires for child care that is more or less consistent with their general attitudes on child-rearing. Few centers I visited achieved this perfect balance, and more than once I was aware that a significant lack in one area—space, staff, curriculum, administration—affected the whole program. Let us look now at how these items actually, rather than theoretically, work out in day care centers.

SPACE WITH ROOM TO GROW

As more and more children come to be cared for in groups, casual and hasty planning, even though well-intentioned, must be unacceptable. As more centers are built or established in renovated or remodeled buildings, architects, designers, and day care planners should begin to accumulate information and experience on how to create effective spaces for young children.[1]

Finding adequate space is the most immediate and difficult task of anyone starting a day care center. Funds for construction are extremely limited, almost nonexistent; in some areas funds for renovation are more readily available.[2] Hence adaptation of existing structures is the primary means of acquiring day care space. Not surprisingly this space is often marginal, unused and unsuitable for more remunerative commercial purposes. This sort of property—basements, empty stores, unused apartments—often fails to meet, or barely meets, licensing requirements, and as a consequence many groups must depend on established institutions like schools, churches, Y's, to allot or share a portion of their facilities for day care use.

State licensing laws list spaces considered unsuitable for day care use; these include floors above the first in non-fireproof buildings, commercial buildings without a private entrance for the day care center, basements below ground level. Usually the most precise and important regulation concerning space is the minimum square footage per child, a critical figure, since enrollment of a center is keyed to the amount of indoor space actually available for classroom use. In most states this figure is thirty-five square feet per child.[3] A center for fifty children would require 1750 square feet, with additional space for kitchen, bathroom, and offices. In addition, most states prescribe one hundred square feet of outdoor space per child; in actual practice, the outdoor space may vary considerably, especially in dense, urban areas. The square footage can include nearby public parks or playgrounds, and the figure can be and often is interpreted to mean one hundred square feet, not for the total enrollment, but for smaller groups at different times. But it is the nature and quality of the space rather than its dimension, both indoor and outdoor, that establish the character of a center.

Few city centers have immediately adjoining outdoor space of sufficient area to meet code requirements; therefore, space requirements must be met by nearby parks or playgrounds. Sometimes this is a convenient and workable arrangement; at other times, it is not. Day care planners, directors, and parents, eager to open a center, can make an unrealistic assessment of the availability and usability of these play areas. In one large city center I visited, the planners had counted on the housing project playgrounds to provide the children with sufficient space and equipment for outdoor recreation. After the center opened, it was immediately apparent that the playgrounds, dominated by older, elementary school and high school children, were neither safe nor enjoyable for the younger children to play in. The center, housed on the ground floor of the project, was surrounded by vast, well-kept lawns dotted with prominent "No Trespassing" signs. The day care director would have liked to use them, but these lawns were jealously guarded by the maintenance crews, who had a running war with her, not because they believed the small children would spoil the lawns, but because they were afraid that one exception to the general rule forbidding walking or playing in the grass would mean the end of compliance by all project residents. In short, there was no outdoor play space. Perhaps a petty and inconsequential miscalculation on the part of the planners, but a telling one for the program. There were almost one hundred children using the center; although divided into smaller groups of thirty, they needed the outdoor space both to run off excess energy and to give teachers a much needed relief from the high-density noise and activities within the center. As it was, the center could count on using the playgrounds only when they were empty—on rainy and cold days. Otherwise, outdoor activities were limited to walks through the project on the asphalt pathways, or quiet play on the grass on days when the maintenance crews were busy elsewhere. With additional funds and some flexibility from the project management, the center might have enclosed its own outdoor space, making it accessible only from within the center. This was not likely to happen. Should this center have been denied a license because it did not have good outdoor space? Certainly not, for in other respects it had organized an excellent program which had compensated for the limitations of the outdoor space.

Although indoor space requirements are more rigorously enforced than outdoor space requirements, indoor space, too, is often inadequate and poorly planned for the needs of young children. While scrupulous attention is generally paid to meeting the law and granting each child his allotted thirty-five square feet, attention to detail commonly stops there. Is the space noisy or quiet? Does it invite attention to individual and group activities or does it encourage haphazard, discordant, and disruptive behavior? Is it friendly or hostile? Do children feel comfortable in it or anxious and disoriented? While architects and interior designers have demonstrated that almost anything can be done with any kind of space, these lessons are too infrequently put to good use in day care centers.

In my observation of day care centers, probably the most blatant offenders in this regard are churches, whose generous inclination to provide space often results in hasty, temporary, and part-time adaptation of a church meeting hall or auditorium. These areas are often large enough to contain an enrollment of fifty, or even one hundred children, but they are extremely difficult to arrange so as to give some spatial limits and coherence to smaller groups. Usually no attempt is made to permanently divide the space at all, since on weekends the hall must be available for church-related events. Hence, easily movable tables or coat cupboards are strategically placed to provide temporary boundaries for each group of children. These arrangements can often be effective and pleasing to the eye. But sometimes they are not. The noise level is usually high and intense, wearing on the nerves of both teachers and children. As well there seems to be a natural tendency of small children to look upon physical barriers such as bookshelves, tables, and coat cupboards as challenges rather than limitations. The phenomenon of the wandering border is frequently observed in such day care centers.

Despite the obvious difficulties these arrangements created for the teachers whose classes I observed, they frequently justified them with passing references to "open classrooms," "unstructured space," and "free schools." There was, in fact, usually little evidence that these were the planned and ordered environments which are an integral part of "open education," nor did their programs suggest a curriculum attuned to learning through the environment. These teachers were using the rumor of new learning theories to rationalize the poor use and planning of space.

Yet expensive and extensive renovations are not always necessary to correct the deficiencies of spatial arrangements. Smaller centers with limited enrollments are more fortunate. Fewer children make less noise, so that small centers can live more easily with the typical concrete block and tile floor construction. Fewer children also create less wear and tear on temporary dividers and boundaries.

One such neighborhood center that I have visited had managed successfully to overcome these kinds of problems. The center was located in a renovated factory building with windows set in on only one side of the room. The day care code required that all class areas receive natural light, therefore no permanent barrier could be placed to divide the space. With the ever-present coat cupboards, tables, bookshelves, and a movable blackboard, the director managed to create two distinct areas for thirty children. Each group had a precisely defined and specially organized area that minimized the disadvantage of one large room, and the relatively small enrollment did not create undue expansionary drives. An immediately adjacent lot, though small and narrow, had been turned into an imaginative and stimulating play area that compensated for the drawbacks of the inside space.

Another center, newly and permanently established within several vacant rooms of a middle-income housing project, with sufficient indoor and outdoor space for an enrollment of one hundred children, had an extremely difficult space problem. Its space was, in fact, better suited to house a cathedral than a day care center. The building was made of poured concrete, which reflected rather than absorbed noise. The center was located on the ground floor of the project and had eighteen-foot ceilings, elegant for the lobby in the front of the building, disastrous for the day care center in the back. Furthermore, the space was long and narrow, with one room opening into another. To reach the furthermost room, children, parents, teachers, and visitors had to pass through all the other rooms. With a minimum of foresight, imagination, and knowledge about day care centers, the architect could have created a more livable and usable space. It did bring out, however, a certain creativity in the director and her staff; they had to devise ways to muffle a disastrous noise level as well as an echo; in addition to that, they had to organize the space to allow transit without disruption of the classes. The class-rooms were enclosed to some extent by use of coat cupboards arranged in a zig-zag pattern; this allowed passage through while discouraging foot races, a favorite diversion of children. Curtains on the windows had cut some of the noise. Carpeting on the floor might have helped but was forbidden by the health code; the director was thinking about putting it on the wall. She was also negotiating with the building management for some structural changes, such as a false ceiling, or acoustical devices to cut down the noise, but these were all expensive. The generous amount of out-door space was partially roofed over by the rest of the building, providing a large amount of rainy-day space. But the ubiquitous concrete and steel made falls and bumps painful. Pits and planters molded into the concrete would have provided areas for sand and water play, as well as tree-planting space for shade and greenery. Unfortunately no one thought ahead about small children who would be using the space.

Children need many kinds of spaces, large and small, open and sheltered, noisy and quiet, social and solitary—spaces that are not very adequately defined by thirty-five square feet. Providing those kinds of spaces ought to be one of the goals of planners and parents who create day care centers, but it is not merely talent for design that is needed but perception about the needs of children in order to meet them even when finances are limited.

STAFFING, OR WHO'S IN CHARGE HERE?

A moderate amount of material has been written about the kind of person who should work in a day care center, the kind of train-ing they should receive, the attitudes and values they may bring to the many different children they will care for. Can a black child from a low-income family find happiness with a white, slightly uptight, middle-class professional teacher? Can a fragile, soft-spoken, and dewy-eyed paraprofessional survive with honor the antics of an active, energetic, noisy 4-year-old boy? Do you *have* to eat cooked carrots when you'd rather have them raw? Faced with fifteen eager and willing children, day care workers are not likely to be meditating on class, cultural, racial, or religious values. Their thoughts probably only go as far as "what next?"

On a day-to-day basis the staffing problems of day care centers seem more mundane. One of the most obvious difficulties is consistent and stable staffing. Absenteeism may or may not be higher among day care workers than among other workers, although frequent contact with young children is known to produce a higher rate of illness among adults. But I rarely visited a center that did not have, or need, at the time of my visit, one or two substitutes working to replace an absent teacher or paraprofessional. Better-organized centers had a list of substitutes on whom they called, but frequently, even by ten or eleven o'clock in the morning, none had arrived. Sometimes the director stepped in, or a parent was temporarily available; more often one day care worker had to do the work of two. And if it was the teacher rather than an aide that was absent, there appeared to be a greater amount of disorganization and disorientation.

The most disastrous example of this problem was a church-run center in a large urban ghetto area. On the day of my visit, approximately twenty-five of the thirty enrolled children were present, plus one aide, the director, and a secretary frantically busy on the telephone looking for substitutes. The two regular teachers and another aide had called in sick at eight that morning. I was asked to leave, since the director felt that I would not get an accurate view of their program under those circumstances.

As day care services become more established and stabilized, a regular system of substitutes, easily and immediately available, somewhat like that in public schools, will have to be organized. Unlike the present system of substitutes in most public schools, and in the few day care centers that have developed such a system, the more experienced rather than the less experienced day care workers ought to be on the list. Presently many workers acquire the experience necessary for a full-time regular job by serving as substitutes. This system may have some merit in weeding out unsuitable people and in providing on-the-job training, but on days when their regular teachers are absent, children need experienced people to compensate for the disorganization and anxieties that are created with unfamiliar faces and different ways of doing things.

This situation was clearly evident in a small city center I visited early one September, which like the school year is often the beginning of the day care year. Thirty children were enrolled with a staff of three aides, one teacher, and a director-teacher. The teacher of the 3-year-olds and the aide for the 4-year-olds were absent. The aide for the 3-year-olds was new and had worked at the center only one week. When I arrived, the director was at her usual teaching task, supervising the 4-year-olds, who seemed happily and busily involved in a variety of activities. Many of the 3-year-olds were new, having been at the center only one or two weeks. They were unfamiliar with the center routine and, not unexpectedly for 3-year-olds, unaccustomed to operating in a group. Supervising these children were a substitute teacher, the new aide, and a third aide who spoke Spanish, for the benefit of the several Spanish-speaking children in the center.

The room was chaotic. The substitute teacher had decided to handle the children as a group, that is, everybody was to do everything together. It was obvious from the 4-year-olds' activities that the total program emphasized individual work and independent activities. Hence, the 3's were being required to behave in a way that, first, most of them were incapable of, and second, that was an unfair introduction to what would actually be expected of them in terms of the center program. Having fifteen 3-year-olds do everything together required, in a number of instances, not that they do everything together, but that they wait their turn in order to participate in the group activity. Wait to wash up. Wait for the teacher and aides to prepare the snack. Wait for everyone to finish the snack. Wait for everyone to go to the toilet. Wait for everyone to be quiet so they could go to the park. Patience is not a 3-year-old's virtue.

The children were unwilling and unable to tolerate the waiting. What they lacked in inner controls, the staff, more or less, tried to make up for with exterior controls—yelling, arm-pulling, shaking, and pushing. The center was a good one if one judged by the 4-year-olds. It was unfortunate, then, that the introduction to day care for the younger children should be so unnecessarily harsh and unreasonable. The Spanish-speaking aide, eventually and of necessity, illustrated what would have been a better strategy for the substitute teacher. She finally took the Spanish-speaking children apart, creating a small group within the group; in fifteen minutes this smaller group was busy and relatively content. If, in the first place, the fifteen children had been divided among the three adults into smaller groups, each child would have received more individual and positive attention. But the substitute teacher was inexperienced and chose the most obvious, strenuous and self-defeating form of behavior control for young children.

The problem was exacerbated by the fact, typical of small centers, that the director was also a teacher. She, too, was occupied and, therefore, not available to step in to give some direction and advice. The best she could do was to assign the Spanish-speaking aide to the 3-year-old group, with the hope that an extra adult would minimize the chaos.

If children need constancy and continuity in their care, they also need consistency. Even more than whether a program was "child-centered" or "adult-centered," it struck me that children seemed most content, relaxed, and purposeful when they knew what to expect from the adults around them. In this regard, perhaps the child-rearing advice meted out to parents by Dr. Spock is equally relevant to the day care center. It is not permissiveness or strictness that is so important to the child as its knowing what adults want and knowing what to expect from them.

In one center, occupying a newly constructed building, this consistency seemed to be practiced even though individual teachers enjoyed a great deal of autonomy in establishing the atmosphere of their rooms. The center's primary goal, aside from providing all-day care for the children, was to encourage and emphasize skills that would prepare children for first grade. The program emphasized reading readiness, language skills, number readiness, and good behavior, such as asking permission, sitting still, taking turns, sharing, etcetera. In adjoining classrooms there were teachers with two very different styles, but both seemingly successful at carrying out the center's overall goals. It was striking that although the classes were so different the children in each classroom knew what their teachers wanted and responded accordingly.

The first class was extremely traditional, with much of its activities adult-centered and adult-directed. The teacher read and acted out a story; the teacher sang and acted out a song. The children were asked to respond in various ways and did so with enthusiasm.

The toys and materials had to be gotten from the teacher. Although the toys were on open shelves where the children could see them, they had to ask if they could use them. While waiting for lunchtime the teacher read a story and quietly indicated to one or two children that it was their turn to go wash up for lunch; she would then send in two more when they were finished. The children responded to her directions immediately and willingly. In the second classroom the atmosphere was much looser, with the children generating many of their own activities. If a child wanted to look at a book or read a story, he took a book off the shelf, and if he could not read, he asked the teacher or an aide to help him. Sometimes three or four children gathered around the storyteller, with the children talking about the pictures and words. In another corner of the room, a few children and an aide had formed a conga line to go to the bathroom. As they danced and sang their way across the room they were joined by more children. Other children stayed with their activities: one group off in a corner playing with trucks and airplanes, another group fixing the chairs and tables for lunch.

Many people might feel strongly that one classroom was better than the other, or they would prefer one classroom over the other. It is true that each classroom represented different values in its child-adult relationships. In the first classroom the teacher was clearly in charge; in the second classroom there was an interplay between children and teacher that encouraged spontaneity and small group activities. In fact this room seemed to be a particular favorite of the maintenance men and cooks, who dropped in frequently during the morning to chat with the children. Even with their different ways of treating the children, it was clear that both sets of teachers and aides were carrying out the goals of the program. All the adults spoke clearly, quietly, and simply to the children so that they would learn to listen, learn to follow directions, and learn to speak in a way that others could understand them. The children, whether they asked for materials or helped themselves, knew how to use things carefully and where to return them when they were finished. They knew how to get along with one another. And, finally, it was clear to them what their teachers expected of them.

This contrasted sharply with two other centers I visited, each like one of these two classrooms. One was group-oriented and adult-centered, with a traditional nursery school curriculum: coloring, gluing, puzzles, etcetera. The other stressed individual and small group activities, was child-centered, and encouraged children to "do their own thing." They were both marred by poor communication and inappropriate adult behavior.

The traditional center was organized wholly on the basis of group activities. Except for nap time and going to the bathroom, there were few moments in the day when children had a quiet time to themselves. Even though physically present, the adults seemed distant and inaccessible to the children. This highly structured program, rather than giving the children a sense of regularity, order, and coherence, as it might have, created an unbridgeable gap between adults and children. Adult expectations were enshrined with a quality of mysteriousness and their persons with an air of aloofness. They were not affectionate, and their attitude was marked by a high degree of condescension toward the children. Nothing was expected of the children except silence and good behavior. The children reacted to directions like a troop of sheep; the adults like disinterested shepherds.

In the second center, the children were encouraged to develop their own activities in small groups. They were all 5 years old and capable of the independence expected of them. Their teacher, however, had an unnerving penchant for organizing group activity in order to improve upon whatever the children were doing. More than once, she destroyed the internal structure of these small group relationships, making strident points about better ways to pile blocks or organize the housekeeping corner. By the end of the morning, the children, instead of being satisfied by their activities, seemed a bundle of nerves from the continuing interruptions and the frustration of their desires to complete whatever they had begun.

In many ways the staff problems that one is able to observe in day care centers seem far removed from those that researchers tend to identify and emphasize. The day-to-day behavior and concerns of day care workers are often remote from larger questions of cultural values and class biases, their relationships with the children often warm and deeply personal compared to the abstract theorizing about appropriate behavior between day care workers and children. During the hearings on the Comprehensive Child Development Act, in fact, several groups questioned the relevance and practical uses of this kind of research. Evelyn Moore of the Black Child Development Institute not only criticized the failure to disseminate and apply research information but also the tendency of this research to label black children as inferior or deprived. In her testimony she said,

> I would like to establish the fact that the Black Child Development Institute supports the need for ongoing research that can be translated into programs which will foster optimum development of black children through the delivery of services. . . . Our thinking is based upon past traditional child development research models directed at black children. A lot of this research ends up being printed in journals and never gets to deliver any service. The results in many cases, we feel, have served to do nothing more than to solidify societal beliefs about the inferiority of black children. They have crippled and done irreparable harm to many black children and their families.[4]

At least in respect to the practical applications of research findings, this was the conclusion as well of Dr. Edith Grotberg. In a volume summing up research findings related to day care, she writes, "While we support research efforts in this country, we have not been too successful in coordinating research results with program activities. This fact is especially obvious in the early childhood field."[5]

It is unfortunate but probably true that little of early childhood research ever trickles down to the practitioner—the day care worker. For many of them, its conclusions would appear obvious or irrelevant. For the research problem is not simply that of broader publication but also the examination of the actual day care scene to identify along with day care workers those areas in which research studies are most needed and would prove most useful.

No one knows, yet, what makes a good day care center work; one knows a good day care center when one sees it. If in broad terms some of this research can suggest and indicate that one way of doing things may produce better results than another way, this information should be available not only to day care workers and administrators but parents too, who have few guides by which to judge the performance of their day care center. For example:

1. Elizabeth Prescott and her colleagues have found that small- to medium-size centers enrolling thirty to sixty children encourage a more affectionate relationship between staff and children, using encouragement rather than restraint as the primary means of discipline.[6]

2. Another study has shown that aggressive behavior on the part of teachers can result in more aggressive behavior on the part of children.[7]

3. A further one that: "Women are not likely to deliberately encourage masculine behavior in children unless they both understand the importance of doing so and are working in a program and curriculum which intentionally includes teaching of masculine activities and preferences."[8]

4. Children have different learning styles; teachers frequently assume that articulate children are better learners than quiet children.[9]

5. Teachers and parents may have different standards for good behavior. "Teachers had higher standards than parents for neatness, noise, care of property, and other behaviors in children that affect the smooth functioning of group conduct. On the other hand, teachers had more relaxed standards with regard to the use of bad words, masturbation, and proper sex role behavior."[10]

6. Day care programs may concentrate on one or two cognitive processes, like language and vocabulary, to the exclusion of others such as "perception, analysis of concepts, improving memory, evaluation, the generation and implementation of rules, building expectancy of success, or reducing fear of error."[11]

All of this research, more like it, and even other research contradicting it, has an important place in staff training and self-evaluation; it also has an important place in parent education and information services. Hopefully it will begin to move out of specialized journals into more popular media, rewritten in less technical language or recast in more accessible form for radio or television.

President Nixon, in his veto of the Comprehensive Child Development Act, suggested another aspect of the day care staffing problem when he wrote: "There has yet to be an adequate answer provided to the crucial question of who the qualified people are, and where they would come from, to staff the child development centers."[12] He is not the first or only one to raise the issue. Jule Sugarman, former head of the Office of Child Development, and organizer of the Children's Lobby, estimates that the number of professional day care workers entering the field yearly will have to increase by 300 percent, from five to nineteen thousand persons, in order to meet future day care needs; the number of paraprofessionals entering yearly will have to increase by 120 percent, from ten to twenty-two thousand persons.[13] Increasing the number of day care workers raises still other questions about staffing.

By what criteria and standards will day care staff be recruited and trained? How will day care staff be held responsible and accountable for their performance? Parents, after all, have to live with their failures and successes at child-rearing. The thorny debate over accountability in many public schools hints at an equally complex discussion in the case of day care workers. What kind of working conditions will attract and keep good workers and, at the same time, provide optimal conditions for good child care? Mothers do not complain, for no reason, that life with small children can be at times arduous, oppressive, and mind-shattering. Is anyone but a mother or father willing to put up with all that, as well as the joy, pleasure, and satisfactions that are part of life with small children?

As any visitor to a day care center soon realizes, it requires an enormously skilled, resourceful, sensitive person with great physical stamina and endurance to work effectively with young children. To be the supplementary parent of a 3-, 4-, or 5-year-old is no easy task. We might idealize the mother or father of pre-schoolers as all sweetness and light, tiptoeing among the tulips, but they would probably last longer if they were six-foot, two-hundred-pound former decathalon champions.

How should personnel be recruited and trained to work in day care centers? Should welfare recipients be made to work in them, as Senator Long, among others, has suggested? Will women and men willingly take up day care as a lifetime career? Will it be a dead-end job or a stepping-stone to other kinds of work? And after day care workers are recruited, how should they be trained? Professional training is no guarantee of competence in working with young children, but a strong "mothering ability" may be an equally dubious qualification. There is safety in regulations and the construction of a certification and standardization system. But as the teacher-training and licensing system in this country so well demonstrates, such a system inevitably locks out nonprofessionals who, through ability and experience, may be eminently qualified to work with young children, and safeguards some professionals who though educationally qualified are disasters in the classroom. In contrast to other institutions, day care must develop hiring, firing, pay and promotion policies of considerable flexibility, based largely on actual performance, even though such flexibility is not a policy that goes well with established work policies of tenure, seniority, and licensing.

Nor will working conditions appeal to the faint-hearted. Day care centers work a staggered shift to cover their ten- to twelve-hour schedule with most personnel working eight to ten hours a day, fifty weeks a year, with annual salaries ranging from $3,500 to $6,000. In comparison, most elementary school teachers work a seven- or eight-hour day, including prep periods and lunch hours, with a three-month vacation and salaries ranging from $7,000 upwards to $15,000. This contrast suggests that good day care personnel may be hard to attract and hold on to; that in order to secure them, conditions may have to be competitive with schools, a move which may indeed increase staff satisfaction without necessarily being good for children.

This in turn raises the complicated issue of unionization. With working conditions as stringent as these, who wouldn't need and appreciate a union? But a consciousness and sensitivity to the needs of children—what will be good for children—may not be amenable to definition by negotiating committees and collective bargaining. The younger the children, the more particularly this is true. Those who propose that infant day care is possible set up a number of provisions for staff responsibility which make it likely that the job will never be one in which hours, coffee breaks, time off, *even* the right to quit can easily be regulated.

It must be granted that unionization has been adaptable to areas which labor's critics had previously declared were "special" and unsuitable for organization. Still, it is not clear that the question of public service unionization, of teachers, civil servants, police forces, etcetera, and the connected issue of strikes have been satisfactorily resolved. What is more, unions, at least in this country and up to the present time, operate within what nineteenth-century political theorists termed the "cash nexus." Till this day, parenthood has not. How do you get paid professional, paraprofessional, and nonprofessional workers to act at least with the same sense of responsibility toward children that most parents do now, out of affection, duty, or fear?[14]

WHAT GOES ON:
DAILY SCHEDULE AND PROGRAM

Daily Schedule

The daily schedule is the structural framework within which a day care program is carried out. The long hours of most centers are dictated by the fact that they provide care for the children of working mothers and fathers. They open very early in the morning, usually between six and eight, which allows sufficient time for the children to be dropped off and the mother or father to reach her or his job. Centers remain open into the evening, often until six or seven, to give parents enough time to travel from their jobs to the center. Despite a day of ten or twelve hours, these schedules can still be inconvenient for many kinds of jobs—factory work or nursing— where shifts may start as early as six or seven in the morning.

The long day requires the day care center itself to operate on a shift basis, with one or two staff members arriving sufficiently early to greet the children, and another one or two remaining at the end of the day to say good-bye. Because the whole group arrives over a period of one or two hours, there is usually breakfast for those who need it and a period of free play until most of the children have arrived.

The mornings are the most active, planned, and structured time of the day, with the initial period of free play followed by the particular activities the teacher has planned: painting or a lesson in numbers or letters, an excursion or a show-and-tell time. The children then usually wash up, go to the toilet, have a snack of juice and crackers, and if the weather's good, play outside. After this there is often a period of structured play, with blocks or in a housekeeping corner, or with paper and drawing material or puzzles and games. By then the teacher will usually have called the roll, often an important group activity since the children will comment on who is, and is not, there. In one center, a teacher was introducing the alphabet to her 3- and 4-year-olds by having one of them call the roll. Since the children could not read, their recognition of the first letter in a name was the clue to the child. Recognizing the letter and calling out the name correctly was greeted with approval by the teacher and cheers by the other children.

As the end of the morning approaches, cleanup time begins: toys are replaced; paper, pencils, and crayons put away; blocks stacked on shelves; housekeeping corners straightened; dolls covered and put to sleep; tables washed; and chairs replaced. Often there are songs and storytelling. In many centers this is a teacher-directed activity, but in others the children suggest and lead the songs or recount a story of their own choosing. In one very lively center the children led the songs, and one little girl rendered a street version of "Hush Little Baby, Don't Say a Word" that her classmates relished, having heard it before themselves and recognizing its shock value for their teacher.

Lunch follows and, after that, rest and nap period. Children are generally required to remain in their cots even if they do not sleep. The quiet is a necessity for both teachers and children: the children to relax and calm down after an active morning; the teachers to relax and do some of the necessary planning and administrative chores. By two-thirty or three, naps are over, a small snack follows, and the children turn to a toned-down version of the morning, often including free play or a final trip outdoors. The activities end as the children are gradually picked up.

Program

The program is the sum of regular and recurring activities in a day care center, including everything from naps and mealtimes to excursions, equipment, educational materials, and the teacher's imagination. It is what happens to the children. The Child Welfare League of America's "Guide for Establishing and Operating Day Care Centers for Young Children" enumerates many of the activities that they think should take place daily:

> Contacts between parents and staff
> Health supervision

Physical care and protection of the child
Supervised play—indoors and out
Vigorous physical activity
Creative arts—drawing, painting, music, and plays
Social relationships
Routines—washing, eating, toileting, and sleeping or resting[15]

Many day care advocates would add specifically "education," even though many of the above have educational aspects. But naturally enough in the daily routine of a day care center it is not usually clear exactly how to label many kinds of activities.

Some day care centers consider developing good health habits of considerable importance and insist, for example, that the children brush their teeth after meals and snacks. Other centers think of preschool preparedness as their chief task and make considerable efforts to have children learn letters, numbers, and correct speech patterns and pronunciation. Other centers seem to emphasize the importance of group relations, encouraging the children to get along both with teachers and other children, to cooperate, and to behave properly.

Despite the fact that good health habits and health supervision have always been one of the paramount features of the day care scene (the bathing controversy in the early part of this century was part of that debate[16]), the fact remains that there is almost no medical or dental personnel available to most centers. Although centers are required to have on record yearly health reports and a record of inoculations for each child, regular in-center examinations or assistance with chronic or special problems are virtually unknown. Many directors with whom I spoke felt their centers would have benefited from affiliation with a child health clinic or having on staff medical personnel to deal with the children's health needs at the center. Long-term and nonemergency health problems, such as dental, hearing, or eye problems, often go untreated, and frequently parents have only limited resources to provide their children with good medical care. One director mentioned, in particular, a need for psychological counseling for some parents and children in her center, but she had no one to refer them to.

In this regard, as in other areas, the Amalgamated Clothing Workers Union Day Care Center excels. As part of its union benefits, all members of the ACWU receive free medical care; when the union opened a day care center for its members, this medical care was extended to all the children enrolled in the center.

> Each child is given an examination and inoculations, and a medical record is begun. A pediatrician has been retained, who visits the center three times a week. A pedodontist [children's dentist] examines each child's teeth and performs all necessary dental work, including fillings and extractions.
>
> Any serious problems are discussed with the parent and then referred to the health clinic for immediate attention. . . . Drugs, eyeglasses, and any corrective measures such as braces, orthopedic shoes, etcetera, are also taken care of.
>
> As a further supplement to the health program, a psychiatric-social worker spends one day per week at the center, and in instances of severe emotional disturbance children have been referred to other institutions, with union financing.[17]

Such an extensive program would not be economically feasible for most day care centers, but certainly some efforts need to be made to make available at each center routine medical checkups and inoculations, and to provide parents with diagnostic and referral services for more extensive problems. At one center I noticed a few children with speech impediments, mild and easily remedied. It is doubtful that the teachers were trained to notice them or prepared to suggest that parents seek professional advice about the problems.

Despite rather specific pedagogies available for curriculum planning in preschools, only two centers I visited had a precise system and theory around which they organized their programs: one was a Montessori day care center, the other the Syracuse Infant Center, which had developed its own curriculum based on the theories of Piaget. Most centers depend on a broad selection of toys and materials, teacher preferences, and the children's own tendencies and capabilities to form their daily round of activities. This eclecticism gives most centers a sense of uniqueness and a character of individuality which would not be found, for example, in most school classrooms. In terms of long-range planning and evaluation, it would seem to have certain drawbacks.

It is a rare center that I visited that knows exactly what its program goals are, how exactly to carry them out, and how to measure their effectiveness against the children's later development. On a month-to-month basis, a teacher may note how well or poorly a child is doing and respond to the child's level of development. This general sense of developmental level is what teachers or directors often refer to when discussing one or another child. It is, only on a slightly more sophisticated level, a version of the parental explanation for a child's behavior by saying, "it's the age," or "he's going through a phase." Most programming efforts I saw might be best described as fluid, with a tendency to flabbiness.

While my observations are not broad enough or long-term enough to say that this situation of variety, individuality, and, along with them, a certain lack of direction, is typical among great numbers of day care centers, it is, for the moment, true that there is no dominant or, according to the fears of some critics, totalitarian child-rearing ideology in control of day care, or likely to be in the near future. One would not, for example, find the homogeneity of Moscow and Leningrad in the day care centers of New York and Los Angeles.

In fact, American day care centers may suffer from the opposite problem—a lack of program direction. There is no one, or even two or three, theories at work in American day care centers. There may be, in many of them, no theories at all, but simply many ways of acting and organizing, with little attention given to pedagogies or theories. A serious and sustained attention to day care programming, particularly upgrading it, would, in fact, be beneficial.

These examples all indicate that a great variety of thought, equipment, planning, and imagination, both good and bad, goes into deciding on a day-to-day basis what happens to children in day care. Without sensitive and competent adults, suitable facilities, good and diverse types of play and learning equipment, and thoughtful curriculum planning, no center can be more than a babysitting or custodial service. If we agree that custodial care—simply looking after children—is not the kind of care our children deserve, and that quality care is what we want (a response clearly linked to how much money we are willing to spend), we still must ask, "What kind of quality?" As we have seen, "quality" covers a multitude of alternatives, including learning, psychological development, social adjustment, nutrition, and mental and physical health, which demand varying emphases, depending on the age, health, capabilities, and temperaments of the children, their family background, economic situation, and parental expectations. "A quality program!" Who could be against it? In a carefully thought-out and arduous process of learning, every day care center will have to create its own kind of quality.

ADMINISTRATION

The character and atmosphere of a center depend mostly on the director, who is responsible for both administrative and child care aspects. It is she or he who carries out the goals of the center, whether educational, social, or play-oriented; who must purchase supplies—food, cots, furniture, toys, art materials, rabbit food, etcetera; who must draw up a budget and follow it; who must hire, fire, and supervise teachers. In effect, the director usually has control over all day care operations. Sometimes these duties are shared with an assistant director, if the center is very large, or with members of a day care board. In a center that is parent-controlled, parents play a more active role. They often hire the director, help in selecting center personnel, and set forth the goals and policies of the center.

Although highly desirable, this parent involvement is rare, partly because centers formerly oriented to helping "problem families" did not see such parents as necessary participants in the work of the center. Many long-established centers have not moved toward bringing parents into its decision-making processes. More recently founded centers seem aware that parent involvement is part of the new rhetoric, if not part of actual operations.

One center, which had been started by parents and was still run entirely by them with the help of a director, shows how arduous and time-consuming parent participation can be. All parents had to attend a weekly meeting to discuss center operations, and each family volunteered a certain number of hours for work at the center, either helping to care for the children or working at some administrative or maintenance task. At another center, recently founded by a local welfare agency, the director discouraged the idea of parent involvement. She felt she spoke for the parents as well as herself when she said that the parents had neither the time nor interest to help at the center. It was not possible to consult the parents about whether this was true, or whether, as is more often the case, they simply were never asked. The director maintained that with jobs, household tasks, and shopping, the parents were too exhausted to do any more than drop off and pick up their children, and have an occasional meeting with their child's teacher.

The presence of parents in the activities of the center may seem a marginal point about administration. It is a presence that, in any case, many professionals and bureaucrats find more bothersome than helpful. Yet it is a crucial ingredient of any day care center or day care philosophy that pretends to be community-involved and concerned with supporting families rather than replacing them. The question of parental and community involvement is, in fact, the single most important, albeit acrimonious, discussion about day care. It asks, in effect, "Who will raise America's children?"

The day care center staff, itself, will have a great influence, and the director is crucially important in creating the center's attitude toward children and their families, but beyond that, bureaucracies and licensing codes will have important influences on the kind of centers there are, on how and to what extent they are funded, on how children are raised. If we insist, as I think we must, that parental and community influence predominate in day care centers, what are the possibilities that this can really happen? At the heart of the problem lies a tension between professionals who are trained to offer child-rearing skills and parents in need of such services. What manner of structures, regulations, and attitudes can be worked out so that having purchased those services and skills, parents do not find themselves without influence over what is happening to themselves and their children?

CONTROL

The solution does not rest solely with negotiating amicable relationships between those who need child care services and those professionals willing to give them, although such a relationship is important. The fact is that the real power lies elsewhere. To a great extent governmental bodies are setting down the conditions under which centers may be operated, and they are backing up their standards with funds. At a time of great scarcity the federal government and to a lesser extent local governmental bodies are able to wield considerable influence over all aspects of the day care question.

There are fewer than 700,000 day care slots for the six million preschoolers whose mothers work. The federal government has paid up to 75 percent of publicly supported day care costs; states and localities have shared the remaining costs. It follows that the federal government has taken the initiative in defining who may use the day care services supported by federal funds. Their priority goes to welfare mothers who are enrolled in work-training programs like WIN or welfare mothers who would be potentially employable if they were free of child care responsibilities to search for work. The remaining slots are then available to working mothers for a fee based on their family size and yearly income. The maximum yearly income for a family of six in New York State, for example, is $9,500 and the fee for one child would add up to $825 a year, or almost 9 percent of the family's income.[18] Many community and parent groups who favor broad-based day care services argue that such narrow eligibility creates day care segregated by race and class, which the government will use to force people off welfare. Furthermore, the fee schedules and upper-income limits penalize the ambitious and upwardly mobile among the working poor and low-income groups by charging them high fees or cutting them off entirely when their income reaches the maximum. Finally, these regulations foreclose any meaningful parent or community participation in setting admissions and eligibility standards. Nor does the problem of government funding and parent control end there.

The advent of more federal funds in the sixties created a mild boom in the ranks of the existent day care bureaucracy, made up largely of social workers, licensing officials, and inspectors, and, where their codes apply, fire, building, and health inspectors. The public demand for more day care and a more efficient system of licensing, added to the increase in federal spending, set state and local governments to organizing, reorganizing, and expanding their day care bureaucracies (which did not always result, as intended, in a more efficient system of licensing). Where a day care office might once have been a minor appendage to the Health or Welfare Department, or, even worse, scattered among a variety of agencies, there has been a consolidation in the creation of unified agencies to supervise day care services,[19] and intended to provide, although rarely doing so, "one-stop service." These super-agencies are intended not only to license but to assist and facilitate the establishment of new day care services. Such licensing and funding functions give them powerful tools over the success or failure of such attempts. As long as these agencies hold power over a resource where the demand far outstrips the supply, they appear to every petitioning group as a two-headed monster designed to impede the expansion of day care. And every petitioning group that demands more efficient service appears to day care bureaucrats to be calling for lower licensing standards.

The image of the two-headed monster has some basis in history. Until quite recently, the primary effect of licensing by the small day care bureaucracy that did exist was to restrict the amount of day care there was. Day care was considered by child welfare organizations as a minor child welfare service, available strictly to children whose mothers could not provide them with full-time proper care, whether for reasons of incompetence, sickness, or, in rare cases, work. And often this care was subsidized by a combination of charity and local government funds. Within these narrow limits, day care was regarded neither as a good in itself nor as a service to working mothers. From this basic social policy flowed the system of licensing and inspection, which, when it was effectively enforced, did raise the standards of care and programming. But because the overall social policy was so restrictive in the first place, it did so at the price of ignoring the fact that licensed and subsidized day care services did not begin to meet the real needs of many people for good child care, particularly working mothers. Their needs were partially met by substandard and often unlicensed commercial centers, but more frequently by neighbors, relatives, or leaving children alone. The cost for these services were unsubsidized and paid for wholly by the consumers. And for the most part people got what they paid for—babysitting.

Licensing officials and local day care offices find themselves, now, in the unenviable position of being responsible for the good, but all too few, centers that do exist, as well as for the bad, and all too many, centers that thrive because there is such a limited supply of subsidized day care. It is, of course, not entirely their responsibility. The supply of good day care remains limited by the amount of money available to subsidize quality care. Changing the social policy that limits the money is essentially a political problem to be solved by legislation, but it is the local day care offices who bear the brunt of complaints and demonstrations. For it is they and not the President or Congress who issue licenses and channel the funds.

Many groups eager to have day care in their neighborhood are often frustrated by the seemingly endless stream of red tape, rules and regulations, inspections and meetings necessary to begin operating a center. Fire inspectors, health inspectors, building inspectors, day care inspectors all troop onto the scene in a process that seems intended to prevent rather than assist the opening of a day care center. People eager for more day care centers argue that the whole licensing procedure ought to be streamlined and simplified so that community and parent groups, rather than lawyers, architects, contractors, landlords, and established organizations, could organize and operate a neighborhood center.

Simplifying legal codes and streamlining the inspections and administrative processes would benefit parent and community groups who want to start a center, but it would not solve all their problems. In some cases, the day care code is exceedingly complex, and without expert advice, including legal and architectural assistance, nobody could begin to understand and carry out what the law requires. The whole process can quickly discourage the nonprofessional. In other cases, licensing procedures themselves present no problem, since in some states and cities they are quite lenient and simple; it is funding and financing that cause difficulties. Money for day care is not easy to come by, and centers that intend to apply for federal funds must meet state and city regulations as well as federal regulations, measures that are often far more stringent than those of city or state. Finally, many other attempts flounder for reasons extraneous to day care licensing itself; zoning restrictions, health regulations, building and fire codes—all these limit and define where and how day care centers may function. Zoning laws that prohibit nonresidential use of land or buildings in a specified area apply, fairly or unfairly, to supermarkets as well as day care centers.

Parent groups or community associations who see children left alone or mothers unable to cope with children, job, and babysitting arrangements are understandably angry over the right of fire captains or health officials to decree, after a building inspection, that

"Parents United" cannot open a day care center in this basement or that abandoned supermarket. It may have insufficient natural light, or be below ground level, or not have a three-compartment sink, or be without a sprinkler system, but to the parents' eyes it appears the cleanest, soundest, safest structure in the neighborhood.

These complexities, anomalies, contradictions, and restrictions will be changed and the whole licensing process simplified and streamlined only when and if there is a change in attitude about day care itself. Without glossing over the legal and social complexities involved in the licensing procedures,[20] the fact that the philosophy underlying these regulations remains primarily child-welfare- and child-protective-oriented says much about the spirit in which licensing officials interpret codes and the consequent difficulties of overcoming their objections.

If every licensing official looks upon every potential day care operator or community group as a monster intent on corrupting or abusing the young, there is not much use in streamlining day care licensing. It is not only the law that is the stumbling block; it is also an attitude, and the conditions that reinforce this attitude. A change in social policy which regarded day care as a normal service available to everyone who needed it, and more importantly, provided the resources to make day care primarily developmental and educational rather than custodial, would probably result in more sympathetic and helpful attitudes.

Nor are groups who are eager to start centers very patient with the bureaucratic mind and attitude that sees day care as an undesirable development, but one, that if necessary, must often meet the standards of twenty and thirty years ago. On the other hand these same groups, in their eagerness for immediate results, often do not think of the long-term needs of a center, and factors such as space, environment, program, and staffing, which will give it stability and usefulness over a number of years. In the unbounded enthusiasm of first efforts, groups will start a center in a church hall or neighborhood storefront, living with the inconveniences because they believe what they are doing is better than what children now have. But the week-in and week-out effort of clearing the church hall for weekend use and then replacing everything for Monday morning, or the daily effort of walking a group of children, two, three, four, or five blocks several times a day to a playground, begins to take its toll of staff and children. What these groups need is some of the foresight and thoughtfulness that bureaucrats and inspectors provide. And what day care bureaucrats need is some of the enthusiasm and positive feelings about day care that people desperate for it so clearly demonstrate.

In all fairness, it should be noted that day care bureaucrats are becoming more concerned with the planned and orderly growth of day care services, although they remain on guard, sometimes over-zealously, against unhealthy environments and unsavory adults—even the children's parents. They are interested in using the funds they do have efficiently and according to regulations. In some areas of the country they remain suspicious of what they consider undesirable entrants into the field, like industrial and commercial interests (although the latter already provide more than 50 percent of the day care slots nationally). In other areas industrial and commercial interests are looked upon more favorably, particularly where they already offer a considerable portion of the day care services. And while day care officials are beginning to applaud the initiative of community groups in organizing day care centers, they remain fearful of any departure from accepted norms and traditions, whether it be in programming, admissions, or building design. Their motto is "safety first."

Parent and small or local community groups are not, however, the only groups interested in opening day care centers. Established organizations and institutions, such as churches, schools, Y's, youth centers, hospitals, and so on, have become, in recent years, interested in sponsoring and running centers, often because they perceive a need in their neighborhoods, and newly available funds make it financially possible to offer extra and unused space for day care services. This combination of altruism and financial self-interest is all to the good for making day care more available; it can, however, short-circuit real parental and community control of day care.

Yet is is precisely *local control* which is intended to restrain the heavy hand of the bureaucrat in the day care center as in the school. Almost imperceptibly, local licensing requirements, federal government eligibility and fee standards, and bureaucratic viewpoints have preempted what so many critics of public institutions like schools regard as basic to the creation of a good day care system: community and parent control within a decentralized system.

This regulatory imperialism appears all the more compelling because it seems so efficient, so logical, so much in the best interests of the children. Yet where community groups make the effort, day care can be diverted from turning into another failing public service institution. How local control can shake up the bureaucratic machinery has been demonstrated in New York City by the Committee for Community-Controlled Day Care. The Committee has pushed the city and state governments back on eligibility standards and fee scales, convincing them to go to battle with the federal government for new standards defined by geographic area rather than income. In several areas the Committee has acted as a counter-bureaucracy, forcing the city to revise or suspend certain licensing requirements, to fund interim or nonstandard centers; it has opened discussion on unionization and community control, and cosponsored, with the city, hearings on staffing qualifications.

The Committee's counterparts in Chicago—the Crisis Committee on Day Care, and the Action Committee for Day Care—are fighting a battle on two fronts. They are pushing a sluggish city government to begin to organize and budget for expanded day care services and a simplified licensing system; at the same time, they must prepare and argue about the role that communities and parents will play in a day care system that will be part of a highly centralized and controlled city government. The passing of time, the pressure of events, and internal frictions inevitably work against the small ad hoc groups who exert pressure for parent and community control. Nor does the volatile nature of grass-roots politics make it easy to organize parents and communities into a unified group who will argue effectively for their children's needs and for the parent's right to remain an important figure in the child-rearing process of the day care center.

Local control will not be easy to implement or maintain. But the question of control is not simply who will run the political boondoggle that is an inevitable part of the day care future, but who will raise the next generation of American children and how will they do it.

CHAPTER **5**

WHAT DAY CARE LOOKS LIKE

According to the Department of Health, Education and Welfare there were, in 1970, 16,600 licensed day care centers in the country, caring for 626,000 children. There were also about 41,000 licensed or approved family day care homes caring for 148,000 children. There are also unlicensed homes and centers of unknown numbers caring for more than one million other children. What do licensed day care centers and family day care homes look like?

COMMERCIAL CENTERS

Well over 50 percent of the care in licensed centers is provided by commercial or run-for-profit day care. They are small business enterprises owned and usually directed by the same person; the "profit" consists largely in the salary available to the director. In some areas of the country, these centers are commonly referred to as ma and pa centers, and are typically small family business enterprises run jointly by husband and wife.

Commercial centers have a reputation for offering only custodial care. Yet their very numbers suggest that whatever the quality of the care they offer, they are filling a real need. Before analyzing the advantages and disadvantages of day care organized on a profit basis, we might look at several examples of commercial centers, both the traditional, single-owner center and the newer variety, established on a franchise or chain-like basis.

The Happy Day Nursery School Center. Happy Day Center is located on a somewhat bleak commercial street on the edge of a residential area of family homes and small apartment buildings. The center is housed in three connecting stores; the display windows have been boarded up so that one cannot see in or out. The interior is lit by fluorescent fixtures, which give it a somewhat dim appearance. The entrance leads into a reception area where the director and a switchboard operator share a small office area. The director is a friendly and cheerful young woman of about twenty-five or twenty-six. I introduce myself as the parent of a 2½-year-old son, interested in placing him in a day care center. Correcting me, she refers to the center as a nursery school, even though it has a full-day program, and then seems somewhat surprised by my desire to see the rooms, toys, kitchen, and play area, although agreeably showing me around. The rooms are all large and high-ceilinged, and the fluorescent lighting suggests that it could be reconverted to a store simply by removing the school equipment. The furnishings—chairs, tables, cots, and cubbies—are all child-sized and rather attractive. The toys and equipment, which are numerous enough, are kept on shelves out of the children's reach.

In the first room a group of eight 2-year-olds is gathered around a table and the teacher is setting their places for lunch. In the second room, the largest in the center, there are thirty 3- and 4-year-olds with three teachers. Despite the numbers the room is relatively calm and quiet. All thirty children have just finished coloring a sheet of paper with a mimeographed picture; they then gather in a corner while one of the teachers reads a story; a second teacher is clearing the tables of papers and Crayolas, while the third brings plates, cups, napkins, and silverware on a rolling cart. She chooses two of the children to help her, and they quickly begin folding napkins and placing the silver around the table. In the third room, twenty-five kindergarten-age children sit around their teacher, who is reading a story; their lunch is waiting on a cart near their tables.

There is a play area adjacent to the center, equipped with traditional playground equipment. The area, however, is quite small and can probably only accommodate about fifteen children at a time.

The director refers to all the women as teachers, though she carefully points out that the kindergarten teacher is certified. All the other women are older and go about their job in a stolid, house-keeping fashion. Their common impression is expressed by the garment each of them wears—an apron that covers them from neck to knees. The order and quiet of the children really arises from a set schedule of activities that is carefully carried out by the women, who do not so much interact with the children as provide and remove materials. Since all activity is group, their work largely consists of counting out sheets of paper and passing them or assigning a child to do it; of placing writing or drawing materials on the table; of cleaning up and putting away. The director describes the children as well-behaved. There is almost no talking and almost no individual or spontaneous activity; with only a little word from the teacher, the children move from one group activity to another. Their behavior reflects what the director describes as the center's educational program. She sees the educational task as largely one of preparing the children for elementary school. For that reason it is important that they learn to adjust to being with other children and away from their mothers, that they learn to obey teachers, and that they learn to behave. She summed up Happy Day's educational philosophy by saying, "At Happy Day the children learn to take orders from strangers."

The critics of commercial centers would probably find Happy Day a good example of what they mean by minimal, custodial care, even though its programming and teacher/staff ratio meet the minimum standard of the licensing code in its area. Its physical facilities in several areas do not. There is almost no natural light, and the artificial lighting is insufficient; there is no natural ventilation, and the mechanical ventilation seems insufficient. From a child development point of view, Happy Day tends toward excessive regimentation of the 2-, 3-, and 4-year-olds, offers little individual attention to the children and its educational program is geared toward producing good behavior rather than cognitive development.

From a parent point of view, however, Happy Day could appear quite attractive. It is not cheap ($25 a week), but it probably is competitive with private babysitting arrangements in the neighborhood; it is flexible and convenient. There are no waiting lists for entrance. Fees are paid on a weekly basis; hence, a mother who finds herself temporarily unemployed can keep her child home without any obligation to pay a whole year's fee or lose the chance to re-enroll her child if she should find another job. Half-day arrangements can be made for mothers who work part-time. There is a bus service. There is a before- and after-school service for older children. And for mothers and fathers who work all day, the good behavior and docility that Happy Day seems able to produce may be a positive selling point, although they are probably mistaken in seeing such behavior as valuable for later educational achievement, which may depend on exactly the opposite values—curiosity, activity, and assertiveness. The teachers are not well trained but they appear competent and adhere to a common-sense approach to child-rearing—no frills, no theories, and no nonsense. None of this is very exciting, but in contrast to the Mother Goose Day Care Center it seems solid, stolid, and reliable.

The Mother Goose Day Care Center. Mother Goose is located on a busy street in the midst of a residential area. In one direction are one- and two-family homes in an established neighborhood; in the other lies an extensive area under renewal, with luxury high-rise apartments mixed with older but well-maintained apartment buildings. The center is housed in a new brick building that may have been intended for a small office building but has been adapted for the day care center. The entrance leads directly into the largest classroom area, where fourteen children of 2½ to 3 are playing. I have made an appointment to visit the center but I see no director or office, nor is there a teacher or adult with the group of children. After about five minutes a young woman appears who seems surprised to see me, even though the door is unlocked and anyone can walk in. She says that she is acting temporarily as director but she is also the teacher of these younger children and must stay with them. She cheerfully invites me to look around for myself, first giving me a brief description of the age groups in each of the three rooms.

The children in her own group are involved in free play, and most are sitting at tables with small blocks and toys. One boy is standing in a corner being punished, but he soon rejoins a small group playing with cars. She tells him he may not play with the cars, but as he continues paying no attention to her, she turns her attention to another group.

The next room, separated from the first by a movable room divider, is empty. The 3's and 4's in this class are out in an adjoining play area. The play area is well equipped, especially with climbing equipment that is set in a sandy area. Although the area has been well planned and appears attractive, the sand is quite dirty and littered with large pieces of soot and cigarette butts. There is no shade, and since it is an extremely hot day, many of the children are leaning against the cool bricks of the building, which itself casts a narrow strip of shade. The teacher finally calls all the children to stand in line; there are twenty-two children in this group. The teacher helps them to shake the sand out of their shoes, a process which takes about ten minutes. Although they are obviously uncomfortable from the heat, the children remain standing in line until all shoes have been put back on and tied or buckled. When they return to their classroom, it is time for coloring. The teacher quickly places plain white paper and crayons on each table and then sends two or three children off at a time to wash their hands. A record is playing, but the general noise level is so high that it is impossible to hear it. As well, the younger children on the other side of the wall divider (which is now closed) are singing, and the children sitting at the tables coloring must yell to be heard. The teacher in this class is quite young and energetic. She is pleasant to the children, but it is clear that she is overwhelmed by the numbers and maintains control only by keeping the children grouped and by immediately trying to suppress any disruptive behavior with a shout. The phone is in this room, and in the course of about fifteen minutes she is interrupted three times to answer it.

In the third room there are twenty children and one teacher. This group is intended for the 5-year-olds, but it is summer and the center has taken in some older children, ranging upward to about 9 years of age. It is clear that two or three of these older children have no significant activities to occupy them, and as a consequence they are disruptive and even unpleasant to some of the smaller children sitting at tables with building blocks and crayons. Their problem in finding something to do is also complicated by the fact that the teacher has organized most of the children into playing store, and consequently most of the toys and materials are gathered at the "store" where no one is allowed to touch them until the storekeeper is ready to open up and sell them. There is a massive buildup of children in front of the "merchandise counter" and naturally there is much pushing and arguing until the teacher shouts, "everyone in line," "Sally will be the saleslady," and "everyone will have a turn." Whatever the point in setting all this up for playing store—learning to count money, or to organize a real-life activity—the energies of the children are dissipated in arguing, waiting, and pushing, so that after a few turns of "buying" most of the store is in a shambles.

The teachers are all young and energetic at Mother Goose, and they do attempt to organize interesting activities for the children, but they are understaffed and overwhelmed. The center does not meet the code requirements for the number of adults per child. Whether teachers favor individual or group activities is not clear since the classes are always on the brink of chaos and disorder. Except for the ubiquitous paper and crayons, there is not enough equipment to go around. Since there is always a question of dividing up or only having a few pieces of any one structure such as building blocks, there seemed to be substratum of small arguments and snatching things from other children. There were also no "gross motor" toys like large trucks or wagons or tricycles, so that the more active children seemed to be reduced to wrestling or picking on other children.

From a child development point of view, Mother Goose appears worse than Happy Day. It is true the children are not excessively regimented; but they seem to receive no consistent direction or individual attention. Those children who do not participate in the current activity do what they please since disciplinary threats from the teacher are not carried out.

The physical appearance of the center and the adjoining play area are attractive. A parent might reasonably believe that his child would be in pleasant, safe surroundings. The teachers are young, energetic, and sympathetic. Yet the overall impression of the center is of chaos and disorder. While some thought has been given to setting up and planning the center and hiring personnel, there is inadequate upkeep and supervision. Mother Goose is an overpackaged Pandora's box.

From an economic point of view, commercial centers have a number of assets. They operate without cost to the taxpayer, often, in fact, using marginal property that might otherwise go unused, and hence they are tax-producing. They either operate at a sufficient profit or they go out of business and are, in this respect, unlike nonprofit centers, which often go on operating without peak enrollment. They must be conveniently located and offer necessary services or they will not attract sufficient customers. Hence they are flexible about full-time and part-time care, before- and after-school care, bus service, and the like. It is often argued that commercial centers are more susceptible to parent pressures, but it is more likely that a parent who does not like the center or wishes to change some policy or other really only has the recourse of removing the child.

The chief disadvantages of for-profit centers seem to be for the children. Although commercial centers are subject to the same licensing requirements as noncommercial centers, it is probable that they will meet only the minimum standards. Furthermore, codes and standards for programming and curriculum, those aspects of the center that most directly affect children, are hazy and unelaborated in most licensing laws. A license, which must be obtained before opening a center, is granted on the basis of the physical facilities and not on programming. License renewals, which might offer the opportunity for examining the program, that is, what happens to the children, are usually granted automatically, often without reinspection even of the physical facilities. The quality of child care in commercial centers is then totally dependent on the intelligence and goodwill of the staff, which, as we have seen in the case of Mother Goose, is undermined by the too-large number of children a teacher must look after.

Franchises

Franchised centers, a new variation on the commercial theme, hope to make the most of the economic advantages of commercial centers without the disadvantages of pinning their profit margins on the quality of the child care they provide. What franchise companies hope to do is develop a model center, working out standardization of methods and techniques for handling the physical necessities, carefully controlling their costs, and hiring qualified personnel to maintain a high quality of child care. The franchising consists in selling the package, much as restaurant franchises are sold, to an interested buyer, with the franchising company providing evaluation and pressures for quality control. The resemblance to restaurant franchises has led to their being labeled Kentucky Fried Children Centers, and a corresponding bad image and bad press.[1] The fact that a Green Bay Packers quarterback has bought a day care franchise instead of a restaurant franchise has, of course, not put worried minds to rest.[2] And yet almost nothing is known about how commercial centers organized on a franchise basis will work out. The prototypes for the franchise have naturally been model centers.

The Woodmont Center of American Child Centers, Inc. is a case in point.* The center is located in Nashville, Tennessee, in an area of middle- and upper-middle-class homes. The building in which the center is located was especially designed and constructed for American Child Centers, and is meant to be duplicated for other centers which it will franchise. Rather than self-contained rooms or classrooms, the center is constructed on the basis of an open floor plan.

The children are divided into groups on the basis of age; each age group has a "home base" area, but there are times of the day when the children are free to move into other areas. Although the children are divided into groups, their activities are not organized on a group basis. "Observers felt that the children were treated as individuals, and had almost unlimited opportunities for learning through individual and group interaction with peers and teachers. The atmosphere is loving. . . . Spontaneous play is respected, encouraged. . . . By encouraging independence in activities, there is time and staff for the individualized tender loving care that is so necessary in filling the lives of preschoolers, despite the large number of children in the program."[5]

"The corporation has used close contact with many academic institutions and consultants to develop an extensive and carefully planned curriculum which ties in closely and successfully with the center's physical plant. Emphasis is given to the child's emotional, social, and physical development, as opposed to social service to the community, services to parents, or simply custodial care."[6] Because it does not provide simply custodial care, the company insists on referring to the center as a "child development center" rather than a "day care center."[7] All observers agreed that, indeed, the quality of

---

* I did not visit this center; my information is drawn from the Abt Associates Report, *A Study in Child Care: 1970–1971*,[3] and "Schools for Early Childhood."[4]

care was very high. Even though, like Happy Day and Mother Goose, it must make a profit, the American Child Centers has shown that it is possible to provide quality care by keeping cost-control down to the penny. As the Abt observers point out, the computerized cost-account system allows a complete and instant inventory, up to and including "the number of leftover cookies at the end of each day."[8] The center also achieves significant savings while maintaining quality care by having two kinds of staff. A formal learning program is emphasized in the morning, while informal play is encouraged in the afternoon. Consequently, trained teachers work only in the morning, while the afternoon activities are supervised by the director with the help of aides.[9] Interestingly enough, the weekly fee for the Woodmont Center in November, 1970, was less than that of Happy Day and Mother Goose—$21.75 a week, with discounts if there is more than one child from the same family. While allowing for the higher labor costs of the Northern city in which the two commercial centers are located, it is interesting that A.C.C. has been able to provide apparently better care at lower prices. Whether this balance can be maintained as the corporation begins to sell franchises is unclear.[10]

Whether or not franchising becomes an important means of providing many communities with day care services, and indications are that with high capital outlay and moderate to high operating costs these communities will be largely middle and upper class, it is fairly certain that some form of franchising and proprietary day care is part of the day care future. The present dominance of commercial centers almost guarantees this. Furthermore, it is not likely that government funds for day care will become available in the communities where franchising is most likely to take hold. Finally, franchisers have shown a considerable amount of initiative in opening new areas for their day care services.

Some franchise companies have developed a delivery system in which their services are sold to companies interested in providing day care as an employee fringe benefit. These companies do not want to run the center themselves, and hire the franchisers to do it for them. Currently the Singer Learning Centers has contracted to run such an experimental program for Ohio Bell and Western Electric. Unlike many franchisers, Singer has committed itself to providing quality care and intends to maintain this quality by running all their centers themselves. Clearly the "for-profit" element in these arrangements cannot be measured simply on a profit-loss basis, since for companies like Ohio Bell and Western Electric the over-all cost to the company must be measured not only in terms of direct costs but of indirect returns in the form of lower employee turnover, higher productivity, and greater employee satisfaction. As these kinds of arrangements reach more and more sophisticated levels, the notion of profit may well shade off into considerations of social as well as monetary profit for the companies involved.[11]

None of these ethereal arrangements means that for-profit day care, whether in the form of owner-run commercial centers, franchises, or chains, has bridged the credibility gap in terms of providing and maintaining quality care and in providing some means of parental influence. And for the few apparently responsible businesses, such as American Child Centers or the Singer Learning Centers, there are many others whose sales promotions and promises of high profits suggest nothing so much as a mentality made to sell quick-food franchises. This image is not helped by recent tendencies of builders and developers to use the lure of a day care center as one means of selling or renting houses and apartments to young couples. Referred to variously as "part of our amenities program" or "a tremendous marketing tool," day care centers have become, for some real estate developers, "one of the most effective merchandising tools since the recreation center with its swimming pool, clubhouse or what-have-you—particularly for tough rental market areas."[12] It is not impossible to provide quality child care under such circumstances, especially in higher income areas where parents are willing and able to pay steep fees, but it is not hard to predict that despite some quality centers, many shoddy ones will also appear, especially in middle- and lower-income areas where parents may become locked into the day care center with few alternatives to changing it if it is not good. Put in the crudest terms: who would want their landlord to raise their children?

NEW SPONSORS FOR DAY CARE

In the nether world between proprietary and nonprofit centers are a small number of day care centers sponsored by industries, unions, and hospitals. None of them are, strictly speaking, profit-making, since it is not the intention of the sponsoring institution to make money; they do exist, however, to provide these institutions with more productive or hard-to-get workers, or, in the case of union-sponsored day care, as a benefit to union members. Like commercial or franchised day care, they are seen as potentially low-quality, since their prime consideration is not child care but providing working mothers with a safe place to leave their children. In the eyes of some critics, the chief interest of industrial day care—finding good workers—is in itself an indictment of their motivations. They argue that a mother, once hired and provided with child care, may find it extremely difficult to leave that job or improve her situation within it. These fears seem not to have been borne out by the few industrial centers that actually have been opened. Such criticisms are even less true of union-sponsored day care centers.

A recent government survey has uncovered all of eleven industrial day care centers, suggesting that despite government encouragement and potential tax benefits, not many companies are rushing to open day care centers for their workers.[13] Whether it is the initial capital investment or the fear of criticism that restrains them, not many companies appear to be anxious to feudalize their labor force by providing them with day care. With few exceptions, most of the industrial day care centers have been established by firms in which the vast majority of employees are women, notably textile and garment manufacturers. Not unexpectedly, the few union centers that exist have been founded by the Amalgamated Clothing Workers of America. One of the more notable and renowned of these union centers rightly refers to itself as "A Rolls-Royce of Day Care."[14]

The Amalgamated Day Care Center is located on the West Side of Chicago, right next door to the Chicago area union headquarters on a large, busy street on which many other union headquarters are located. The location is not considered ideal by the union or center staff, since it requires that the parent bring the child from home to the center, and then the parent must go on to the factory. At night the trip is reversed. Thus travel may consume a considerable amount of the parent's time. The union hopes that in building additional centers they will find sites more convenient to the parents' factories.

But for many parents the effort to reach the center is worth the excellent care the children receive. The physical appearance of the center suggests that the union has spared no expense in building and furnishing a facility that is bright, cheerful, well-designed, well-stocked, efficient, and completely child-centered. The building itself is long and narrow, thirty-five by one hundred and five feet, with two inner cores providing office, kitchen, and toilet and washroom space. The long side walls provide storage from top to bottom; cots and toys on lower shelves are within the easy reach of the children. These storage areas are enclosed by large sliding doors painted with super-large letters and numbers that are part of the children's everyday learning activities. At the back of the center is an outdoor, roofed play area, well-equipped for vigorous activity; there is also a roof playground similarly well-equipped, making it possible for the entire enrollment to play outside at the same time.

The center has a capacity for sixty children, with children divided by age into four groups of fifteen each. Although the center was constructed as one large room with four distinct areas, the staff has found that the total openness encouraged too much running around and chaos, so plexiglass partitions were put up to create more enclosed spaces. The children remain free, however, to explore other areas. The day I visited, in mid-August, there were only fifteen or twenty children, with the rest on vacation. One group of smaller children were listening to a story being read to them, while a larger group of older children were busy with three teachers at a variety of individual activities. With such small numbers it was difficult to get a sense of the total program. The children are said to come from intellectually unstimulating homes, so there are efforts to rouse their curiosity with individual activities and small experiments. The day of my visit, the older children had been discussing flies, and there they were, especially imported, flying around the room. Catching and swatting them was ultimately part of the lesson. The atmosphere created by the director, staff, and children was warm, friendly, and casual. The director, Mrs. Tuteur, obviously proud of the center that the union had created for the benefit of its members, was quick to suggest that yes, this was a good center, but there was room for change and improvement. One of her own feelings was that the children might benefit from a more structured environment which would better build their own internal controls.

"Our situation may be ideal for a British Infant School, but I'm not sure that this is what these kids need." One could not help but reflect that her criticism was a luxury of those who run good programs and have an abundance of resources at hand.

As of 1971, the center was spending about $2,800 per year per child, but since it was the first year of operation and the director had been given a free hand to buy what she needed, it is difficult to gauge whether this figure is realistic. In any case, the parents pay nothing and the cost is met by the union from funds provided through collective bargaining agreements with employers for social benefits to union members. With these funds the union also supplies free medical care to its members, a benefit also extended to the children in the center.[15] The Amalgamated Day Care Center is a remarkable example of a collective effort by a union and its members to provide a quality service to those of its members with small children.

NONPROFIT DAY CARE CENTERS

Nonprofit day care centers are operated under a variety of auspices and financed in a variety of ways. Formerly the auspices under which centers were run offered some clue to the quality of services offered, but as funding has been met more and more by federal financing, most of these centers have had to conform not only to their local regulations but to federal requirements as well. The effect of federal funding has probably been a raising of standards. Where it once might have been difficult to distinguish between the quality of for-profit and not-for-profit day care, in many areas the nonprofit care is of much higher quality than that offered in many commercial centers.

In this category there are centers run by voluntary organizations such as settlement houses, religious organizations, Community Chest, etcetera; public day care centers run by cities or local government; and private nonprofit centers, usually attached to private schools. The benefits of not-for-profit (except for private) centers are, of course, that they are subsidized by the government and that these funds, along with parent fees which are arranged on a sliding scale according to income, provide enough money so that the care children receive is not dependent on what parents can afford but what is a good program for children. Although, as we shall see, funding is not the sole clue to a quality program.

The Self-Help Day Care Center, originally part of a settlement house, is now located in a housing project in the midst of an urban ghetto. The project is about ten years old, appears well-maintained, and is clearly the most attractive housing in the neighborhood. The day care center is housed on the ground floor of one of the buildings; another building houses a youth center and summer day camp for older children. The ground floor was built for use as a day care center and exhibits all the benefits of a well-planned and intelligently designed space. Although usable and adequate outdoor space is a commonplace of good day care planning, relatively few centers have such space available to them. The Self-Help Center is a rare exception, for on each side of the center are two large play areas; the younger children in two adjacent rooms sharing one of the play areas, and the older children, 4 to 5, in three adjacent rooms sharing another play area. It was a scorching hot day in the middle of July when I visited the center, and the children were all outside playing. A part of each play area was roofed over, providing shade and a cool place to play; on rainy days it served as an umbrella. The play areas were fenced off by high and unattractive cyclone fences, but the trees along the outside moderated the harshness somewhat and provided additional shade.

Mrs. Walters, the director, has not yet arrived, and her secretary, who is also the receptionist, invites me to look around. The classrooms are large and well-furnished with a multitude of toys, games, art materials, counting and sorting devices, etcetera. All the children are outside and remain there through the morning; in effect, while there was material characteristic of a good program, I saw no program in operation. In each room there was an aide straightening up and cleaning who also kept her eye on any child who might wander in from outside to use the bathroom or get a drink of water. In one room a child whom the aide says does not get to bed on time at home is sleeping on a cot. The center is licensed for one hundred children, but it is vacation time and many are not there; those outside are riding tricycles, or scooters, or are sharing a rocking boat; there is a slide and jungle gym, and in one corner a sandbox. The teachers in both play areas were gathered in a group, talking, and neighborhood teen-agers hired for the summer were the organizers and supervisors of most of the activities. With the teen-agers the ratio of adults to children is about one to five. During the year each group of twenty children is supervised by one teacher and two aides, a ratio of one to seven.

Mrs. Walters arrives and invites me in to talk with her. She is a friendly, down-to-earth woman of about 45. As I soon discover, she is also a sophisticated observer of the day care scene, both in her own center and around the city. In her twenty-four years working at Self-Help, moving up from aide to director, she has probably heard of every theory about day care and child development there is, but, nonetheless, runs her own center on a premise that she feels meets the needs of the families that use the center.

She began by asking, "Is our center primarily child-welfare-oriented or child-development-oriented?" She responded to her own question by saying that first and foremost the center gave families an opportunity to get out of this neighborhood by allowing mothers to work to supplement the family income. Given the housing conditions in the neighborhood, the social conditions, and the poor public schools she felt this was a laudable endeavor, thus the center basically was neither child-welfare- nor child-development-oriented but simply the means whereby a family could better themselves. But to some extent, of course, the center was child-welfare-oriented. Many of the children who used the center lived in dirty, smelly, rat-infested tenements, so the center at the least was a safer, cleaner, better place to be. Although there was a "formal academic program" for 5-year-olds only, the director noted various ways in which learning did go on among the 3's and 4's—a view supported by the materials I saw in the classroom. She was proud of the fact that some of her 5-year-olds were beginning to read, and that the 3's and 4's seemed brighter and more curious than many of their peers in the neighborhood. The public schools in the neighborhood are overcrowded and on double-shifts. Whatever learning experiences that children had in their preschool years, the director thought were valuable, and she hoped they would carry over. "No more excuses from the public schools that these kids are culturally deprived and can't learn. They are learning right now."

Her optimism notwithstanding, Mrs. Walters felt that the day care center had several problems she believed stemmed from external sources rather than internal difficulties, but problems which made life more difficult for both herself and the parents. Self-Help was the only day care center in the neighborhood, and there was a long waiting list and strong resentment from those who could not get in. Project residents were given no special preferences, including use of the play areas. The cyclone fences were designed as much to keep the center children in as to keep neighborhood children out. This is a rather common problem in centers that do have adjoining play areas. The equipment and appearance of center playgrounds are often more attractive than the neighborhood facilities, and the centers have neither the funds nor staff to allow other children to use their facilities. This problem was a general concern of the staff in those few centers that do have play areas, for they realize the need for play areas and children's centers is great, and the fact that one child is selected over another is often arbitrary or due to chance. By way of solution to some of these problems, neighborhood parents had organized to open another center; the process was arduous and discouraging, but Mrs. Walters was hopeful that their efforts would result in one or more new centers being opened.

The quality of medical care was a problem in the neighborhood as well as in the center. A visiting nurse came once a week to check on health records, inoculations, and general conditions, but she could only advise the staff and parents; for any medical needs they had to use clinics or see their own doctors. The center would benefit from direct medical assistance, and Mrs. Walters would like psychiatric services, in particular, available to the children and their parents. In the course of her work there she had often observed children, some whom she believed had minor brain damage, some with behavioral problems, who would have benefited from psychiatric help, but the center could offer none.

An infant unit in the Self-Help Center is also needed by many parents, who while they may have one or two children in the center must still find someone to care for a younger child at home. Mrs. Walters herself was in the process of investigating the possibility of adding such a unit to the center.

Self-Help was meeting the needs of the many families who were able to use it, but many more centers like it were badly needed in the neighborhood. In addition, facilities for children, playgrounds and parks, were desperately short. Mothers who remained home with their children had few outdoor facilities to which to take them. It is Mrs. Walters' opinion that Self-Help provides families with a means of upward mobility, and may contribute to a sense that the center is an enclave for a fortunate few, but in the face of the neighborhood's many problems it is difficult for Mrs. Walters and her staff to show a more community-oriented concern.

Self-Help is a good example of an established center that has benefited over the years from additional funding, new theories, a greater variety of early-learning materials, and yet maintains an orderly and consistent sense of what it is doing. And perhaps it has been instrumental, as Mrs. Walters says, "in getting people out of this awful neighborhood."

On the other hand, keeping people in the neighborhood and organizing community resources is one of the objectives of the *Helping Hand Day Care Center.* Helping Hand is located in what has been described as one of the worst slums in America; while some sections of the area are overcrowded, whole blocks in other sections are full of abandoned and burnt-out buildings. Typically the center is located in an old but well-kept abandoned parochial school building. Helping Hand has been open less than a year and shows all the loose ends characteristic of recently founded centers. Despite this, the center has certain organizational assets that have gone a long way to smooth over what might have created a disorderly and chaotic center.

Helping Hand is one of the few centers I visited that decided to adopt a specific educational method of its own. It is a Montessori day care center. The benefit of having chosen a specific method— the distar method was also considered—consists in the ready-made structure it provided for the parents and director for choosing equipment, hiring teachers, organizing the classroom, and, in general, providing themselves with the educational tools to match their ideas about the kind of center they wanted for their children.

The two classrooms, providing space for thirty-five children, have been adapted for Montessori use, with the walls lined by low shelves where children may find and select their own tasks. The day of my visit is the first in which several new children have joined the group, and it is clear that the Montessori structure operates to facilitate a peaceful entry of these children into the school. The children who have attended the center before are busy with their own work, and the teacher and her aide are able to spend a lot of time with the seven or eight new children. The order and self-discipline of the Montessori method are also carried out in the noneducational aspects of the program. Before going to a nearby park to play, each child finds a partner and goes to the door of the classroom to wait for the other children to gather in line. The teacher insistently and patiently repeats her orders to several children—both those running to the door of the school, eager to get out, and others still in the classroom who have not found a partner. This procedure is described as part of the parents' and school's effort to give the children a sense of self-discipline and a recognition that they are part of the group.

Mrs. Brown, the friendly and enthusiastic director of the center, placed great emphasis on the parent support of the center, both for the school program itself and for the larger educational program of which the day care center was part.

The Helping Hand Day Care Center is supervised by an educational task force that, in conjunction with a nearby Catholic elementary school and high school, hopes to develop a total education program from preschool to high school for the community children. Eight of the sixteen children who spent the last year at Helping Hand will go to the kindergarten at the elementary school next year. The task force is made up of parents in all three schools; the parents from Helping Hand were involved in overall planning as well as being involved in the day care center. Mrs. Brown cited the parents' interest in the center by noting that they had helped to build much of the furnishings and regularly replenished the school's supply of found materials. These were widely used to supplement the school's supply of Montessori equipment, which is expensive. While purchasing much of the more complicated sorting and counting equipment, they had themselves constructed many of the simpler items from materials the parents had contributed.

Helping Hand has benefited from the fact that it has strong external support from the community in the form of the educational task force and from the government in the form of a grant that has met its operating costs, and strong internal structure from the Montessori ideas of educating young children. At the end of its first year, it was probably in better shape than most day care centers after one year. It still had problems to resolve and some of them

WHAT DAY CARE LOOKS LIKE 139

result from these very organizational supports. At the end of its second year the special government grant would probably be reduced, requiring the center to adopt a sliding fee scale according to income. The city welfare department, with federal funds, could meet some of the costs for ADC families, but obviously the change-over from a full-funded free center to a partly funded, paying center will require additional work and perhaps even a search for additional funds on the part of the educational task force and the staff and parents of the center.

The Montessori method, too, poses a few difficulties for the center. One is the cost of the equipment. Another is the tendency, common probably to all wholistic theories of education, to use the theory of what should happen to describe what is happening. Thus, are the children at Helping Hand acquiring the internal discipline and external discipline that their parents and the staff want, or are they learning to submit to a mindless regimen? This is one of the evaluations that the center will have to start to make if it hopes to effect its educational plan. Despite its drawbacks, it is an important resource for the parents of the community. Not only does it offer parents the opportunity to work while providing a potentially good child-development program, but as part of a total education project it offers some hope that the promise of early childhood education will be sustained through a child's high school years.

Helping Hand and Self-Help are both located in ghetto neighborhoods, and their total enrollments were from black or Hispanic families. Like many centers with similar enrollments, the directors of both centers, although assuming the need for child development, were highly conscious of the importance of day care for the parents of these children. In a two-parent family, the only way out of poverty is for both parents to work—a goal which could be accomplished only by providing day care for preschool children. The centers provided a dual service—safe and healthy surroundings for the children of working parents and a preschool education.

This merging of parent needs, child welfare, and child-development goals within a day care center typifies many of the directors' descriptions of their centers. In another urban center, located in an economically and racially mixed area, the director tended to emphasize the welfare and protective aspects, although the children's activities were developmentally oriented. In terms of teacher-child involvement, this center perhaps more than most exhibited a warm and strong attachment between teachers and children, with a high degree of interaction in play, games, stories, singing, etcetera. Many of the families who used the center were described as multi-problem families for whom the neighborhood's overcrowded housing presented additional difficulties. Several of the children in this center had minor physical or language difficulties, exaggerated, or even caused, by the lack of physical or psychological space within their own homes. In other families the presence of several small children made it a necessity for the mothers to be able to send one or two children to the center in order to cope with housework and to spend some greatly needed time resting and caring for an infant. In these homes preschool children would likely have spent the day in front of a television set; at the center they were with other children and in contact with adults who had the time and energy to play, talk, and be with them.

Clearly one of the chief advantages nonprofit day care has over commercial day care is its ability, through higher funding, to provide better quality child care as well as good educational programs. Of course, not all nonprofit centers do this, nor can they. For many nonprofit centers do not receive public funds, or if they do receive government funds the amount is so restrictive that in many respects they are not better than commercial centers. And yet in day care as in most other areas of life, "money isn't everything." In their report *Windows on Day Care*,[16] the National Council of Jewish Women cited a center which, despite a lack of any funding and almost no equipment, was described as "a most unusual center—an example of what concerned members of every poor community can do, armed with almost no funds but with a deep desire to improve their conditions and an equally deep love for children." The goodwill and hard work of many members of this community and the leadership of one couple compensated for many of the amenities, services, and equipment that money *can* buy.

The Fifth City Preschool in Chicago, described in the Abt Associates Report,[17] although it is not without funds and equipment, is another case in point. Located on Chicago's West Side in one of the city's roughest neighborhoods, the Fifth City Preschool has been organized by the Ecumenical Institute as part of its community reformulation project. "The Fifth City experiment is designed to make the community capable of mobilizing its own leaders and resources to care for the needs of its own people." To this end it has designed a unique curriculum and educational methodology and developed a system of staff training for its day care center, whose target is the "total child" and whose aim is "the promotion of a strong self-image as the basis for the emergence of an orderly self-structure out of life's chaotic data." The parents pay nothing; the cost to the center is $1300 a year per child. A large amount, yet according to government figures, sufficient to provide only custodial care.* This is yet one more example that highly motivated and well-organized groups and communities can provide quality care, compensating for a lack of adequate funding. The Abt Report observers described the center in this way:

> . . . The facilities are inadequate in the extreme, made livable only by the imagination and hard work of staff and parents. Almost all equipment is donated or homemade.
>
> The spirit and atmosphere of the place, despite its grim environment, is overwhelming. Songs and rituals are a large part of the program, and the children sing at the beginning and the end of the day, before and after meals, in classrooms, while marching from place to place. The living style of the Institute pervades everything; it is an entire world, very much isolated as an enclave of hope in a failed city, and yet to a large degree part of the surrounding neighborhood. The Institute's members are predominantly White, in a totally Black neighborhood. The majority of the children in the preschool, however, are Black, except for the children of the Institute staff (13%). Six of the 19 teachers are from the community. The parents are constantly in and out of the buildings, bringing kids and taking them home, or participating in parent activities; the ethnic mix is cheerful and cooperative.
>
> Children are at the center from 8:00 A.M. to 4:00 P.M. A few stay until 5:00 P.M., or whenever someone picks them up. There is always somebody to watch over the late-stayers. The center is open 47 weeks a year, with a two-week vacation and three weeks of staff training. The general tone is hectic—28 children, frantic schedule revisions to cover teacher absences, the director functioning at full tilt inside and outside the center, parents and teachers and Institute staff coming and going, and little children everywhere.[18]

* See the Abt Report for a fuller discussion of the curriculum.

Something Different is a preschool with the traditional time divisions of half-day sessions for children from 3 to 5. Out of this program has evolved a day care component. The new interest in day care has encouraged a good amount of experimentation and searching for new ways to offer day care services, and Something Different is a notable example of this creativity and resourcefulness. Something Different is located in an old school building in a densely populated neighborhood which is part of an economically and racially mixed area. It started out as a private nursery school in the early 1960's and over the past ten years has evolved a variety of programs for young children. About three years ago an all-day program was introduced to meet the needs of working parents or parents, particularly of only children, who felt a longer day would benefit their children and themselves. Although the school is private and supported largely by tuition, it has always had a large scholarship program to make it accessible to everyone in the community. When the all-day program began, the administrator and parents realized that many families in the new program, who were then on scholarship, and many low-income families in the community, but not in the school, would be eligible for subsidy from the city government because it had become, in effect, a day care program. Along with other such preschools in the area, Something Different worked out a purchase-of-service plan (also called vendor services) with the city day care office, whereby the day care fees for low-income families were shared by the city and family on a sliding-scale basis. The results have been to give the school a high degree of racial and economic integration and to provide an excellent day care program for many families.

There are forty-two children in the program, and thirty-five of them have part or all of their fee paid by the city's day care office. In other respects they are indistinguishable from the rest of the student body, even to the structure of their day. Rather than creating a separate structure for the children who remain all day, the school worked out a schedule whereby these children spend one-half of their day in a regular classroom and the other half in a classroom designed for use by the all-day program. The program works like this: the all-day group of children has been divided into two groups: one-half of them spend their mornings in the special classroom and the other half is dispersed throughout the four half-day classes. At noon, the two groups exchange positions. The children who have been in half-day classes gather together and come to the all-day classroom; the other children spend their afternoons in the half-day classrooms.

One fall afternoon I visited Something Different, which is housed in a small, unused school building. The special classroom for the all-day program is on the top floor and is graced with twenty-foot ceilings, giving the room a large, airy look. Taking advantage of this height the school has built a large loft in one corner of the room. The afternoon group was just beginning to arrive, having spent their morning in the school's regular half-day classes. The program in these classes has some schedule and a good deal of structure—the school was originally organized with a Montessori orientation and has moved on to an eclectic selection of materials and a varied curriculum. My observation of the half-day classrooms suggests that structure and schedule vary considerably from teacher to teacher. Because the half-day program is structured and cognitively oriented, the school decided that the all-day class should be more loosely organized, with more emphasis on free play, physical activities, art, and music.

The afternoon began with the children coming in, hanging their coats up, and gathering around their three teachers on a rug in one corner. After an active morning for the children, the teachers tried to establish an atmosphere of calm and quiet conversation by gathering everyone into the group in a very warm and affectionate way. There was a quiet song. Some children sat in the teachers' laps, others gathered with their friends, everyone sat cross-legged on the rug. The children talked about their morning. One of the teachers asked if anyone had brought anything beautiful. A few children had brought something, a stone or a small toy. This was passed around for everyone to look at. After about ten minutes of talking and a few songs, it was time to eat lunch. The children washed up and each settled at one of the three tables placed around the room. A teacher sat at each table; children opened lunchboxes and got help with tight Thermos bottle caps. There were three teachers for the group of eighteen children present that day. At one table the children talked among themselves; at another the teacher continued her questions about the morning's activities. As each child finished (and they ranged in age from 3 to 5) they packed up their lunchboxes, threw away papers, and washed their places. After finishing, the children wandered around the room looking at the rabbit and the fish, or a book, or yesterday's drawings.

When everyone was finished each child got his mat and blanket from the storage area in one corner of the room, and took them to the place where they wanted to lie down. A few of the children went up to the loft with a teacher and for forty or fifty minutes a sort of quiet fell. There was hushed conversation and some shushing by the teachers who walked around, preparing the afternoon's activities.

After the noise reached normal levels, the teachers judged nap time over and had everyone roll mats and fold blankets. Since the children had been on a trip the day before, a quiet afternoon of playing or painting was planned. In the meantime someone had given the class two gerbils in a small cage. The children were eager to see them and someone opened the cage. This effectively precipitated the major activity of the afternoon.

The gerbil ran under a free-standing bookcase, which meant it could run out in four directions. About ten of the children occupied themselves with figuring out ways to recapture the gerbil. There was talk about how scared he must be, so the children decided they had to be quiet and move gently. Someone retrieved a carrot from their lunchbox to lure out the gerbil. Meanwhile, five or six children had gone to the loft to play with blocks which were stored up there. A few others gathered around the dress-up box, which was filled with some masks and old clothes.

After about a half hour of suppressed excitement and quiet suspense, the gerbil was captured and one of the children suggested writing a story about it. The whole class then gathered around a large paper taped to the wall and began, collectively, to write a story called, "The story of what just happened: the story of the gerbil who ran away and how we got him back." The process of writing the story involved the children remembering, finding the right word, thinking about how the sentences should go, and how the story should proceed. What happened first, then second, and then . . . ? Toward the end children began to wander, and the head-teacher started urging children to sit down and be quiet. There then occurred a moment which symbolized, I think, the emotional rapport between children and teacher. One of the children asked, "Are you happy? How do you feel?" And the teacher, recognizing her growing annoyance with the children's declining interest, replied, "I am happy, but I'm tense, I'm getting nervous." She then asked if everyone could help by listening to whoever was talking so that they could finish. The children took her seriously and settled down to a few more minutes of writing the story. After finishing, the children dispersed to a variety of activities: painting, playing with the rabbit, block building, playing with Lego blocks, listening to records, looking at books. One of the teachers mimeographed the story, and several of the children illustrated and colored their copies to take home.

The loose structure and relatively free schedule allowed the children to choose most of their own activities. At the same time the three teachers were sensitive and attuned to an individual child's need for help or support. For example, at the end of the painting session, one little girl decided she wanted to give the tables a good washing with soap and water. One of the teachers reminded her where the pail was, where the soap and sponges were, and helped her to carry the pail filled with water. At another point, two or three children painted lips on pieces of masking tape and put them over their mouths. One of the teachers encouraged them to show with their bodies, since they could not talk, how it was to be sad, happy, joyful, mad.

The spirit of the class then was one of spontaneity and warmth, with a remarkable degree of teacher sensitivity to drawing the children out into new experiences and different ideas.

St. Ann's Day Nursery. Not all nonprofit centers are so conscious of the newer ideas about day care and child development. Some have an other-worldly air about them—St. Ann's in more ways than one. The St. Ann's Day Nursery was founded almost a century ago to serve the population of a combined residential-industrial area in a densely populated urban area. Where it once served the children of Irish immigrants who lived and worked in the neighborhood, it now serves the children of Spanish-speaking immigrants. While many factories remain in the neighborhood, the tenements that once housed their workers have disappeared. Present-day nursery children and their mothers or fathers must travel from outlying areas— the children to the day nursery, their parents to the factories.

The day nursery (it holds on to the older designation) is housed in three connecting buildings. The buildings front on a busy thoroughfare, noisy and dirty with the truck traffic for nearby industries. A step inside is a step backward in time.

The center is staffed by a religious order that specializes in teaching. Although the order has been involved in running the center for many years, one of the older sisters remarked that many of the younger sisters who, unlike their predecessors, are trained kindergarten and elementary school teachers seemed more and more reluctant to work at the center. Since they were now permitted to choose their own work rather than being assigned, many of them chose teaching in elementary schools rather than the nursery school. It was not hard to discover why.

The center is open from 7:30 A.M. until 6:00 P.M. and does not have a shift schedule. The sisters are all on duty for the entire ten-and-a-half-hour day, with a brief respite at the children's nap time. Their long hours do not seem to affect their relationship with the children: the sisters are, as tradition has them, bright and cheerful. The facilities, too, are as one might expect—although worn, clean and highly polished. It is a work situation, however, not likely to attract nuns with professional training.

St. Ann's reminded me in some respects of Happy Day: the children were expected to behave and the program was organized with that end in mind. Unlike Happy Day, the children were treated with warmth and genuine affection. The program is totally group-oriented, with the evident good behavior characteristic of group-oriented programs that really work. The children stand and say "good morning" when an adult enters the room; they virtually sit or stand at attention when their work is being looked at or when they are being spoken to. One group of 3-year-olds was painting or playing house; the children painting politely offered their work for my inspection, and those playing house stopped to explain who everyone was. A group of 4-year-olds led by a sister and a young woman was just beginning a music lesson. The young woman, very pleasant and very soprano, sat at an old-fashioned, upright piano, while the sister had the children gather in a circle for a song which required a great deal of body movement and which the children performed with great glee, although they seemed to require minute directions from the music teacher who starred at the piano. Another group, 5-

year-olds, was having what their teacher termed a "free period" before lunch. They were all seated at little tables, working on simple puzzles which she expected them to do without assistance from herself or the other children.

The center was not offering simply custodial care, but clearly it was not overly concerned with the education of young children. It provided the children with warm, affectionate attention and the means to keep them occupied for eight or nine hours a day (which it seemed to do on a great amount of found materials rather than an extensive supply of toys or educational materials). The children, however, did seem timid and perhaps overburdened with the cares of "being good." St. Ann's would obviously get no stars from early childhood educators. Like Happy Day, it seemed to be a center where parents would feel their children were safely cared for and learned to behave. Furthermore, the fact that the staff were nuns meant the children were introduced to the religious values of their parents. Curiously enough, no allowance was made for the fact that the children came from Spanish-speaking homes. The sisters spoke only English, and when the children responded in their shy fashion, they spoke English too.

The center was funded almost entirely by its board of trustees, made up of a number of wealthy men who, as a charitable activity, took it upon themselves to maintain the center; if parents were able, they were asked to pay a small fee, because it was thought this would help them feel they were contributing to keeping the center open.

St. Ann's is a throwback to earlier days, based upon an attitude of benevolent authoritarianism toward the children and paternalistic charity toward their parents. These are not "modern" values nor values particularly desirable for running a center. Anachronism though it may be, there is no gainsaying that the center meets the real needs of people today in an old-fashioned way.

Obviously the development of a national system of day care or the widespread development of day care services cannot depend solely on the goodwill and imagination of generous people. Yet all the examples of nonprofit centers suggest that most such centers address their efforts to larger social goals and purposes than simply the care and education of preschool children. In many centers these social goals may be only vaguely defined with no particular effort to formulate a precise means of putting them into effect. In other centers, the importance of larger social goals may be an overriding feature of the center. In one such center, the parents themselves had founded the center and were firm believers in parent control of day care; not only did they spend a considerable amount of time working out an organization and structure whereby they were involved at all levels of their own center but they ultimately involved themselves in a struggle with other centers against a local government attempt to limit parent control over eligibility requirements.

As the first chapter suggested, a variety of groups want day care for a variety of reasons, many of them contradictory. The government funds that have been available for day care have as their larger social purpose the reduction of welfare rolls—by providing day care for women in work-training programs, or offering day care on a sliding scale to some of the "working poor" or those who would be on welfare if the mother did not work, or if at least two adults in the family did not work. Many directors recognized the funding of day care centers to cut welfare as a legitimate reason for government funding, and yet few expressed any desire or willingness to enforce the conditions of such funding on their parents.

Most directors felt their responsibility was met by having the mothers or parents fill out the center's forms, including those listing income; it was not, they believed, their responsibility to check on either the accuracy of income figures nor what the mother did with her time, or, in fact if she had a job. If the task of policing regulations had to be done, they felt it had to be done by welfare workers and not by the day care center, whose responsibility was caring for children and supporting the parents. One director, who found herself in a tight position, expressed deep resentment for the "social welfare" tasks assigned to her center, which was sponsored by the housing project in which the center was located. The center was funded by the local welfare department on a sliding-scale basis for the use of project residents. The director was required to report to the housing project office the names of the children using the center and the employment status of the mother. If the mother was employed and off welfare, the housing project was entitled to a higher rent, while at the same time the employed mother was also usually subject to a higher fee for day care services. As a result, the center, though offering good care with fine equipment and a stimulating educational program, had difficulty recruiting children for its program. The director found that while many mothers wanted to work, the jobs they were able to find were low-paying or temporary; hence, they preferred to leave the children with relatives or a neighbor in order to avoid the bureaucratic hassle of having to apply for a rent decrease when they lost their jobs and had to go back on welfare. To some extent the center was getting around this problem by providing permanent jobs in the center but obviously in a center intended to care for one hundred children this was only a minor solution to the problem. The director ended her complaint with a note of resentment and frustration: "If day care is good for children, then it's good for children period, and they shouldn't come around talking to me about jobs and welfare."

Another director, who is running a good child-development program, expressed a similar sentiment when she remarked that running the center without government funds would, of course, be impossible, but that many of the mothers who did have children in the center had enough to cope with without also trying to hold on to a job. She probably reflected the older social welfare attitude when she admitted that, despite rules and regulations, she encouraged many mothers *not* to go to work but to use their time and energy caring for their infants or younger children and keeping house.

Some of the nonprofit centers, in contrast to almost none of the commercial centers, not only offer good child-development programs but also address themselves to larger social goals, even though these may not be the same social goals emphasized by the larger day care lobbies. It is clear that Senator Russell Long would find few day care directors sympathetic to his point of view. On the other hand, not many directors would find the "away with the family" viewpoint of the radical feminists to their liking either. Although there are significant exceptions among some of the day care people I talked to and among those that have been interviewed in newspapers, the majority, when talking about larger social goals, expressed themselves in terms of building a community, fostering pride and self-sufficiency among both parents and children, and encouraging family solidarity rather than replacing it. Even in those centers where most children were from one-parent families, the staff and directors did not talk in terms of the center as a replacement for the missing parent or an alternative family but as a support and a means for one parent to maintain a family with the child. And several directors, summarizing their sense of what the day care center was like, often compared the center to a large family and then noted several ways in which, of course, it could never be a family, but was only family-like. It is safe to say that day care centers do not for the most part see themselves as anything like a substitute for family, but more like a place where things that used to happen in large families with many siblings happen again. They are family-like rather than family.

INFANT DAY CARE

Infant day care, although it was a regular feature of day care centers at the turn of the century, was one of the first kinds of care to be done away with as standards were raised.[19] The identification and diagnoses of maternal deprivation, hospitalism, etcetera, in the forties and fifties strengthened the existing opposition to the institutionalization and even part-time care of infants outside of their own homes, and although many of the assumptions, premonitions, and prejudices against infant care outside the home have been shown to derive not so much from maternal absence or institutionalization as much as from lack of proper care and stimulation, there remains a great deal of concern about widespread care of infants in day care centers, as well as a number of practical barriers.

The pleas for infant day care stem from many of the same conditions that have made day care for preschool children so necessary: inadequate care in the home or by neighbors when mothers have to work, and health or social problems that make it impossible for a mother to care for her infant full-time. Where a mother may have secured good day care for her preschoolers, she is often unable to work because the same kind of care is not available for an infant. The tendency of many centers, especially those responsive to parent needs, has been to shift the minimum age downward from 3 to 2½ or 2 years of age, or to make admissions dependent on the child being toilet-trained, in effect lowering the admission age for some children. But these exceptions are not a sufficient response to a widely expressed need.

While many people argue that an infant is best cared for in its own home by its own mother, the fact is that many infants whose mothers must work are cared for in unlicensed day care homes where the conditions are often detrimental not only to the babies' physical well-being but to their proper emotional and social development. Furthermore, there are many mothers, often unwed teen-aged girls, who are unprepared to care for their own infants and who need support, advice, and instruction in the proper care of infants and young children.[20] It is in response to these extreme but common enough situations that a very few experimental and model programs for infant day care have been developed and funded by a variety of government and private grants.

One such project, the Syracuse Children's Center, has been extensively written about and analyzed. One of its founding directors, Dr. Bettye Caldwell, has written widely to answer many of the objections to infant day care and to day care in general.[21] And, indeed, a visit to the Children's Center showed it to be as impressive as many observers and writers have found it to be.

The Children's Center has been in operation since 1964, and since 1966 has been housed in a church building that has been adapted to the center's needs. The physical plant might be best described as straightforward and unadorned; every piece of equipment has a use, and there appears to be little recourse to gadgets or gimmicks. The obvious focus of the center is on interrelationships and activities between the children and teachers. The children begin attending the center at 6 months of age, although an extensive home-visiting program, including pre- and post-natal services, puts many of them in contact with the center before they actually attend. From 6 to 15 months the babies are at the center for one-half day and from 15 months to 3 years for a full day. After 3 they "graduate" to a Syracuse University-sponsored nursery school program. During their enrollment with the Syracuse Children's Center, a home-visiting program is in contact with the child's family, not only explaining what is happening at the school but putting the family in contact with information and services, that its present director, Dr. Ronald Lally, hopes will create "a climate in which the parents and caretakers can feel better about themselves and can see themselves in positions of responsibility and pride with regard to the education of their young children."[22]

The center program has been devised to provide the infants and toddlers with the environmental stimulation that will encourage their cognitive development in a normal fashion. What that means in practical terms is that the infants, on the day of my visit, were in their rooms with two infants for each adult (this can vary up to four to one). The six infants in this class were doing a variety of things. One was starting to eat with the help of a teacher; another was having a diaper changed; two others were examining a colorful ball; another was holding onto the back of a chair trying to pull it out; and the sixth was looking at a mirror. All very normal and unexceptional. But it was clear that the teacher's attention was purposeful and directed to describing, encouraging, and explaining in very simple language to the children what was happening. The chatter was very much like that that most mothers indulge in when talking to their infants.

"What a good boy."

"Who is in the mirror?"

"Is that Tommy? It is Tommy."

"Push the ball" (with a pushing motion).

"Hold on to the chair."

But all this conversation was the instrument of the center's program to give the experiences and information, words, toys, smiles, songs, gestures, that many of them do not receive a sufficient amount of in their homes. A little later, in a second room, a group of toddlers was being put to bed for their naps. A regular routine of washing, trying the toilet, diapering, and tooth-brushing was in operation. Throughout the process the teachers talked to, cuddled, held, helped, and sang to the children.

The scene appeared in many ways quite artless and even easy to replicate, but when questioned about the duplicability of the center, Dr. Lally responded with some hesitation. He felt the Children's Center could be duplicated, given the almost total lack of infant day care services available, but under ideal conditions, where a community's infant care needs would be specifically tailored to provide a variety of services such as drop-in care, good family day care, nursery schools, and emergency care, widespread infant day care might not be so necessary. In contrast he emphasized the importance of the home-visiting program, which was working to facilitate social and economic changes within the Children's Center's families. This program, he believed, was easily duplicated, and in the long run, if the family learned to help and support its children, home visiting could prove as valuable as the infant program itself.

In fact he has written that intervention even in the lives of very young children may not have the lasting effects that was first thought, unless their home environment is able to sustain the improvements made in the children's cognitive functioning. "I have moved from the somewhat glib position that changes in the cognitive functioning of primary grade children from these families could be made by minimal intellectual intervention in the lives of these same children during their infancy and toddlerhood, to the position that comprehensive and extensive intervention must be provided for the child and his family if any meaningful and permanent changes might be forthcoming in their lives."[23]

Dr. Lally and his associates have underlined the importance of the family in sustaining the improvements made in the children's cognitive function, but for the purposes of the debate over infant day care the important point of their findings is that good group care of infants and toddlers does not have a deleterious effect on their development and, in fact, in a select group of infants it enhances their development. So, from a psychological point of view, good infant day care may be beneficial to some children and, at least, not harmful to other children. There remain, however, several difficulties. The two most crucial are staffing and cost.

Both Dr. Lally and the director of a very small infant center in New York City pointed out the difficulty in finding and selecting personnel who are able to work well with infants and toddlers. It is with this age group that professional credentials are an almost meaningless indicator of the competence and quality of a care-giver's skills. Dr. Lally pointed out that you can teach the cognitive skills necessary for working with infants but you cannot teach affectivity. "Cognitive abilities apart from affectivity is useless at this age level." The other director put it in more concrete terms when she remarked that women with mothering abilities are few and far between, and even then it was no easy task to find them. Finding people who will work well with very small children is one problem for infant day care centers—a problem heightened by the realization that the individual care-giver at this age level has a crucial influence on the emotional development of his or her charges.

A second crucial and perhaps insurmountable problem is that of cost. Good infant care can cost between three and five thousand dollars per year, per child. Much of this cost is based on a low child-adult ratio, absolutely necessary for adequate care and sufficient attention. These costs are prohibitive for most families. Without extensive government subsidies, it is hard to see that there can be any extensive system of infant day care. The danger may well be that in attempting to provide some measure of infant day care, government funding will increase the demand for it without beginning to meet the real needs. For that reason improving the quality of what is referred to as family day care or home day care has a high priority in providing an alternative to the care of infants and toddlers in a day care center.

FAMILY DAY CARE

While the discussion of day care services usually focuses on group care in centers, most children in day care are cared for in what are called family day care homes. In 1970 there were almost 41,000 approved or licensed family day care homes with 148,000 children. Since most day care homes are not licensed, the actual number of such arrangements was estimated to be 1.8 million children cared for in 450,000 homes.[24] The uncertainty of the figures rises from the rather casual arrangements typical of family day care and the uneven enforcement of state licensing laws. Most people, in fact, simply call family day care "babysitting," although under the definition of many states, the care of two or more children unrelated to the care-giver in his or her own home is considered family day care.

Family day care can range from the casual to the elaborate. It may consist in nothing more than a neighbor keeping an eye on school-aged children after school. Or it may be quite involved, with the care-giver watching several children from more than one family and ranging in age from a month to 5 or 6 years. Although most states have some kind of licensing procedures for such arrangements, the vast majority of family day care homes are unlicensed and unsupervised; even where there is licensing and it is enforced, there is often little or no follow-up supervision or conditions for relicensing.

The numbers of children cared for are sufficient to indicate that family day care, whether or not it represents an ideal form, merits a great deal of interest and further exploration as an alternative form of day care. Because it so obviously approximates at least the physical arrangements of the American norm in child-rearing—women and children in the home—family day care is often cited by those who consider centers too institutional as a preferable means of supplying day care, especially for those families where special and/or intense care is needed. Infant day care is one obvious area; part-time, drop-in, and after-school care are others.

Before looking at the advantages and disadvantages of family day care, a description of two family day care homes I visited might illustrate the possibilities as well as drawbacks of this kind of day care. Both were licensed homes and had been for a number of years, submitting to the yearly inspection and relicensing procedures required by the state.

The first home was located in a semi-rural area on what had once been a family farm but which was gradually being closed in by the development of the surrounding area. The head of the family was Mrs. Carson, an energetic and articulate 80-year-old widow, who with her two unmarried daughters raised chickens, sold eggs, and maintained a small vegetable garden for their own food. At various times they had taken foster children as well as caring for children on a daily basis. At the time of my visit they had two foster children and three children for day care. The three day care children were brought early in the morning by their mother and the school bus picked them up at the farm; the youngest returned from kindergarten at noon and the older two after school. Their mother picked them up at dinnertime on her way home from work.

Since it is carried on in private homes, it is difficult to make first-hand observations of family day care, so I eagerly accepted the invitation of a licensing official to accompany him on his rounds, although it meant I was only able to observe and not question Mrs. Carson or her daughters about their ideas on day care. It was clear, however, from their conversation and the appearance of the house and farm, that the younger Miss Carson, who took charge of all the children, thought that a farm was the best possible place for children to be raised and that she knew exactly what she was doing. There were obviously many things for the children to do, from helping to feed the chickens, playing with a dog and cat, to swinging on an old tire hanging from a tree, to playing with a number of toys on the back porch, to traveling with Miss Carson on her daily round of errands. In a real sense the children in Miss Carson's care were receiving an old-fashioned upbringing. There was a certain distance between adults and children; the children were to be seen and not heard. There was a great deal for them to do and a great many things for them to see and watch—"stimulating environment" is the phrase that might appeal to an early childhood specialist.

Another day care home contrasted somewhat with this "stimulating environment." Located in an older and somewhat rundown residential area of a small city, this day care home was run by a 65-year-old widow who supported herself on a pension and the fees she charged for caring for three children: two sisters of 4 and 8, and a boy about 2½. The 8-year-old went to school and the 4-year-old attended nursery school, half-day. Mrs. Baskin cared for them after school and the little boy was with her all day. She appeared a kindly and responsible person, who characterized her own method by saying, "I have a system and a schedule and I keep to it and it works." Her house was spotless and tidy, and the amount of bric-a-brac suggested few concessions to the children's presence. They were permitted to sit and watch the television in the living room or they went outside in a large fenced yard to play. On a rainy day there was a small enclosed porch for them. There were no toys or books, drawing materials, or paper. Mrs. Baskin thought it was the parents' responsibility to supply these, and since they didn't, the children played with whatever they found around the yard. The children were spotlessly clean and well-behaved, and quietly followed us around when Mrs. Baskin showed us the rest of the house. She noted in the course of the conversation that she only took quiet children who knew how to obey; they quickly learned her rules and then everyone got along fine. This family day care home supplied responsible care, but little else; Mrs. Baskin acted essentially as a good babysitter with little interest in providing activities or interesting things for the children to do. The fact that the parents of the two little girls sent them to nursery school was an indication that they were conscious of Mrs. Baskin's limitations, though prizing her regularity, accessibility, responsibility, and insistence on good behavior.

Compared to these two settings, some family day care homes have been found to be quite minimal, even dangerous for the children. Cases cited in *Windows on Day-Care* and in Maya Pines' book[25] suggest that many family day care homes are overcrowded, unhealthy, and sometimes do not even provide custodial care. The women who run them take up family day care often as a last resource for earning some money, and they have neither the resources, facilities, nor energy for coping with the numbers of children they take in order to make a living.

> When Mrs. —— opened the door for us, we felt there were probably very few, if any, children in the house, because of the quiet. It was quite a shock, therefore, to discover about seven or eight children, one year old or under, in the kitchen; a few of them were in high-chairs, but most were strapped to kitchen chairs, all seemingly in a stupor.
>
> It wasn't until we were in the kitchen that we heard the noise coming from the basement. There we found over twenty children huddled in a too small, poorly ventilated, cement floor area. A TV with an apparently bad picture tube was their only source of entertainment or stimulation.
>
> When we went to look at the back yard, we passed through a porch, where we discovered, again, children, children and more children. The children were literally under our feet. Pathetically enough, it was necessary for Mrs. —— to reprimand one child for stepping on another.
>
> Mrs. —— takes care of two families—six children—which the Bureau of Children's Services subsidizes. The other children (41, for a total of 47 children) she takes care of independently, receiving two dollars per day per child. She told us that she has been doing this for twenty years and seemed quite proud to be able to manage as well alone, with no help.[26]

Many family day care arrangements are the result of desperate situations—both for the mothers who must work and find care for their children and for women who must work and find child care their only possibility. With both, what is best for the children can often only be a secondary consideration, in spite of their own wishes to do the best for them. No surprise, then, that many mothers who must place their children in family day care homes are not happy about it, even for very young children. Many say that if a day care center were available and convenient to use, they would prefer it over the theoretically homey, personal, and small family day care home.

> The mothers' preferred group day care because they were convinced that it is reliable, and this was their first concern in planning for their children during the day. They also believed that the staffing pattern, the daily routines, and the administrative structure of group day care as provided in the centers guarantee better care. To these mothers, not even the advantages offered by a capable day care mother known by the parent could compare with those offered by a professional staff trained in child care and the program of a day care center, which always provides that children are fed properly, are taken outdoors, are given play material, and receive health care.
>
> There is another important reason the mothers, especially those who lived in slum areas, favored group day care. These mothers, mainly Negro and Puerto Rican, preferred group care because it offers their children learning opportunities. In group day care children learn by being with adults and with other children, by being read to, by being taken on trips, by being stimulated by their teachers. Group day care, the mothers emphasized, offers more than just custodial care; whereas family day care is a babysitting service that does not offer, nor did they expect it to offer, any type of intellectual experience.[27]

Does its present unpopularity mean that there is no room for family day care homes in the overall expansion of day care services? Whether it is popular or unpopular, whether it is good or bad, family day care will remain an important part of any system of day care, if only because group care in centers will probably never be expanded to a point where it can meet fully the needs of families in search of child care. Furthermore, the capitalization costs for building or renting a center that might only be used part-time, for before- and after-school care, for drop-in, for emergency care might be better spent in training family day care mothers and supplying them with materials. Infant day care, too, will long remain a need whose high cost will severely limit its expansion, even for high-risk babies.

The more realistic question may be: What can be done to improve family day care?

One start has been made with a family day care program in New York City where both the "teacher mothers" and the "career mothers" are given a considerable amount of help and support from a family day care center in their own neighborhood.[28] The staffs in these sub-centers are organized to provide mothers who wish to care for children with the advice and actual help necessary for them to provide good care. This includes educational aides who assist the day care mother with planning activities and trips; staff help in providing care if the mother has to have some time off for schooling, shopping, or a doctor's appointment. The career mothers, that is, the mothers of the children who are in family day care, are assisted either in acquiring the training necessary for a good job or help in finding a job that will use the skills they already have. One of the many positive effects of this system has been to put family day care mothers in contact with other adults to whom they can talk about their difficulties and their accomplishments with their day care children. This has given them a new sense of confidence and self-respect in their own abilities to do a good job, to earn a steady income, and to have opportunities for job advancements. For the whole system encourages the acquiring of skills and interest in new jobs by promoting "teacher mothers" to educational aides who work through the centers and on upward. The effect on the children has been to provide them with the consistent and stable influences of a good day care home. The mothers of the children often for the first time have been able to obtain good training and good jobs, thus fostering their own sense of accomplishment.

The whole system is hampered by a lack of funds, funds for toys and materials which the day care mother often has to supply out of her own meager salary. In 1971 the program was being supported by city, state, and federal funds to the amount of eight million dollars or $2,287 per child per year. On an operating basis, this is not far from the $2,500 per child per year in New York City day care centers. Yet it meets the special day care needs of infants and schoolchildren who would otherwise have no provisions for day care at all. And it gives both "teacher mothers" and "career mothers" opportunities that they might not otherwise have had.

CHAPTER 6

WHAT IS IT LIKE TO USE

DAY CARE? MOTHERS TALK

ABOUT DAY CARE

It would broaden our understanding of what day care is like and what it does if we turned from the perspective of what day care looks like to what it is like to use day care. The two mothers in the following interviews talk about, in a sympathetic but not uncritical fashion, the whole range of benefits and problems that come with having their children in day care centers. In addition to raising all the practical issues involved, they demonstrate in their concerns and questions an unusual sense of their responsibilities and rights in relationship to the center. They are not passive receivers of a service but active participants in an alternative form of child-rearing.

Barbara Dwyer and Janet Schwartz are two young, white women in their early thirties and late twenties respectively. Each has one child—both of them girls. Socially and educationally they are middle-class; economically neither are, or have become so only recently. Day care centers have provided both of them with the chance to lead productive working lives. Each one is without a husband, and is the sole support of herself and her child. In this respect they fit the traditional child welfare establishment description of the mother who needs day care; in other respects they do not. They are not apologetic about their use of day care but have, in fact, aggressively pursued their right to use it. It is not, for them, a second- or third-rate arrangement but an essential and valued part of their ability to carry on with the raising of their children.

In many ways alike, their day care experiences have been very different. They are both independent-minded and active women. They might be described as "liberated women," except they display none of the frivolousness or privilege sometimes attached to the term. They are both serious people up against the economic reality of supporting themselves and their children. Barbara Dwyer has been deeply involved in a community- and parent-run center. Janet Schwartz has her child in an established, rather traditional day care center. To judge from the children, Miranda and Annie, both day care centers have contributed to the development of two lively, intelligent, and energetic children. Their mothers agree with that assessment, although both raise other and larger questions about how their day care centers are operated.

What kind of education for young children? How does and can parent control work? What is the proper role of the community in the day care center? Can there be class and race integration when and if there is real parent control? These mothers have strong opinions about how day care should work, some of them quite opposite those of day care professionals, some not. For example, they both favor strong parent and community influence in the running of their day care centers, even though this means they must also face the inevitable problems and conflicts that go with all activities where there is strong community interest. Most day care professionals would minimize the role of parents and community in favor of an efficiently and professionally administered program. On the other hand, these mothers are in agreement with many professionals, including educators and child psychologists who believe that pushing children into reading and math before they are ready can be detrimental, rather than helpful, to a child's future educational performance. But despite their articulate disagreements with the way their own day care centers are run, one certainty does spring from their conversations: two educated, sophisticated, and critical women have discovered that day care, despite its problems, meets their need for good child care. Without day care neither would be able to work; without good day care neither would be able to continue work with a sense of confidence that her child was well cared for.

BARBARA DWYER AND MIRANDA

Barbara Dwyer is a serious, thoughtful, hard-working woman of about 33 years of age; she seems possessed of a great amount of disciplined energy. If the year in which I interviewed her were not 1973, one could imagine her, without much difficulty, a frontier woman living in a sod house on the Kansas frontier. By profession she is a nurse, by political inclination a grass-roots activist. After finishing her nursing education she spent several years in the Civil Rights Movement in the South, using her nursing and organizational skills. She left the South when the Movement became all black and returned to live and work in the large Midwestern city where she had gone to school.

Deeply committed to improved public health services and preventive medicine, she worked as a visiting nurse, as well as with a number of groups trying to improve health care in ghetto areas. She lived in the same integrated, semi-slum area where she worked. In the spring of 1969 she gave birth to Miranda and shortly thereafter broke up with Miranda's black father, with whom she had been living since her return to the city. Faced with the responsibility of raising Miranda and of supporting the two of them, she decided to finish a degree in nursing education. That effort and her return to work required her to use a variety of child care arrangements which, by and large, she thinks have been good experiences for Miranda.

> Miranda has always been taken care of by other people, and she has always been with other children. From 3 weeks after she was born until she was 7 months old, she stayed every day with a family in the town where I was finishing school. We returned to the city when she was 7 months old, and between then and about 28 months she was in two family day care homes, both of which I would describe as essentially custodial.
>
> The first one wasn't too good. She was the infant in a house with three or four other children. She spent most of her time in a playpen. Nobody played with her. She was never taken out. After three months I found another place that was still custodial but so much better. Here, there was a lot of maternal affection and warmth and a lot of socialization with adults and other children.

It really was an extended family, with uncles, aunts, cousins, older brother and sisters in and out. The family was Spanish-speaking and Miranda learned Spanish, which I thought was great. She really thrived there. It did have some drawbacks. She wasn't learning much and there was no attempt to develop skills, no paper, pencils, or toys, except for what I brought. She could do whatever she wanted, there was no discipline. The television was on all day. She did go outside a lot to help with the shopping or the laundry. Although people played with her, no one read to her or encouraged her learning things.

Barbara believed that educationally oriented group care was better than these family day care arrangements, but despite a good deal of searching around had not found a center that would take Miranda until she was 3.

One cold evening in late January, 1973, she recounted what had obviously been a consuming interest of the past three years—helping to organize a community- and parent-controlled day care center in her neighborhood, one that Miranda would not have to wait to attend. Barbara and Miranda live in a neighborhood that has been touched by several waves of urban renewal, leaving in its wake large clusters of new low- and middle-income housing projects, and a residue of old but solid apartment buildings and houses. They live in one of the apartment buildings. There is a large Spanish-speaking and black population, as well as some poor and middle-class whites, in the area. Some of them are long-time residents, others are like Barbara, relative newcomers who feel strongly about breaking down racism and social class barriers and see living in the community and organizing structures within it as one means of doing that.

In January of 1970, when Miranda was almost 9 months old, Barbara heard about a community attempt to organize a day care center. Provision for such a center had been made in the last renewal plan and was supported by many community organizations, but the impetus to finally organize it was lacking. Although there was a site for the center and the landlord was renovating it, the months of work needed to make it a going program could only come from people with a certain amount of self-interest in the project. Those who needed day care and those who needed jobs were the most likely prospects and, indeed, Barbara soon joined such a group.

After a few meetings there was a group of ten or twelve women who could be depended upon to attend regularly. They were all community people, that is, everyone lived in the community. But there were essentially two groups, white middle-class, at least educationally although usually not financially, and black working class. Not everyone in the whole group needed day care. As it turned out, several people needed jobs. And that was always one of the goals of the center, to hire community people to staff the center. But in these early discussions that was a secondary consideration; perhaps somewhat naively, everyone agreed our first goal was quality child care.

Of course, we had larger ideas and reasons for being there. There were others like me who had been in the Civil Rights Movement and others who had worked organizing in ghetto areas. Many of us started out with big ideas, not only about organizing a community but politicizing and educating it. For example, one of the things we looked forward to was the day when the kids from the center would start going to the local public school. The day care center would have created a bloc of parents who knew what education was all about, who were organized and who knew how to get things done. We felt this could have a tremendous influence on improving the school, especially as more and more kids left the center for first grade. We also hoped that having a multi-ethnic center would begin to lower the level of racism in our society. Getting little kids together was the place to start. We were very proud that our center, long after many others had given up, remained integrated—racially, culturally, and on a class basis too. We were also democratic. Everyone could participate.

The effort, as Barbara described it, was not easy. The group had to deal not only with the financial and administrative problems of organizing and opening the center but inevitably with the racial, cultural, and class differences that characterized the group. It proved rough going. Under the best of circumstances it is not easy to organize and start a day care center. With the melange of ideas and people gathered around this group, that their center ever opened is nothing short of a miracle. They did have several assets that helped to ease the way: a guarantee of city day care funding if the center became operational; contact with a local and very fine teachers' college that was prepared to act as educational consultant and provide staff training; and the ground floor of a renovated apartment building.

We spent hours and hours, and meeting after meeting, discussing educational philosophy, setting up rules, writing by-laws. What age children should the center take? How should we group them? According to age or "family style," that is, in mixed-age groups? How young should we take them? Everyone wanted infant day care, although the Board of Health did not approve. We were struggling with the city over how many children, how many teachers, how much money. We talked about whether socialization or education was the most important thing. We decided both were.

In the beginning few of us knew anything about early childhood education. A few people knew about Montessori and traditional nursery school curriculums. But nothing significant. Finally some money came through. We hired High Point Teachers' College as educational consultants because we liked their ideas about education and curriculum planning. They organized a staff-training program for us. Before the center opened, most of the staff took this course and continued with it on a part-time basis at night, after we opened.

We had to get an architect and a lawyer. We had to get incorporated. One very old man from the community took this job up and he was very good at handling a lot of administrative and architectural stuff. And the three women who were eventually the cooks were very involved in designing the kitchen and selecting equipment for it. We also hired some student architects and with our equipment money we paid them to design and build all our equipment. We saw movies of equipment and environments. We had big discussions and they built models. Unfortunately that was a mistake. Many of the things that they built were unsafe or fell apart. And since that was our initial equipment money, there wasn't much we could do about it. We were left without much usable equipment or equipment money.

We saw a lot of movies about everything—education, equipment—and we discussed, discussed, discussed. But it was the white middle-class people that did the discussing and everyone else sat around listening. At the time I didn't understand why, if they didn't want to talk about setting up the center, so many of these black women came, but I guess it was really the jobs they were interested in.

Although they didn't talk then, when the time came they did have strong opinions about who should be hired and not hired. The whole group of ten interviewed people, a procedure which presented a lot of problems, but everyone thought this was very important. We had to go out of the community for head teachers because no one local was qualified. Head teachers had to have degrees in early childhood education and state accreditation. There were people in the community who did qualify as assistants and aides and they filled most of those positions. Anyway hiring head teachers was really a struggle. The black and Puerto Rican women did not like the people whom the white, middle-class women liked. The white middle-class liked nonrigid, nonstructured, nontraditional teachers. The black and Puerto Rican women liked just the opposite: traditional and structured teachers. It really wasn't even a race thing, because we interviewed several young black women who were more than qualified, but they were "hip" and the black and Puerto Rican women invariably voted against them. Their idea of education was very traditional, formal, rigid, and (in my opinion) uptight. They wanted people who looked and acted like teachers. The selection was pretty much a compromise, although in fact the staff we started off with was pretty good.

The center was supposed to open in January, 1971. That was impossible. We finally hired a director in December, 1970, because all the parents were working and the administrative and planning stuff just got to be overwhelming. The director was very young and very sweet. Even though she was kind of "hippie," everyone liked her and it was because she was sweet, agreeable, and just very open with everyone. She had great educational ideas but unfortunately very few administrative skills. We went ahead hiring staff and they went to the training program and began setting up their classrooms. The staff was being hired on majority vote, and there didn't have to be any quorums at the meetings; whoever showed up for interviewing could hire. And in fact there were more traditional people around than nontraditional.

Despite this the initial staff was warm and good with children, everyone was very child-oriented. The center was not tightly run and had an easy comfortable environment. Everyone didn't get the precise people they wanted but in the end we got people everyone liked. We finally opened in the spring of 1971.

One of the basic decisions of the group was to include very young children. They first enrolled infants as young as 12 months.

Although this was against local day care regulations, the community felt there was a strong need for group care for young children. This brought the parents into some conflict with the staff, who had, at first, been willing to include young children in the center. However, the day-to-day difficulties of caring for infants in a setting which included all other age levels proved overwhelming, and there was a revision of policy.

> We had decided on "family" structure, that is, all age levels in each room. In order to do this well, we decided that there should be a gradual buildup of kids. We only opened three rooms at first, although there are now four. Each couple of weeks we enrolled a few more kids, until we had a full enrollment of seventy-three. We also decided to take 1-year-olds and there was one of them in each class. We were still pursuing the idea of infant day care, but we couldn't find a place in the neighborhood that met code requirements. The 1-year-olds have turned out fantastically, and their parents are really happy.
>
> Unfortunately the staff hasn't been so happy about it. Some of the teachers felt they couldn't handle all the age levels in their classrooms. They felt they couldn't handle all the different requirements of 2's, 3's, 4's, and 5's. Maybe it was a bit much. The 5's did help the 2's and 3's a lot. The 5's would play house and the 2's were the babies; but often the 3's and 4's did not play with anyone. It was hard to find activities that all the children could participate in. As it turned out, by the end of the year there were more 5's in one room and more 2's in another. The teachers and family worker tended to make more homogeneous placements than the parents or board wanted. After lots of discussion the board did change policy. We took no more 1-year-olds and created a 5-year-old room and a mini-room for the 2-year-olds. Recently the city has complained about our taking 2-year-olds, and the staff is all for limiting enrollment to 3's, 4's, and 5's.

Despite these disagreements between parents and staff, Barbara has no doubts that the children have done well. She is particularly happy that Miranda began attending in the fall of 1971, at 2 years, 6 months. She thought the first year was particularly good. But she referred to the difficulties the center has had in the past few months as creating difficulties for Miranda and the other children. And clearly part of the difficulties arose from the staffing problems that

168 WHO'S MINDING THE CHILDREN?

were created by the center's dedication to hiring community people.

Within the last month there have been lots of problems and things haven't gone too well, but really before that everything went well as far as the kids were concerned. I must admit that Miranda was somewhat favored by the teachers, she talked a lot and related to them. She gets to hold the teacher's hand when they go to the park. She gets to go on special errands. I finally talked to the teacher because I thought this wasn't fair to the other kids and probably not very good for Miranda. There have been a few things she's brought home, incidents, language that I've talked to the teacher about, and it's usually worked out. The past few months there's been a big push to get the kids to learn the alphabet, to learn to read and while Miranda loves looking at books and things like that, she doesn't like sitting at a table learning the ABC's, so she just goes off in a corner by herself. Since August she has had no head teacher; although the assistant is quite good, the aide is not. The aide has a lot of problems and she's very militant. She's absent a lot, but everyone has felt she should stay on. She has so many children to support and when she is asked to take her job seriously she defends herself and accuses everyone of trying to keep her down because she's black. Unfortunately she is very punitive, harsh, and rigid in the classroom. But she thinks of herself as pulling herself up by her own bootstraps. She is absent almost as often as she is there. Somehow she has always managed to stay on, though she has been put on probation a number of times by the board. She is the most extreme example of the problem of a number of community people who work there. They are heads of multi-problem families; things are always happening to them.

As a result the center has an incredible number of substitutes every day. On an average there are four or five subs most days and some days there are no regular staff members at all; *everyone* is a sub. This, too, has created another problem, because the subs are other community people. Some of them think these jobs are theirs by right. In fact, one of them said recently that if she didn't sub twice a week, she couldn't make ends meet. So there is a big competition to be called for subbing.

In the past few months things have gotten to the point where the day care center meets staff needs instead of the children's needs. The idea of providing community jobs seems to have overwhelmed the desire to provide quality child care. Sometimes the last staff member there at the end of the day will ask a parent to stay with the remaining children so she can go home. Sometimes there's no one there at eight to let the first children in. And every time there's a job opening, someone has a friend who needs a job. We have a new janitor who was somebody's cousin and he got hired. Now he wants to work at night so the kids won't interfere with his work. But one of our staff policies at the beginning was to have everyone, maintenance, kitchen, and secretarial help, be interested in children, be willing to show them what they were doing. We meant to have all the staff participate, to care about children. Well, if he works at night the kids will never see him; his working at night would defeat our purpose.

Part of the staffing problems that plague the center rises from the difficulties the center has had in finding and keeping a director. This problem is certainly not unique to this center, although here it has become the focus of other struggles going on between different groups of parents and staff. The first director left after a year amid charges of favoritism; several teachers left with her. For seven months, one of the staff worked as acting director. The discussion about, and selection of, the second director exacerbated many of the differences in the center, particularly the racial ones, and precipitated the crisis that the center is going through now.

Selecting a new director was a real bone of contention. Staff wanted a big input into that decision, and the parents felt they should have it. But then, it was impossible to come up with criteria. The personnel committee, which had always been very active, was given the job of screening people for the board. We interviewed many qualified people, but class and cultural problems really began to come out. I was the only white, middle-class person on the committee. I had a hard time. Obviously many of the people who answered our ads were white and middle-class. I didn't like a lot of them. The ladies from the suburbs didn't please anyone. But people, white or black, whose educational philosophy I liked didn't make it with the rest of the committee, and their attitudes weren't always reasonable.

For example, we were supposed to interview the director of a nearby day care center who was thinking of changing jobs. Well, the personnel committee called her an hour before they wanted to interview her. She said she couldn't come then because they were having a cleanup day at her center. She said she was a mess and really wasn't prepared, could she come another day? Whoever talked to her said not to worry, to just come as she was. Well she did "just come as she was." She had on blue jeans, a work shirt, and loafers with holes. Half of the committee refused to talk to her because she came looking like "white trash." What could you do with that kind of situation? She didn't have a chance, though her educational and administrative experience was good.

Part of our problem was an extremely militant woman who had joined the committee as we were beginning our search for the new director. We remained open to the community and she had a nephew in the center, so I guess she had a right to be there. This woman had worked in a very structured, formal day care center run by a Baptist minister. He ran a tight ship. She thought we needed a strong director just like him, someone who would take total responsibility. Never mind that that would mean the end of community and parent control, the end of me *and* of her. Anyway, she was very hard to work with. She didn't like whites. She thought the center should only take poor blacks and Spanish. Her standard was that anyone whose children wore Buster Brown shoes was too rich to be in the center. Ironically enough, her nephew was the best-dressed kid in the center. She was difficult. She would call meetings and not tell me. And after we had meetings that I knew about, she would hold a meeting after the meeting and change decisions and recommendations. During the summer of 1972 I took a short vacation with Miranda. When I came back the personnel committee had hired a new director. They had never taken it up with the board or the staff or the parents.

The personnel committee simply presented the new director to the staff. In the end everyone was so happy to have another director that the irregularities of hiring him were overlooked. He came with good references, both educational and administrative. He was a young, black guy, about 25. He was like a minister in a way, and everyone stood in awe of him—at the beginning. He did work out some administrative procedures which we very badly needed, and he did bring some consistency to staff policies. But he never visited a classroom, and the staff began to feel he wasn't supporting them or providing them with guidance. He wasn't developing any curriculum. People used to joke that he moved to the other side of the hall when he saw a child coming.

He went to school at night and started bringing in his schoolwork to do during the day. Then the parents began to question what he was doing. Although, I'll admit, on one item he had a lot of parent support. Many of the black and Spanish parents wanted formal classroom situations. They were anxious to have their kids learn numbers and letters; they wanted them to be able to read before starting first grade because they were afraid they wouldn't learn afterwards. He thought black ghetto kids should be reading at 3. Many of the parents also wanted a lot of control in the classroom. They wanted the kids to learn to behave, to learn to sit still with their hands folded. This has meant, in terms of classroom activities, that formal lessons have become a big thing, memorizing letters and numbers. The educational program has become more and more formal and more and more rigid. There's a thing against having the kids enjoy themselves, or doing the things they like to do. Through his influence the center got involved with some reading program, which aside from the questions of whether it was good for kids of this age, was totally inappropriate to our kids. All of the books in the reading program present white, rural America. No blacks, no urban scenes. They were crazy.

At the beginning of the winter the city found that he was not qualified, and they refused to continue his salary. He left. This really caused a fall in morale. Because even if he was having problems, he did bring some coordination and consistency to the place. We don't have a director now and I don't know how we are going to hire one. Two of the parents are sharing the job of acting director *until* and *if* we pull things together.

After almost three years of operation many of the center's problems have caught up with it. And yet in one way it is highly organized. Any threat from the outside has brought instant unity to the center. Threats from the city to cut off funds have resulted in every parent turning out for well-publicized demonstrations at the city day care office. Despite all its difficulties the center has always been funded, which has been a cushion against its falling apart. Somewhat proudly, Barbara commented on the fact that they really didn't have to have demonstrations any more; all they had to do was call and threaten one, and their money came through. In that sense the center is very much together. In other ways it is not.

Class, cultural, and race problems have really come to the fore. It tends to be the difference between middle-class whites and now some blacks, on the one hand, who want loose structure and informal learning, and working-class blacks and Spanish-speaking, on the other, who want formal, rigid structure. Although 60 percent of the center families are Spanish, they exert very little pressure and, at least, educationally follow the lead of the working-class blacks. Since we were intended to be parent-controlled, this is a real problem. For a long time all our meetings were bilingual; Spanish-speaking parents who could speak both Spanish and English translated; then they got tired of doing it and refused and none of the rest of us could speak Spanish. So these parents either don't come to meetings or just sit there when they do.

Another real problem is that the majority of staff people live in the community and everybody knows everybody's business. Staff is particularly hard on nonworking parents. The staff really has a kind of negative welfare mentality. It is very much against people who are not working or going to school using the center. The possible value of the experience for the children seems to give them little thought. We do have a policy of taking children whose parents work. But people lose their jobs or they get sick or just take a day off. The staff resents working, even though they're getting paid, when the parents aren't working. The board finally passed a rule that said when parents aren't working they should pick their children up at 4:30.

At the present moment, January, 1973, I feel that the center may be detrimental to some of the kids because of all this turmoil. It may be especially hard on the 2's. But up until now the kids have done really fantastically well. And however else the parents disagreed, they did agree that the children seemed to be growing and developing. My own feeling is that it has been good but it could have been so much better. But low staff morale, backbiting, and general discontent may begin to really affect the children in a bad way. I am thinking about taking Miranda out, though I really don't want to. She has two more years before first grade and I don't know where I can find a place. But it's not just that. I feel I was very, very involved in an important effort at community organization and I would like to see it come together, and I guess I would like to remain a part of it. Everyone has always acknowledged it was a struggle. Everyone also felt it was healthy and productive disagreement. We were especially proud that the whole center was integrated, everyone was glad about this. Although now, there is a lot of open racial antagonism between

blacks and whites. The blacks say the whites want to run everything and have their ideas dominate. The whites agree and draw
back; then the blacks say the whites won't contribute, won't
help, won't take responsibility. I've gotten to feel like the typical
benevolent, condescending white liberal.

Although feeling somewhat defeated after the events of recent
months, Barbara appreciates that many of her difficulties arise from
the fact that Miranda is in the center and subject to an educational
program that a majority of the parents favor and Barbara does not.
She admitted, when I asked her, that parent and community control
were important goals for her and the center had to a considerable
extent succeeded in building a center on that basis, although the
continuing frictions could lead to demands for strong leadership and
a consequent decline in community and parent involvement. If
Miranda were not in the center, Barbara might be in a better position to appreciate and applaud the amount of parent and community
control that does exist. She is, furthermore, extremely sensitive to
the racial and class problems that are an inherent part of her
dilemma. And while she may be willing to give way on most points
in those conflicts, she has some confidence in her sense that the
educational program the parents want could be self-defeating, even
though she understands their anxieties about whether their children
will learn to read at the local public school. She feels that the rigid
and formal program at the day care center, in demanding behavior
and learning far beyond the children's age capabilities, could turn
the children against learning and school.

> In an unexpected way, at least unexpected for me, I guess the
> community has been organized and there is a day care center.
> I just don't agree with the way things are going. I am afraid
> after a time they will find a strong director who will take total
> responsibility and make things run smoothly. I am afraid they will
> follow city regulations and exclude 2-year-olds. I am afraid the
> program will become very formal and traditional. But I just hate
> to give up.

JANET SCHWARTZ AND ANNIE

Janet Schwartz is 28 years old; she is pretty and lively, with a friendly and easygoing style of conversation. Like Barbara Dwyer, she has measured up to a difficult situation. Unlike Barbara, who gives all appearances of having chosen many of the difficult circumstances in her life, Janet has had hers thrust upon her. Certainly the most critical of these was the fact that her husband died when Annie was 3 years old. That was four years ago. Throughout my conversation with her, she frequently referred in various ways to the two years afterwards as ones in which concerns about future security, about being able to support herself and Annie, about assuring Annie's safety and well-being, were foremost in her mind. She had never finished college and felt she had to, if she were ever to find a good job.

> Annie was 3 years old when my husband died. At that time she was in a part-time summer play group and I was working temporarily. After he died, I realized that I would be the sole support of Annie. There was a little life insurance and Social Security, but essentially financial support was now up to me. The best plan seemed to be for me to return to school to get my degree, which I did in September. My parents offered to pay the tuition for a private nursery school for Annie. That was open from 9 A.M. until 3 P.M., which gave me the time I needed. At the end of that school year I had a chance to go on for graduate work. I had no idea what I would do with Annie. My parents couldn't pay for the nursery school again and neither could I. What's more, I really didn't like it. All the kids were so much alike and their parents were very proper and prissy.

Like many people, Janet had never considered a day care center for Annie. And when she was more or less forced to begin looking at them as her only alternative, she found long waiting lists and a reluctance on the part of the centers to take Annie, because Janet would not be working but going to school.

> The dean of the graduate school where I planned to go suggested that I apply to a day care center. I was reluctant. I thought of day care centers as places where kids got dumped. I did visit

some day care centers in my neighborhood but none of them would take me. Then the dean of the school called a friend of hers who was the director of a center and that paved the way for Annie to get in, even though they had a long waiting list. I met the director and visited the center. Really I was very impressed. It was much different than I expected and I was impressed with the director's ideas about education. The center wasn't, after all, a dumping ground, but very educational. Though later I found out it did have some drawbacks.

The center was very structured and scheduled; there was something planned for every minute. At the time, I thought the structure would be very good for Annie, since our life was rather unstructured. Most of the kids in the center were black and Spanish. I was afraid Annie might have some identity problems. In fact, she did have a little trouble joining in group activities, but the center handled this very well. They were sympathetic and found ways to encourage her without forcing the issue. Anyway I met her teacher and had a brief interview. Actually all she said was, "Don't worry if Annie gets hurt." I don't know what made her say that. I guess the kids were very physical. In contrast, Annie was very verbal and not physical at all. I thought the vigor and movement of the kids would be good for her, and it was. I liked the kids; I liked the heterogeneous quality of the place, and as far as the kids went, it was a great place for Annie. The teacher also asked me to come to her if I had any problems and not go to the director, but that year it was never necessary. Annie was then 4 years old.

The only other problem with her starting was really something that had nothing to do with Annie. The center had a rule that I had to be available for the first two weeks. It was a rule for everyone. I didn't think it applied to Annie, who was really very independent and had already spent a year in school. The first few days she only went a few hours anyway. But I felt that they were applying a rule that just didn't fit our case. And as it turned out, she did adjust. After the first week they decided I didn't have to stay. Frankly I really resented having to stay. I was terribly anxious to begin my own work and just when everything seemed settled they had this rule.

I also had an interview with the social worker who took information about my financial situation. On the basis of their sliding scale I only had to pay two dollars a week, which was really great, because then I didn't have anything but Social Security.

In terms of Annie's needs the day care center was exactly what Janet wanted and she was initially happy with what she found there. She was, as she said, even relieved because she felt some of the responsibility for Annie's care was being shared. She did find some things different from Annie's old nursery school.

> Annie adjusted very well. And once everything was settled, I really felt relieved. I felt I could get on with my life. I worked and went to school part-time. I realize my psychological need for feeling secure and safe was intense—knowing that Annie was well taken care of just made everything so much better. And I did feel she was safe and secure. The classes were very structured, and at that point in our life that was good. The teacher was very warm and motherly. The assistant was a man and just great; he had so much rapport with the kids and he was very creative with them. He played the guitar and that was one thing that really drew the kids together.
>
> The first year I had no contact with other parents. I felt alien. Most of the people lived right in the neighborhood; I lived a little outside of it. And there really was no encouragement on the part of the center for parents to interact. There wasn't even a list of names and addresses if you wanted to call another parent. Annie's old nursery school had encouraged all of that, kids visiting and playing with one another. Of course, at the day care center the parents worked all day and the kids were in the center, so there wasn't that much extra time. I would drop Annie off at nine on my way to school and would pick her up late in the afternoon. The director and social worker thought I should only use the center when I was actually at school and doing schoolwork. I got to know some of the staff that way. They would be in the playground when I would come and I would talk to the teachers, though, in general, the teachers didn't seem to have too much contact with the parents: only when kids were dropped off and picked up. And I guess I had teaching in common with the staff.
>
> After I was around for a while I began to notice that things weren't as great as I first had thought. But I never lost my good feelings that Annie was safe and well taken care of.

After having been around the center for a while, two things began to make Janet uncomfortable: the education program and the attitude of the director toward the parents—an attitude which Janet

considered condescending. Despite her own feelings and observations, she realized that most of the parents either approved of the
program and director, or were reluctant, if they didn't, to do
anything about it. As Janet herself appreciated, it was dependable,
safe, and educational. The parents, she believed, were concerned
about their children doing well later on in school. If the education
program put their children ahead of the game, so much the better.
Feeling little support among the parents for her criticisms, she never
felt easy about bringing them into open discussion.

> The center was very education-oriented, big on numbers and
> letters and learning to read. Very formal. I think the director
> staked her reputation on sending bright kids to the local public
> school. There really wasn't a lot of equipment and many of the
> things they did have were worn out. They didn't have a big
> equipment budget. Much classroom activity depended on the
> teacher's initiative and creativity. The outdoor equipment was
> really not good. And it was all on asphalt. In fact, that was what
> the parents first got organized around, buying rubber padding
> for the playground.
>
> Anyway the second year, when Annie was 5, she had a teacher
> for the first several months who was just fantastic. She was really
> creative and very child-centered. But she didn't get along with
> the director, partly, I think, because she really wasn't so structured
> and was much more informal and spontaneous than the director
> liked. She would let things happen instead of making things
> happen. The director kept telling me and this teacher that Annie
> should be pushed more; that she should be learning to read; that
> she had great potential. The director felt Annie wasn't working
> hard enough. The teacher and I disagreed. Who cares if a 5-year-
> old can read? I felt she would read when she was ready. But
> that's not what the director thought. She would come into the
> classroom and interfere, she would even take Annie aside and
> work with her, which the teacher objected to. This teacher
> finally left.
>
> The teacher who replaced her was incredibly academic and,
> in my opinion, hated kids. Annie even complained about her.
> This teacher fitted in perfectly with the director's idea about
> pushing the kids. In fact, the new teacher once said to me, "This
> is a child who needs to be pushed. This is a child who plays too
> much." Well, I talked to the director, but since she agreed with

the teacher she did nothing about my complaint. I found out that some of the other parents were dissatisfied but everyone felt you had to accept it. They felt they had no choice.

The director is a little hard to describe. First of all, she was very friendly and I feel she went out of her way to be nice to me. But she was also very condescending to the parents. She was a white liberal who thought she was helping out a lot of poor people. I'm not sure the parents even noticed, or cared. She always kept her door open, and if you wanted to talk to her she always welcomed you. You know, coffee, cookies, small talk. Or, if you had a personal problem with your child she was always eager to help. Although the time I had the "learning to read" problem with Annie's teacher, she really wasn't very sympathetic and defended the teacher. I don't think many parents ever went to her with complaints about the staff.

She did try to keep them informed about funding problems and city-wide day care problems. Once the social workers went on strike and our social worker had a special meeting for the parents. She explained what it was all about, even though she wasn't going on strike. She didn't agree with the issues. I thought it was nice that she and the director explained the situation.

Sometimes the director would take parents with her to meetings about day care problems and issues. Within the center itself her views generally prevailed. If there was a petition to be signed or information to be passed around, she just asked people to sign or read without going into details about alternatives. I guess most of the parents were willing to accept her view of matters. And she did run a responsible, safe program, so that parents, who probably weren't used to sitting around talking about education or children, just felt she was doing a fine job.

Janet's views of more parent involvement got a push from a group in her own neighborhood that was organizing a day care center. And while there was a reorganization of parents at Annie's center, it did not result in more parent involvement with the center's program. At the same time, Janet's own reservations were strengthened when she was asked by the director to substitute at the center; she had a chance to observe the teacher, kids, and program at close quarters. Her one attempt to bring some of her concerns into the open at a parents' meeting ended in the director closing the meeting without responding to her questions.

I guess my own view started changing, or anyway became broader, when I got involved with a community organization that was setting up a day care center not far from my house. There I saw parents, just like the parents in my center, being very involved, talking about day care, organizing staff and programs, thinking about policies and regulations. I began to see how important it was for parents to be involved and how they could be involved if given half a chance. I later worked at this center for a while, and I know parent control can cause a lot of difficulties, but in the long run these kinds of problems are better than the kind of problems that got ignored or overlooked by the parents at Annie's center.

I didn't think of switching Annie to the other place. The new center was just getting organized and I felt that she was safe and secure where she was. That's what I cared about, that and the family atmosphere in her own class. I was getting out of it what was most important for her at the time.

During our second year there, the parents' organization at Annie's center was reactivated. In fact, the director encouraged me to get involved, and she was very friendly even though she understood that I was dissatisfied. She suggested that we raise money so that the parents could go on a trip with the kids or things like that. Some of the parents thought the money should be used to put rubber padding on the playground. But the director said that was in the budget, that the center was entitled to it, and that she would get it, although she never did. The parents ran a great bazaar. They made lots of money but I've never been sure what the money was finally spent on.

As far as other parent activities went, there wasn't much. The director encouraged the parents to be friendly, to get to know one another, but *nothing* as far as educating or informing the parents about child development or education, or anything that had to do with the center, like the teachers she hired, or the program. I substituted there several times and I remain convinced that it was safe, secure, and educational, but it did have problems. I thought it was overstructured. I once subbed in the 3-year-old room and the kids were so scheduled that they could tell me exactly what they should be doing every minute and exactly what they were supposed to do and not to do. And one of the things they couldn't do was cry. As one of them said, "We are not allowed to cry." That seemed a bit much for 3-year olds.

As well there was a large turnover of staff, and they also had a subbing problem. It was hard to find substitutes; sometimes they had regulars, but in emergencies they often had to call an agency. I think the substitutes were very hard on the kids. And especially in such a structured situation, the minute the teacher wasn't there everything fell apart and subs didn't really know how to pull everything together. If more parents had been available and had known about the program, I feel most of them would have made better subs than the ones the center got. The other problem I noticed when I subbed was that the teachers didn't communicate very much with one another.

The teachers were selected by their academic qualifications. I am sure all the head teachers had degrees; but they were not selected on the basis of the relationship they established with the children. I think Annie summed up the problem when she said "L—— (the director) is practically the president of the whole place." It really was her show.

Janet is fortunate in that the center has an after-school program. After Annie started first grade, she was able to stay in the program. The center picks the children up after school every day and they can stay at the center until six o'clock. Janet works full-time now and she is greatly relieved that Annie has a place to go. She is also happy that an advisory group was elected this year, although she feels the director is reluctant to really consult with it, and that the action of establishing the group was a *pro forma* action on the part of the director to follow city regulations. But there are several parents now who are interested in becoming involved, and they may have some impact on the center.

Annie started in the after-school program last year. Last year it seemed somewhat disorganized. Even though L—— is technically in charge of it, she doesn't really pay much attention. This year there is a special director for the after-school program and the program has become quite good. She really works with and supports her staff. She's been very good at developing activities. She has introduced a sports program for the boys and that has cut down on a lot of aimless wandering and fighting among the boys, freeing some of the teachers to do more creative things with the girls.

This year an advisory group was also started. The city day care office sent a notice that all day care centers had to have one, or, as the director said, "We'll lose our funds." That was the way she handled all problems with the outside world. Sign this, sign that, or we'll lose our funds. And that's exactly the way she handled the advisory group. But I think parents may take their advisory responsibilties seriously. More parents talk after meetings and ask questions about how this works and how that is done. I don't know whether they are more conscious of their own interests and that of their children, or whether they are different kinds of parents, more informed maybe.

There are also new family workers. One of them is really militant and big on parent participation. She has pushed this advisory group and encouraged parents to sign up and run for the places. One-half of the group had to be parents. There were several meetings so that all the parents could understand what the advisory group was about; then there was a meeting to introduce the people who had agreed to be candidates. The first meeting after the election, committees were formed. But I hear now, that the director hired a new teacher without consulting the staffing committee, so it looks like, unless the parents push it, the director will not willingly consult with them.

This will be Annie's last year there and I suppose I am not as interested as I once was. But if a real organization gets going, and parents can work themselves into a position of some influence, maybe other people won't feel as frustrated as I did about making my opinions known. After my experience with the community-run center where I worked for a while, I do appreciate the value of how smoothly and easily things run at Annie's center. There is obviously a value in having someone in charge. On the other hand, I now see that parents who have organized and run their own center have had something special happen to them and their children. They are really in touch with things, they understand what's happening to their children, and that makes a great difference.

Barbara Dwyer and Janet Schwartz raise a whole range of issues that surround the day care question: education, administration, staffing, parent and community control, and economic and racial integration. The two women talk about the inevitable uncertainties from opposite kinds of experiences. Parents and communities cannot run a day care center alone. Lacking some degree of consistency, continuity, and coordination, a day care center seems to pass, as Barbara's has, from crisis to crisis. But without some measure of parent participation and even parent power, a day care center must be, as Janet's is, dictatorial, minimizing parent concerns and interest. In its effect, this kind of policy has to reduce the role of the parent in his child's rearing.

In addition to the administrative dilemma raised by both centers, the programming problem brings the desire for racial and class integration in face-to-face conflict with the educational perceptions and consequent opinions of different kinds of parents. Barbara and Janet are, in their centers, of the minority opinion as far as educational policies go. It is doubtful that if Janet's center had more parent participation there would be any moves toward the less structured, less formal program she favors. Barbara and Janet's middle-class status confers on them a sense of assurance and confidence that early reading and good behavior are not necessarily key ingredients for happiness and success in adult life—and that, in fact, their children will, in time, undoubtedly learn both how to read and how to behave. The working-class parents in their centers do not share that view. For them, learning to sit still and learning to read may be the important first steps in acquiring the discipline and self-control that go hand-in-hand with making it in our society. If parent control is to have any relevance and parents are to have a choice in educational programs, it may turn out that class integration is an unattainable goal. Racial integration, where black and white middle-class and black and white working-class live in proximity, is perhaps more likely to occur. Parents should have a right to choose a program, an educational philosophy that most nearly meets their understanding of the needs of their children and of themselves.

III

Day Care Debated

During the middle sixties, day care worked its way up from Point Zero to become "a major issue" with high priority on the national agenda. During the late sixties and early seventies the will for reform died and with it the attempt to remake day care into a child development service available to every child who needed it. Throughout the 91st and 92nd Congresses and most of Mr. Nixon's first term, day care was the focus of a major conflict between Congress and the Administration. The precise issue under discussion was the Comprehensive Child Development Act which, after two years of Congressional hearings, debate, and compromise, Mr. Nixon vetoed on December 9, 1971. Mr. Nixon's veto did not close the discussion, but gave substance and organization to what had been until then a rather disorganized and sloganeering opposition. Not only were the provisions of the bill—things like costs, control, and the effects on the family—called into question, but broader supports for the new popularity of day care—such as early childhood education and working mothers—were given new attention and criticism.

The veto that precipitated the renewed debate about day care actually originated, in a convoluted way, with a day care proposal by Mr. Nixon himself, but one that he eventually dropped. The day care bill he vetoed, the Comprehensive Child Development Act, was quite different, however, from his own proposal, which went with the welfare reform measures he originally introduced to Congress in the fall of 1969. During the following two years, Mr. Nixon and Congressional liberals kept day care on a political seesaw, with each side striving to control the definition of day care services and their future growth. The battle for a new definition of day care implied in the Comprehensive Child Development Act suffered a major setback with the Nixon veto. Since that time Mr. Nixon has instituted by administrative fiat a policy diametrically opposed to that favored

185

by Congress and has settled on one that embodies the narrowest "patchwork" definition of day care, which favors custodial rather than quality care.

In the following chapters I have laid out the elements of the political debate, the resolution of that debate with the veto, and the questions of social policy and social values which the debate sometimes touched upon but never finally resolved.

CHAPTER 7

POLITICS AND POLICIES

Throughout 1970 and 1971 the United States Congress was the scene of a revolutionary discussion on day care, child development, and, though no one said so publicly, on the future of child-rearing in America. The hearings, in Senate and House, were, in themselves, a comprehensive short course in day care and child development.[1] The Comprehensive Child Development Act which came out of these hearings was a piece of social legislation designed to be as basic and popular as Social Security or veterans' benefits. It provided "the legislative framework for eventual universally available child development programs for *all families who need and want them*,"[2] and offered a variety of medical, nutritional, and educational services for children from infancy—from preinfancy, to be exact, since the bill included prenatal programs—to fourteen years of age.

The provisions for day care in the Nixon Administration's welfare reform bill, the Family Assistance Plan, were clearly outclassed, although ironically, it was the Administration's bill that largely set off this round of legislative interest in day care. While the Family Assistance Plan languished in the hostile Senate Finance Committee, day care itself blossomed into a Congressional flower. What Congressional liberals had managed to do was extract the one apparently pure issue in the whole welfare reform package: kissing babies.

The flurry of legislative activity in favor of day care after the introduction of President Nixon's Family Assistance Plan in 1969 indicated that everyone from the President to a bipartisan group of Congressmen favored some form of nationally supported day care. For some this meant a consolidation of day care services divided among the Departments of Labor, and Health, Education and Welfare, the Children's Bureau, and the myriad state, county, and city governments that participated in a variety of federally funded day care projects. For others it meant the establishment and control of a federally funded day care system that would be used to rigorously cut welfare rolls by sending the welfare mothers of young children to work. For still others it meant a redefinition of the whole idea of day care and its expansion beyond a custodial and welfare-oriented institution to a quality educational and developmental service for young children. Thus their argument was not over "should we?" but "who ought to do it?" "for whom should it be done?" "how should it be done?" and "how much should the government pay?" —all questions over which reasonable men might disagree. The hidden question and the unspoken debate centered around a deeper issue: Would day care become a quality institution, a normal part of American life, or would it remain a substandard service stigmatized by its association with welfare and custodial care?

The drama began with Mr. Nixon's announcement on August 5, 1969, of the Manpower Training Act. Linking the success of training and employing welfare mothers to the availability of day care services, Mr. Nixon called for "greatly expanded day care facilities which would be provided for the children of welfare mothers who choose to work." Mr. Nixon went on to note, however, in words that would subsequently be quoted back to him *ad nauseum*, that

> these would be day care centers with a difference. There is no single ideal to which this Administration is more firmly committed than to the enriching of a child's first five years of life, and thus helping lift the poor out of misery at a time when a lift can help the most. Therefore, these day care centers would offer more than custodial care; they would also be devoted to the development of vigorous young minds and bodies. And as a further dividend, the day care centers would offer employment to many welfare mothers themselves.[3]

Apart from the paternalistic tone used regarding the poor, there was nothing in Mr. Nixon's original definition of quality day care (developmental rather than custodial) that essentially differed from that finally embodied in the Comprehensive Child Development Act. But his justification for day care, tied as it was to removing women from the welfare rolls, aroused the suspicions of many liberals, who felt that as long as day care was tied to welfare it would never be significantly more than custodial. In short, it could never be any good. Whatever Mr. Nixon's first idea of day care, it did not last long. The legislation that was finally sent to Congress under the rubric, the Family Assistance Plan, made the strategic error of only vaguely outlining the day care services that would be provided welfare mothers. The lack of detail gave the impression that the Administration: 1) did not really know what kind of day care it wanted; or 2) was not really interested in day care "with a difference"; or 3) wanted minimal day care services so as to be able to take the last legitimate excuse from welfare mothers who said they wanted to work but could not find anyone to care for their children. In general, Mr. Nixon proposed care for 450,000 children at an annual cost of $386 million, available solely to welfare mothers in training or those who found jobs.[4] When and if their incomes rose above the allowable maximum, they would, of course, no longer receive free day care (making it necessary for them to pay for day care or to quit working so they could stay home to care for their children and—go back on welfare).

The vagueness of the Administration's proposals persisted until the spring of 1971, and is believed to have reflected a battle within the Administration itself, between the Office of Management and Budget and the Department of Health, Education and Welfare. The Office of Management and Budget wanted federally funded day care to be strictly limited to families who fell under the income provisions of the Family Assistance Plan, i.e., welfare families. Health, Education and Welfare, especially the Office of Child Development, was interested in a broader clientele and a child care system more like that envisioned in the Mondale-Brademas legislation; it was particularly sensitive to any possibility that custodial care would become the trademark of Administration-sponsored day care. Dr. Edward Ziegler, head of the Office of Child Development, summed up this intramural battle when he remarked, "This Administration is having a heck of a time in coming to grips with what its philosophy is on day care."*⁵

The lack of a clear Administration position, and the fact that many Congressmen did not like what they did see of it, resulted in the introduction of a number of day care bills, many of them with bipartisan support; the major ones were those that Representative Brademas introduced in the House in the spring of 1970, and Senator Mondale in the Senate in the spring of 1971. These bills were introduced independent of any welfare reform measure, but it was clearly the hope of many Congressmen, particularly Republicans, that whatever day care measures did pass through Congress could be made to fit whatever welfare reform legislation the Administration itself could get through Congress.

The Mondale and Brademas bills were similar in that they attempted to set up a comprehensive system of day care available to people on welfare, to the "working poor," and to middle-income families who would pay fees on a graduated scale. The precise level at which free day care ended and day care for a fee began was a figure over which the bill's supporters later argued with the Administration. The Administration wanted the figure set at $4,500—in effect, excluding the working poor from free day care; Congress wanted the figure set at $6,000, making a good number of the working poor eligible for free day care. Both versions of the bill, although allowing state sponsorship, tried to bypass state control through provisions that would allow smaller government bodies or nongovernmental groups to be the prime sponsors responsible for running day care programs. Among these groups the legislation suggested were: community action agencies, Head Start agencies, community corporations, parent cooperatives, migrant worker groups, labor unions, Indian tribes, employers of working mothers, and public and private educational agencies and institutions.[7] Mondale and Brademas also talked about developmental day care with a

* But before the extremely hostile Senate Finance Committee, Dr. Ziegler had no trouble articulating and minimizing the Administration's interest in day care. "What the Administration's child care program envisions is helping those children whose mothers must work, 'plus other children who have enormous problems' . . . The Administration is talking about 'high risk' children . . . 'I would deter the nation from spending vast sums for all children for preschool training. . . . The great value of preschool training has been oversold.'"[6]

strong educational component, what they described as quality day care, distinguishing it from custodial day care. Finally, their broad definition of child development services included a variety of medical, nutritional, and educational services for young children far beyond anything the Administration had dreamed of doing under the aegis of its Family Assistance Plan.

After a series of compromises in a Senate-House Conference Committee, the Comprehensive Child Development Act finally passed on December 6, 1971. In hopes of receiving a Presidential signature on the bill, the Conference Committee had attempted to take into account some of the Nixon Administration's disagreements with the bill, particularly those dealing with the question of prime sponsors and maximum income allowable for free day care.[8] In retrospect, perhaps the bill's supporters, both inside and outside of Congress, were too optimistic about President Nixon signing the bill, especially since his Family Assistance Plan had gotten nowhere in Congress. In any case the momentum behind a major social innovation seemed to be steadily building when on December 9, 1971, President Nixon stuck out his foot and day care went sprawling.[9]

In commenting on Nixon's veto of the bill, more than one liberal editorialist conjured up the image of shooting Santa Claus.[10] There were some reasons for their irritation. Nixon had gone beyond nuts-and-bolts criticism of the measure to do some conjuring of his own, claiming that the Comprehensive Child Development Act "would commit the vast moral authority of the National Government to the side of communal approaches to child-rearing over against the family-centered approach." This was a deliberate overstatement and undoubtedly a concession to the Agnew-Thurmond right, which had branded large-scale day care as a plot to Sovietize America. One conservative columnist predicted that the Brademas Bill "contains the seeds for destruction of Middle America; and if Richard Nixon signs it, he will have forfeited his last frail claim on Middle America's support."[11]

There were other exaggerations in the Nixon veto message, such as a twenty-billion-dollar price tag; but it was the accusation that the bill had "family-weakening implications" which dominated Nixon's attack, and which was all the more perplexing since in almost two years of Congressional hearings on all the day care bills, not one of the Administration witnesses had mentioned this problem. When Mr. Nixon declared that, "There is a respectable school of opinion that this legislation would lead toward altering the family relationship," he was undoubtedly correct, but why had the Administration kept that school of opinion to itself during the period when the bill was being formulated? (There was testimony on the subject, of course, from those who *favored* the bill because they believed it would indeed alter family relationships—for the better.)

The problem with the President's veto message was the Administration's own plans for day care—plans which unfortunately have won out. For not only did the broader definition of developmental day care services and the more generous eligibility standards of the Comprehensive Child Development Act go down to defeat, but the old system financed through Title IV-A and IV-B of the 1967 Social Security Act underwent drastic revisions, limiting strictly the overall federal expenditures allowed for day care. Title IV-A and IV-B had granted funds on a three-to-one matching basis. States, localities, or private voluntary groups who could meet 25 percent of their day care costs could have federal funds for the remaining 75 percent. The funding was open-ended; no ceiling was placed on overall federal expenditures or on the amount any one state might apply for. In passing the Revenue Sharing Act of 1972, Congress did put a limitation on those expenditures, indicating that revenue-sharing funds could be substituted by those states that wished to use their money in this way.

The Title IV-A and IV-B programs were focused on welfare and very low-income families, and control was vested in state governments, features which were not, after all, so different from those vague ones presented along with the Family Assistance Plan and which were reinforced by the Department of Health, Education and Welfare guidelines issued in 1973. They are features which Dr. Edward Ziegler characterized in testimony before Senator Mondale's subcommittee: "I think in many instances we are paying for service that is harmful to children."[12] But in the same testimony, Dr. Ziegler and Steven Kurzman* insisted that the Administration's plans for day care were better than this, although in terms of structure, financing, and per capita expenditure it was difficult to distin-

* Assistant Secretary for Legislation, Department of Health, Education and Welfare.

guish between the FAP proposals and those now in effect. In short, the Administration seemed not to be willing to go beyond minimal day care services for a relatively small number of children whose mothers would agree to participate in work-training programs.

It is this background which accounts for a certain skepticism about the President's demand that day care be "consciously designed to cement the family in its rightful position as the keystone of our civilization." Is it the middle-class family which is about to be "cemented" while the lower-class family is sandbagged? When the President says that, "All other factors being equal, good public policy requires that we enhance rather than diminish both parental authority and parental involvement with children," does that initial qualifying phrase mean "except in cases of welfare mothers or lower-income families"? In the hearings Senator Mondale conducted, it was the Senator, not the Administration's witnesses, who expressed concern with intervention in "the most sacred institution in American life, the family." (Senatorial rhetoric is no more constrained than Presidential.) What was at issue was Mondale's insistence on local control and parent participation, which the Administration opposed in favor of a scheme that, as Mondale quite accurately pointed out, would give Governor John Bell Williams control over day care policies for black children in Mississippi. And for anyone who cared to look further, it was obvious that FAP day care services would do more to undermine the family with their attempt to coerce the mothers of preschool children to work than the Comprehensive Child Development Act, which was being established on a totally voluntary basis.

As Gary Wills wrote at the time of the veto, apropos of Nixon's own plans for day care, "The generous American spirit thinks that those ignoble enough to be poor have forfeited that right [to be free]. If they can ask for a dole, it is only because they are slavish in soul. They must be forced out to the employment line, there to 'redeem themselves from poverty,' earn back their children, and reenter the status of full citizenship."[13]

That Mr. Nixon, blessed with a talent for understatement, should refer to the family not only as the "keystone" of the nation or of society—an elementary cliché—but of the *civilization*, only encourages further questions. *What* civilization? Or for that matter, what *family?* Philippe Ariès has instructed us that the family and home as we think of them today, separated from the world of community and work, are inventions of the last few centuries: they have existed over a relatively limited time historically and a relatively limited area geographically. The flux is greater than ever today. Whatever model the President may have in mind as *the* family, he had better use quick-drying cement. A mere assertion, or a veto on day care, does not a keystone make.

What made the veto message all the more annoying to those who supported the bill was that on some points the President was clearly right. That the Comprehensive Child Development program was "truly a long leap into the dark" was another Nixonian hyperbole; a leap into the dark is a "bold initiative" when it is decided to visit China or restructure the economy. What the President was getting at, however, was that the measure was a major social innovation— "the most radical piece of legislation to emerge from the 92nd Congress." The bill's supporters preferred to minimize its novelty, describing it in terms of services already offered, as an improved, educational version of the babysitting working mothers must currently utilize, or as an extension downward of the public school system. The bill, said one Senatorial spokesman for this point of view, "is as American as apple pie." But Nixon's estimate was not only more accurate, it also reflected the reverberations such a development would have throughout the social system.

Each version of day care politics has its own set of social policies and priorities. One clearly falls within the "patchwork" definition we discussed in Chapter 1, and it is now clear that it is this version of day care, with its narrowly defined goals and rigid eligibility standards, that the Nixon Administration favors and is intent on implementing. The Congressional version was not without its patch-work elements, but it went beyond that in an attempt to meet the child care needs of the working poor with quality rather than custodial care.

Political battles sharpen our sense of issues; they do not encourage dallying over complicated questions of social policy and, even more important, the values that social policies embody. In battle, values are invoked, not examined. Nixon hails the family and fiscal responsibility; Congress calls upon the needs of children and local control. And it is these values that we should now examine.

THE LARGER DEBATE:
THE SEVENTIES MEET THE SIXTIES

Is President Nixon right? Despite his "holier than thou" veto defending family, fiscal responsibility, and administrative efficiency, might not Mr. Nixon have raised the right questions—even if for the wrong reasons? The veto message did not detail precisely what reverberations the Administration thought the Comprehensive Child Development Act would have. Concern over control, cost, and the family predominated, and it was these issues that critics concentrated on in elaborating the potentials for disaster. And their criticisms did not stop there but went on to scrutinize the total rationale upon which the new interest and popularity of day care during the sixties had been based, resurrecting questions of early-childhood education, maternal deprivation, and working mothers that day care advocates had seemingly laid to rest. The ensuing discussions suggested, not that day care critics or day care advocates had the winning arguments (in many cases their positions were not, in the final analysis, mutually exclusive) but that the pendulum-like quality of most of our political discussions and activities has finally overtaken the discussion on day care as well.

In general, many day care critics favor the traditional patchwork child welfare rationale for providing day care for children from welfare families and children from negligent or inadequate families. They see broad-ranging day care services for "all families who need and want them" as a threat to the healthy and necessary intimacy of the mother-child relationship, the family, and the social order. Such day care is fearfully seen as the vehicle for introducing a number of unspecified but probably undesirable values, summed up in the phrase "community-centered versus family-centered" child-rearing, which would ultimately provide the State, or the Expert, or an Unrepresentative Group, with the tools for an intolerable degree of social control, going beyond the acceptable limits for a democratic, individualistic society.

On the other hand, many day care advocates are critical of certain forms of day care—for two examples, commercial development of day care systems, and custodial care for children from welfare families. But they see broad-ranging day care services as a necessity for meeting the child care needs of many kinds of families, for providing children with the opportunity to be with a variety of other children in a child-centered environment, and providing them with happy, sane, and intelligent childhoods. Moreover, they recognize what many day care critics do not: the economic well-being of many families depends on a working mother who, in turn, must be provided with decent child-care alternatives. Whether they are reformers or radicals, advocates strongly suggest that many of the conditions of our present social system need changing, and they see day care as one instrument for encouraging those changes. Underlying this view is the assumption that education, including preschool education, does make a difference in a child's later ability to establish an economically and psychologically secure adulthood. They see day care as a means of creating a more democratic society in which every individual has been more equally equipped.

The chief issue which divides critics and advocates is the degree to which day care should become a normal part of American life, the degree to which it should cease being a "necessary evil," in short, become a legitimate child-care option for middle-income as well as low-income families. Involved in the disagreement are differing perceptions and opinions about the role of women, the effects of day care on young children, the condition of the family, and the long-term fiscal and social costs of day care.

Early Learning and Maternal Deprivation

Throughout the fifties and early sixties there was an accumulation of convincing evidence that a child had reached the halfway point in his development by the time he reached first grade. Instead of being a time when the child, for all his emotional sensitivity, was intellectually somnolent, the preschool years were recognized as a period of intensive and concentrated learning. These findings stimulated increased interest not only in early learning itself, but in the conditions and environments which most encouraged this development.[14] Inspired by such optimistic mottoes as Jerome Bruner's, "Any subject can be taught effectively in some intellectually honest form to any child at any stage of development," Head Start centers and private nursery schools had been established and developed, both of them considered one way of meeting and encouraging this intensive learning period in young children. Some of these children had come from homes which fostered and allowed an atmosphere that met a child's early learning potential; others of them had come from homes where poverty, indifference, or simple lack of information inhibited and prevented a child's proper development. For some children, nursery schools and Head Start centers had reinforced their home environments, underlining the fact that for some parents, preschools were used not only for learning purposes but as well for broader social, economic, or psychological reasons. But for other children nursery schools and Head Start centers had been seen as vital necessities for their proper development; and when and where Head Start became a full-day, year-round service, it had in some measure acted as educationally oriented day care. Day care where it existed had not been long in following suit, attempting to implement programs for early childhood education, though often enough limited resources and staff made this an extremely difficult task.

The whole promise of early childhood education had been tied to a general belief that an improvement in educational services at all levels—preschool, primary, and secondary—would not only improve educational performance but would also begin to equalize the quality of adult life by preparing people to take good jobs, by equipping people to compete for higher-paying jobs. Educational reform had been, during the sixties, thus linked to a widespread and powerful political belief that poverty and racism, or, at least, their most blatant effects, could be minimized in coming generations. There had been educational innovation and experimentation at all levels, but early childhood education—which theoretically nipped the problem in the bud—had been the particular beneficiary of this attitude, and the establishment of Project Head Start had been the particular focus of governmental efforts at working on the preschool level. The spillover from the Head Start effort plus the growth of private nursery schools had redefined the meaning of good day care services. A warm, loving, and solicitious environment was no longer enough for maximally *good* day care; some further concern had to be shown for the child's cognitive development. Hence the expansion of day care services had become linked to the cause of early childhood education and development, finding specific legislative expression in the Comprehensive Child Development Act.

Educational research done for day care purposes was not designed to prove anything about ultimate adult status, job, or income. In fact, it made no vast claims about the future at all. Rather it was intended to examine the question of whether day care presented the same problems of maternal deprivation as did total institutionalization. On a pedagogical level such research asked, what kind of educational programs should be developed to meet the educational needs of the day care population, for the most part low-income, minority families, and what kind of language, attitudes, and behavior on the part of day care workers produced a good environment for children.[15] This research addressed itself to "how to" questions rather than to possible long-term gains associated with the total rationale for early childhood education. Obviously it was hoped that a good educational program in a day care center would, like Head Start, produce better educational performance in primary school. But in the meantime, there have been some questions raised about whether Head Start and early education produce anything in the way of improved cognitive performance at the primary school level.[16] All evidence seemed to suggest that by the end of the first grade, children who had been in Head Start did no better on tests than children who had not participated in such programs. Whether they would have done even worse than they had is an intriguing and untestable proposition. Such tests do not, of course, measure intangible results like behavior, or emotional and social development, or even broader effects like changes in parental and community attitudes toward learning and schooling. Obviously cognitive effects and the ability to test cannot be the only measures of success or failure, but unfortunately in political terms such results translate into decreased interest and most likely decreased funding.

The veto of the Comprehensive Child Development Act, whatever the bill's final limitations and problems, was as much a symbol of a decline as anything else. Hand in hand with poor test results, the decline in the political willingness to eradicate poverty and racism jeopardized the attempt to incorporate good educational programs into day care services. Until other rationales are produced and politically justified, it may be extremely difficult to convince Congressmen and taxpayers that vast expenditures for providing educational components to day care services are warranted, although the effort to cut welfare rolls will continue to make day care necessary.

The publication in the fall of 1972 of Christopher Jencks' monumental study, *Inequality*, drew the complexities of the problem in bold relief. After a thorough review of available data relating to access to education, distribution of educational resources, heritability, and environmental factors in IQ scores and family backgrounds, Jencks and his co-authors concluded, "None of the evidence we have reviewed suggests that school reform can be expected to bring about significant social changes outside the schools."[17] In other words, educational reforms were not likely to produce a more equitable distribution, either of income or competitive advantage in gaining good jobs. Jencks does not advocate, as many parsimonious Congressmen and taxpayers might, drastic reductions in educational expenditures. He does argue that schools should become an end in themselves, a pleasant place for both teachers and children.

> If we think of school life as an end in itself rather than a means to some other end, such differences are enormously important. Eliminating these differences would not do much to make adults more equal, but it would do a great deal to make the quality of children's (and teachers') lives more equal. Since children are in school for a fifth of their lives, this would be a significant accomplishment.
>
> Looking at schooling as an end in itself rather than a means to some other end suggests that we ought to describe schools in a language appropriate to a family rather than a factory. This implies that we will have to accept diverse standards for judging schools, just as we do for judging families. . . . The ideal system is one that provides as many varieties of schooling as its children and parents want and finds ways of matching children to schools that suit them. Since the character of an individual's schooling appears to have little long-term effect on his development, society as a whole rarely has a compelling interest in limiting the range of educational choices open to parents and students. Likewise, since professional educators do not seem to understand the long-term effects of schooling any better than parents do, there is no compelling reason why the profession should be empowered to rule out alternatives that appeal to parents, even if they seem educationally "unsound."[18]

Day care services would obviously fit comfortably such a description and profit from such a degree of diversity and parent control, although the twists and turns of Jencks' argument may well lose some present admirers of both educational reform and an expanded day care system. For the force of his argument does not necessarily lead to his conclusions, nor even to the more radical alternative of closing schools and collapsing the present day care system, but to under-financing and custodial-type arrangements. His conclusions, in fact, pose a particular challenge to day care, which has never enjoyed public support or the relative largesse of funds granted the nation's educational systems; rather, day care has been struggling to move from custodial to developmental services. And, in recent years, it has benefited from a generally favorable climate of opinion toward innovation and reform at all levels of education. Although Jencks takes care to note that there are minimum levels below which schools and school financing cannot go, a change in the over-all attitude toward the value of education may well leave day care in its present limbo, foreclosing any hopes for educational or developmental services.

Quite apart from questions of early childhood education, concerns remain about maternal deprivation and the long-term psychological effects of day care, particularly for young children. Despite the experiments and theorizing that have been done on the relevance of maternal deprivation to the day care question, analysts and psychiatrists continue to express deep-seated concern about early separation of mother and child. Throughout the sixties there were attempts, as we have seen, to explore the differences between maternal deprivation and mother-child separation, that is, the difference between the absence of maternal care and its effects on the child (although, in some cases, the mother may be *physically* present, but emotionally absent) and the temporary, daily separation of mother and child where the child receives good, substitute maternal care. These studies had centered particularly on group care for infants and toddlers, that is, children below the age of 2½ or 3.

The findings were positive, producing convincing evidence that a good day care program could be developed that was beneficial for infants from homes where there was inadequate maternal attention.[19] Good day care could compensate for poor home conditions. There remained two unanswered questions: 1) Would day care be good for infants and toddlers from adequate homes, where they received good maternal attention; and 2) Would day care be good for children from 3 to 5. In fact, the latter question has been of little real concern since it is felt that by the age of 3 most children have reached a sufficient degree of independence or autonomy to be able to leave their mothers temporarily without any great degree of difficulty. And, in fact, popular wisdom has it that, if by the age of 3 a child has not reached a healthy degree of independence from its mother, a play group or nursery school might be useful for reducing an often unhealthy dependency on the part of both child *and* mother.

Nonetheless, both questions remain of considerable concern to many people, particularly psychiatrists and analysts. (And they would be of concern to everyone if minimal and custodial-type day care were to be the rule rather than the exception.) Their generally reluctant and conservative approach to the question of expanded day care services was probably best advanced by Dr. Dale Meers, whose conclusions rest not on observation of American day care centers but on day care centers in Eastern and Western Europe.

> The early years from birth through three appear developmentally as the time of maximum psychiatric risk, and failures of psycho-biological adaptation are manifest in a progression that includes marasmus, autism, childhood schizophrenia, and an extended range of poorly understood pathologies. . . . Since these severe pathologies are not directly evident in present Day Care populations of the Communist world, or in the experimental nurseries of the U.S., many academically oriented child development researchers presume that mental change is an all or nothing phenomenon. . . . The clinician is less fearful of gross pathology that might derive from Day Care, than of incipient, developmental impediments that would be evident in later character structure, such as flattened feelings (schizoid personality), a-social attitudes (psychopathic tendencies), defense against emotional intimacy (fear of marriage), etc.

> In emphasizing the potential damage of early Day Care, there is a danger of implying that there is little risk for the three to five year olds. From the psychoanalytic viewpoint, the maturational vulnerabilities of that age span include (only) the risk of phobic, hysteric and obsessional neuroses and these risks certainly should be taken into account. Nevertheless, the child who is emotionally

secure in his third year exudes intellectual curiosity and evidences a hunger for experience with his contemporaries and, in this instance, part-time Day Care offers delight and a momentous learning experience, i.e., so long as the option for daily attendence remains, more or less, with the child.

Given the present state of our ignorance about psychiatric damage, massive Day Care programs appear all to much like Pandora's box.[20]

Dr. Meers ends by recommending that day care be reserved for use only by the most disadvantaged and neglected children in the population. His opinions probably represent the most negative case against expanding day care services; there is a considerable range of psychological opinion between his views and those which see day care as an unalloyed good.

Even Drs. Urie Bronfrenbrenner and Jerome Kagan, both of whom see day care as potentially workable, have nonetheless raised questions about our national capabilities for providing good day care—day care that does not divide parents and children, does not separate children and adults, that does take a thorough look at the kind of social values it is promoting, day care that would meet the differing needs of children not only according to their age but according to their cultural background.[21]

Psychologists, psychiatrists, educators, and other professional experts can provide evaluative tools for measuring the quality and effectiveness of day care services; their findings can and should influence the whole question of expanding day care. But the question is finally a political matter to be settled in a political way. One can be utterly cynical and predict that politics in the narrowest sense will prevail, that Administration fiat will dictate in favor of the "patchwork," minimal and custodial. But, in fact, the future role, size, and place of day care is a political question in the broadest sense, raising matters of basic value, control, economic and social cost, and family life, to which citizens as well as officials and experts must respond.

Control

Day care represents a tremendous force for political, social, and economic control. Depending on how day care is financed and regulated, it will be a bonanza, boondoggle, or bust for a wide variety of people and governmental bodies. Therefore, the fear of *the wrong people* in control of day care looms larger than most of the other frightful possibilities, even among those generally favorable to the expansion of day care services. On the right, the conservative journal *National Review*, which supported the Nixon veto, predicted: "It is not likely, to put it mildly, that the moral, religious and social attitudes of those implementing the program would reflect the main-stream of American life, or traditional values."[22] On the left, the Radical Education Project foresees the day that a nationally controlled system of day care would be used to force poor people into a system of slave labor while their children were cared for in custodial day care centers.[23] Whether control of day care is vested in the federal government, or in state and local government, in bureaucrats or experts, in parents or local communities, in the public school system, private franchisers, or in industries, there are those who see any one or two of these groups as detriments to *quality* day care, as well as exploitative and un-American.

Federal government intervention in the crucial years of early childhood and its intrusion into the sacrosanct child-rearing responsibilities of the family are, in themselves, notions alarming enough to convince many people that the expansion of day care services is an invitation to total social disorder and chaos. The complaint among conservatives was that the Comprehensive Child Development Act was a liberal conspiracy to Sovietize American youth. A less paranoid view doubted it would turn innocents into Red Army recruits, although it shared with conservatives certain suspicions about control from the top by impersonal and anonymous bureaucrats. Such liberals, in fact, favored federal funding with a large measure of parent and community control. Ironically enough, the conservative side of the argument, at least in the case of the Comprehensive Child Development Act, fell on the side of greater rather than lesser federal centralization in the cause of fiscal and administrative responsibility.

The federal government does not constitutionally trade in social disorder, but in this case a social institution was being created from the top—an institution intended to deal with young children. It readily conjured up images of Washington bureaucrats dictating feeding schedules, prescribing play equipment, and issuing lists of approved social values. But even without these conspiratorial fears, many critics would raise objections to federal control of day care. In comparison to day care, other human service institutions— schools, asylums—"just growed" like Topsy during the nineteenth century. Even now when there are federal standards and financial support to these institutions, states, local communities, small groups, and individuals often maintain a powerful influence over them. Would that be true in the case of day care? There is little merit in having day care "growed" like Topsy, nor is there much chance that it will; neither are critics on both right and left happy with the prospect of the federal government funding, controlling, and setting standards for day care. On the other hand, they must face the reality that without federal support there will never be extensive day care and that without federal money whatever day care there is will never be very good.

The editorial in the *National Review* charged that the Comprehensive Child Development Act went "far beyond the concept of the 'day-care center.' The Federal Government . . . would become the most important, and ultimately the strongest arbiter of child-rearing practices in the United States." The dominating position of the federal government in national affairs, its money and administrative power, would eventually control early childhood care, standards, and studies, and, if the government were so inclined, it could significantly undercut all parental responsibility for child-rearing. The editorial went on to charge that the agents of the federal government, i.e., day care workers, would come between parent and child. "The child's values and attitudes would be shaped by the social workers, educationists, psychiatrists and so on who would be interposed at the earliest possible moment—even during the first eighteen months—between the child and its parents." The editorial drew to a close with a quote from Senator James Buckley, one of the bill's strongest opponents, who invoked the image of Big Brother before his Congressional colleagues by declaring, "I believe that the American parent is not yet prepared to delegate the development of his child to the white-coated bureaucrats who will inevitably dominate the program."[*24]

---

* In Congressional debate Buckley's remarks went even further. Apropos of the Comprehensive Child Development Act he said, "I cannot escape the haunting fear that if this measure is enacted we shall be taking a final, fatal step down

The fear that the federal government would be Super-parent is magnified by the premonition of some critics that all too many parents are eager to turn their child-rearing responsibilities over to others. Opening day care centers would present them with the opportunity. And proposing day care centers at public expense only inflames the opposition of irate taxpayers, who see a great political giveaway to irresponsible parents at the expense of hard-working and responsible ones. But if the federal government was judged an unsuitable organizer of day care centers because of its power, remoteness, and potential for totalitarian control, proponents of community-controlled day care found the alternative suggestion of putting them exclusively in charge of state governments even less to their liking.

The Nixon Administration was adamantly opposed to community control; it wanted federal funds channeled through state governments, which would be the "prime sponsors" of day care in their own states. The federal government would then have no more than fifty administrative bodies to monitor, regulate, and fund. In contrast, the Comprehensive Child Development Act had tried to bypass state and even some local government bodies and grant funds directly to the prime sponsors, be they private nonprofit organizations, voluntary organizations, school districts, ad hoc day care groups, *or* governmental bodies.

The Nixon Administration charged that such a system would never work and predicted that an army of federal inspectors and bureaucrats would be necessary to run it. Nonetheless, many groups opposed state control of day care for a number of good reasons. Attention was focused primarily on the South, where it was feared that state governments controlled by whites would use federal day care money to the detriment of blacks, forcing them into undesirable and low-paying jobs in exchange for day care. Northern states controlled by a nonurban legislature might not be any more inter-

---

the road which leads to a completely controlled existence of the kind portrayed by Orwell's *1984* and Huxley's *Brave New World* and, most recently, by the work of B. F. Skinner. Rather than breeding that race of wise and just philosopher-kings dreamed of by Plato, however, we are more likely to end up producing a race of docile automatons." One suspects the desirability of Plato's vision over that of B. F. Skinner's is a function of Plato's distance in time from Senator Buckley.

ested in providing quality day care to largely urban populations. The lingering liberal distrust of state governments stems from those bodies' generally pro-rural, anti-urban attitudes, a characteristic which has long caused supporters of progressive social legislation to look to Washington. The case with day care has been no different. Furthermore, most state governments have not shown great initiative in establishing day care services, even when the federal government was willing to pay for 75 percent of their costs; California is probably alone in the support it has given to developing a statewide system. Existent systems elsewhere are most often the result of efforts by city or county governments, voluntary groups, or day care associations. Finally those groups who favor community and parent control of day care see state governments as being the least likely of federal, state, and city to grant the autonomy necessary for their idea to work.

Everyone is agreed, at least in public, that some degree of local control is required if day care is to meet the needs of the communities in which it is located. But the consensus ends when it comes to defining the extent of local control, and even more so in defining who exactly constitutes "local." Is a state, municipal, or county government "local"? Or is a community group or organization "local"? Or are the parent-users of day care services "local"? City officials may exercise "local control" because they channel funds and select sites, but parents may exercise "local control" by refusing to use such day care or by making the day care service meet their own needs irrespective of governmental rules and regulations. "Local control" is a shifting notion and a switchblade slogan, depending on how it is being used and who is using it. Can there be local control on the municipal and state level if the federal government sets program and staff standards? Can there be local control on the community level if eligibility and fee scales are established on the state level? On the other hand, if a community on the basis of "local control" decided it wanted only custodial care, should higher bodies be required to fund it?

Under Title IV-A and IV-B, states and local governments contributed 25 percent of day care funds and it was they who spoke for local interest, a position which has been enhanced by the fact that some day care funds will now come out of general revenue-sharing funds. The notion of "local" in the Comprehensive Child Development Act had a more diffusive and less governmental orientation. Under its provisions, the prime sponsor was required to have a Child Development Council with at least one-third of its members economically disadvantaged parents, and in each locality a Local Policy Council composed entirely of parents or their representatives.[25] This, of course, posed a threat to many large city governments, accustomed to the power and patronage that went with funneling federal funds for projects under their control. Local community groups within these cities, especially those who argued strongly for community control of day care, saw the city governments as their potential adversaries in securing federal funds, and have made it known that parent and community participation will not be merely advisory to the city governments. In ghetto areas especially, where the local government has often ignored or minimized previously existent needs, community groups are vociferous in their demands for real control over their own day care centers.

Not unexpectedly, these community and parent groups are seen as a mixed blessing by everyone else. Despite cries of "Sovietization," no serious observer of the day care scene expects the federal or even local governments to become the child-rearers of America. These community groups are the key ingredient for community- and parent-centered day care; their presence and interest is taken with great seriousness when they go along with establishment planning and thinking on the subject of day care. Yet when they speak up, they are seen as a threat to the natural order of things. In this respect, they are no different from the poverty groups in the sixties who were tolerated as long as they let professionals or government officials define their needs, but were immediately proclaimed revolutionaries when they began to articulate their own ideas. When they are most effectively acting as a grass-roots organization, most clearly making their needs known and demands heard, they are seen as a group of raggle-taggle irresponsibles who do not really know what is best for their children. In other words, bureaucrats seem to think that if community people were really in charge, we would have abysmal day care services.

About the only sentiment that unites these groups contending for control of day care (aside from "doing what is best for the children") is their common opposition to any kind of day care which would be eligible for federal funds but whose only control would be the profit margin. Franchised and commercial centers and some kinds of industrial day care, where there is no effort to meet any but the most minimal standards and with no provisions for parent control, are what they have in mind. In circumstances where a family might have recourse to such centers, but where fees are met by public funds, neither parents nor officials have a handle by which to enforce higher quality standards.

Despite the apparent uncertainty over who controls day care, some things are certain: the federal government will have to supply the funds; state and local governments will be responsible for inspecting and licensing centers; parents and communities will have to work hard to get good day care. Yet another question of control is raised by critics. Who will be in daily charge of the children? What kind of people will they be? Here the contrast is drawn between, on the one hand, highly skilled teachers who work in cooperation with other professionals, such as family workers, psychologists, and medical doctors, and on the other hand, paraprofessionals, who are more likely to have had on-the-job training, perhaps not less skilled than the college-trained teachers but without degrees and, perhaps, without resources for consultation and advice. Although everyone wants what is "best for the children," many people argue that what is best in this case is not necessarily the professionally trained, but the warm and loving.

One critic of the Comprehensive Child Development Act put the differences this way:

> Great numbers of good day care centers are urgently needed, but the notion of Sen. Mondale's that "good" means armies of psychiatrists, psychologists, psychiatrically trained counselors, medical specialists, etc., is self-defeating and archaic.
>
> Let's hope Congress will back up and run the hill again, this time providing sufficient funds for medical and dental care; good beds, food, recreation; and most importantly, for warm, intelligent child-care counselors concerned with early childhood development.
>
> Too many good programs—OEO, medicare—have been choked by too high administrative salaries and unrealistic staff requirements. Excellent child day care centers, like public schools, should be a way of life in our country.[26]

The distinction between the two types is drawn sharply—more so than it will be in reality. Warmth and love are not the singular province of the nonprofessional nor is he or she necessarily lacking needed skills, or sufficient training; a professional may be warm and loving, but even a professional might not be trained in the proper care and education of young children. This division concerns many who see the total professionalization of child-rearing as a disaster and, on the other hand, those who see a total disregard for professional skills in dealing with children similarly. The effects of putting children in unskilled hands is clear: part of the lingering distaste for day care flows from a remembrance of the time when unskilled child care workers were the rule rather than the exception. Since we have so rarely accomplished it, the consequences of putting young children in the hands of professionals are less clear but this, too, raises ticklish problems.

Will day care promote the professionalization of child-rearing? If the past is any clue, the authority of the "amateur" parent seems to decline in proportion as the role of the professional child-worker grows. If the professional's authority is continually enhanced by research and studies in child development, what future has parental authority or influence? As quality day care services become available, these early learning theories and child development patterns will more and more become the basis for child-rearing techniques. The parents of the future may not only not know how to teach the "new math," they may not know how to develop optimal crawling techniques. Will the elaboration of an esoteric body of knowledge about children set new standards about how children should be raised—standards that can only be met in day care centers? The coercive aspects of expertise can be more compelling than those of the law.

Costs: fiscal and social

Since labor costs are the single largest item in the day care budget, about 75 percent of the budget, the resolution of the professional/ nonprofessional dilemma may not be a matter of warm distinctions but cold cash. It may be that the question of daily control will finally come down to cost. The immediate costs of day care have been closely analyzed; the long-term costs, including day care's impact on the total economy and its social costs, have been only cursorily examined.

Several studies have constructed detailed budgets showing that good, acceptable, or minimal day care will cost on the average $2,320, $1,862, or $1,245 per child.[27] Multiplied by the six million children whose mothers work and who are presently said to need day care, the cost comes to an annual expenditure of between seven and twelve billion dollars.* The obvious first question critics raise is: Should that kind of money be spent on day care? Will it be money well spent? They argue that the national budget cannot possibly afford that kind of outlay. And, they go on, even if we could afford to spend seven to twelve billion dollars for educational and social purposes, wouldn't it be better to spend it improving present educational facilities on the primary or secondary school level, or in creating higher-paying public service jobs that could raise a family's income without having the mother work, or even more radically, paying all mothers to stay home and take care of their own children?[28]

Part of this concern for costs and working mothers is related to concerns about mother-child separation and the attenuation of family ties. But a significant part of this concern rests on a question of social policy: in simple money terms, which will cost less, welfare payments or day care costs for low-income families? In a situation where she is offered subsidized day care, what is the likelihood of a welfare mother finding a job that would raise her family income above what she receives on welfare? On the basis of his analysis of the WIN (Work Incentive) program in Washington, D.C. (which has been training welfare mothers for clerical jobs), Gilbert Steiner calculated that in a four-person family the net gain for a working mother over her welfare counterpart would amount to twenty-two dollars a month. It is a sum that could only appeal to the highly motivated or to women who expected to move up the ladder. The difference in cost to the city was more marked and

---

* It is not likely that all six million children are in need of day care services, but it is difficult to estimate how many actually are. Government estimates tend to fall between one and two million, numbers which reflect the population that might be eligible for government-subsidized day care. Those who take a broader view, seeing all working mothers in need of some kind of day care, make far higher estimates.

more favorable to the day care side of the equation, if the mother had fewer than four children of day care age. For example, a working mother with two children in day care and one in elementary school would save the Washington, D.C. Department of Welfare about fifty-six dollars a month. Steiner is doubtful that the use of day care can significantly reduce welfare costs, unless a rather cheap variety of day care is used. He specifically makes note of the attempt to use other welfare mothers as babysitters, a suggestion that has been roundly criticized for both its coercive aspects and the potentially damaging effects on the children who might use it. Steiner himself believes that the use of day care or its expansion will "have little effect on the number of welfare dependents and no depressing effect on public relief costs."[29]

In a similar study done in New York City by Blanche Bernstein and Priscilla Giacchino, the findings showed the same consequences for day care. In order to meet the vast need for day care and to keep costs within reason, they concluded that day care centers should meet only the minimum standards set by HEW for federal funds, rather than the uniquely higher standards that New York day care centers are, by and large, meeting. In other words, developmental or educational components ought to be minimized in favor of custodial care.

> . . . Without abandoning the long-range goal of enriched pre-school programs universally available for all, the public interest would best be served in the short range by reaching more children with good day care, rather than fewer with a highly enriched program. One immediate means of implementing such a policy is to serve more children in existing day care centers, thus expanding the ratio of children to staff and lowering the per capita day care cost, in addition to developing new facilities and programs.[30]

Their solution is, in a sense, no solution at all; they are merely suggesting that we revert to the kind of day care the country had until early childhood education made a dent on the "good babysitting" notion. It was precisely to get away from that notion that the Comprehensive Child Development Act was proposed; it is precisely that concept of day care that a decade of activists have argued against, in favor of educationally and developmentally oriented day care. And it is precisely that form of day care which critics like Dr. Meers find so dangerous. The questions of cost that both studies raise are legitimate, if the only purpose of day care is removing people from the welfare rolls. If day care has other purposes, then that question must be measured against a broader view of day care policies.

It is this broader view which day care advocates have taken. For them day care is not simply a way of cutting welfare costs, but of establishing new priorities while meeting old necessities. Children, they think, should come high on the list of priorities, particularly the children who are now the major users of day care services. In their view there is little merit in providing children from welfare homes with custodial care. In a sense they are twice penalized; not only have their mothers gone to work, but the children are not receiving quality substitute care. But the advocate view of day care sees a far broader clientele than welfare mothers needing day care. There are blue-collar women who are not eligible for government-supported day care and must often resort to care far worse than that offered welfare mothers in day care centers. There are middle-income women who could perhaps meet the cost of day care but whose incomes make them ineligible. For the most part a tit-for-tat cost analysis between welfare and day care does not interest those who favor quality day care.

Another matter of cost does trouble them, however. They are fearful that while a vastly expanded system of day care may come to pass legislatively, largely for welfare reasons, sufficient money to implement its provisions will never be spent. All too conscious of Congressional failure to appropriate, or Administration refusal to spend funds actually authorized by legislation, groups like the AFL-CIO and the National Urban League, and educators and bureaucrats like John Niemeyer and Jule Sugarman, in testimony before the Mondale Committee, stressed the need for full and continuous funding. The National Urban League, in fact, suggested that a three- to five-year funding cycle be adopted to provide greater stability to programs whose yearly existence hinges on the result of annual Congressional appropriation fights.[31] The fear in some quarters that day care will cost too much is balanced by the fear in others that not enough will be spent to provide quality services. Speculating about the costs of day care can be a heady business, for we are talking not only about the direct costs of day care services but also about the social costs and social savings that might accrue from such a system.

It has been argued that part of the payoff for spending on quality day care will be a reduction in the amount of money spent on welfare, special education, child welfare services, and, perhaps, even on the cost of prisons. While providing day care to reduce the cost of other welfare and educational services has never been a major argument for most day care advocates, there is something like a long-term *quid pro quo* implied when people argue that extended day care services will alleviate numerous social and educational problems. These savings, if they exist, are far in the future, and taxpayers bitten by the promises of poverty programs and special educational services are justifiably suspicious that day care will increase their taxes rather than reduce them.

And in terms of the national economy and job market, the awkward question has been raised as to whether the economy can absorb the additional number of women who would go to work if they did have day care. George Gilder, writing in the *New Leader*, raised one aspect of this problem.

> We must recognize that when we allocate money to one plan we may well deprive another, and that when we subsidize work-force entry for one group (middle-class wives, for example), we directly or indirectly reduce jobs, wages and vertical mobility for others (black middle-class men, for example). Furthermore, when we persistently direct our energies and subsidies toward diminishing the dependence of poor women on male providers, we needlessly intensify an already powerful trend: We exacerbate the social, economic and psychological crisis of young males, extend it to new classes and generations, and undermine familial constraints.[32]

Mr. Gilder's argument focuses on a real question of social policy, although he fails to take into account the number of women who already work because they must support their families and the changing social attitude which does not see the right to work as the province solely of the male citizen. This is a classic male, liberal argument, not without its validity or seductions, but it's finally unjust because it asks women to pay the price when they can't afford to and because it assumes that it is always somebody else's turn, not theirs.

Women, including the mothers of preschool children, are working in ever greater numbers. Many of these mothers work because they are the sole support of their families. Others work because their husbands' salaries alone do not provide sufficient family income. The vast majority of these mothers attempt to make suitable arrangements for child care and yet find few alternatives available to them. In other words, acting in a conscientious fashion and not leaving young children to their own devices, many working mothers find that the care available to them does not meet a desirable standard. There are also those mothers who remain home and support their children through welfare.

But not only does the prospect of more women working raise the likelihood of higher male unemployment, as Mr. Gilder points out, it also suggests the possibility that day care, rather than improving the economic conditions of the poor, might actually exacerbate it. Is it possible that the use of day care by middle-class women earning a second salary in their middle-class family might increase the gap in family incomes between the poor and rich, forever closing off the chances for a more equal distribution of income? People with similar educational backgrounds tend to marry each other. The professionally trained woman who goes to work and doubles the family income from twenty to forty thousand dollars has increased the gap, absolutely, between her family's income and that of the high school-educated woman who goes to work and doubles her family's income from six to twelve thousand dollars a year. This argument does suggest that some rather intricate social planning, including perhaps a change in tax laws, must accompany any calculations about the true cost and economic consequences of day care.

In ending his excursion into the economics of day care, Gilder returned to an old refrain: day care could "undermine familial constraints." For many critics that possibility raises the ultimate question of social control—or the lack of it. Their concern about costs, control, white-coated bureaucrats, and irresponsible parents palls before the possibility that day care might actually destroy the family. It is over this issue that they find themselves in complete disagreement with some day care advocates, in fact, a small minority, who consider the decline of the family as we know it a positive step in social evolution. The possibility that day care might actually do away with many of the constraints of family life is for some feminists, futurists, and social thinkers one of its more obvious benefits. By and large this is not a position that attracts most day care supporters who, nonetheless, have a tendency to deny the tremendous impact day care might have on the family. But day care, depending on its quality and its extensiveness, can be expected to have an important influence on the family.

CHAPTER **8**

LARGER QUESTIONS: DAY CARE,

THE FAMILY, AND SOCIETY

Day care will not destroy the family. Day care will not replace the family. Day care will not become the arbiter of child-rearing in America. Depending on the degree of its future development, or lack of it, day care will have a substantial impact on the family. The extent and nature of that impact hinges on many decisions yet to be made about the control, financing, administration, and programming of day care services—decisions which President Nixon's 1971 veto of the Comprehensive Child Development Act postponed but did not resolve. The possibility that these questions may never be resolved, that the present, small, piecemeal and inadequate system will continue, is, in itself, a decision too, one that will have consequences for family life as powerful as those that could flow from a decision to expand day care services. The rigid limitation of government-subsidized day care, for example, could encourage the growth of custodially oriented for-profit centers where the child care is often poor and where the only parental control is through the cashbox.

The questions one ought to pose about day care's effects upon the family are not those most frequently asked nor those coming from our most illustrious public figures.

The question is not: Shall America have day care? We already have day care. The question is: What kind of day care shall we have? Excellent, good, or bad?

The question is not: Will day care destroy the family? In their one hundred years of limited but effective existence, day care services have never attempted or unwittingly managed to do that. The question is: Will day care support family and community or will it continue to be an instrument of government social policy offered and withdrawn solely in response to Washington's attitude on welfare and regulation of the poor?

"Excessive emphasis on day care centers," says one critic, "can weaken the family at a time when it needs strengthening." Day care, adds another, could "undermine familial constraints." And President Nixon feels day care would replace "family-centered child-rearing with community-centered child-rearing." These fears, and others much like them, expressed by so many opponents of day care, are related not so much to concern for family life *per se* as to concern that day care might become an acceptable child care option for families who by traditional definitions have no need for day care, namely those families who are apparently effective agents of social control, those families who are considered to be effective transmitters of prevailing social values, those families where the mother assumes the major role in child-rearing. Any attempts to legitimize day care, be it through legislation or a change in public opinion, represents, especially in regard to "normal" families, a potential for social change that men like President Nixon, critic George Gilder, and columnist William Shannon find unacceptable. In a time of rapid and often unintended political, economic, religious, and social changes, the possibility that The Family, like God, Country, and The Dollar, should become hidden, unstable, or devalued is a calamity they hope to forestall.

It is true, nonetheless, that the effect of day care upon the family and children is ultimately the most important question that will be asked about it. But the questions posed as the critics have posed them, in scatter-gun fashion, are never sufficiently focused to give a clear and fair indication of how to find an answer. Will day care weaken the family? Will it undermine family constraints? Will it replace family-centered child-rearing with community-centered child-rearing? These questions lead us nowhere on the kind of emotional energy fueled by the threat that the answer is "yes."

Furthermore the unstated assumption in all these questions—that the family is in good condition—is a hotly debated issue. Like most institutions in our society, the family is passing through a time of troubled and often unexpected changes. To some, these changes augur a radical reconstitution of the family unit; to others, these changes, while disquieting, appear to be only mild adaptations to the increasingly technical and affluent nature of our society. Wherever the future of the family may lie, however, the condition of the family, with or without the advent of widespread day care services, would be a cause for concern and discussion. Finally, all those criticisms made against day care on behalf of saving the family have lost sight of the fact that day care proposes only to provide child care services, relatively limited and circumscribed ones at that. Even within the perhaps narrowing confines left to its responsibility, child care is only one aspect of family life. While children may define certain areas of family life, they do not cause the whole of it; the future of the family depends more on the needs, desires, and actions of adults than on the possibility that day care services will be available for child care.

Calmer considerations would rule if one remembered that the existence of day care and its effects upon the family have been a recurrent and perplexing issue from the moment when the first nursery opened its doors. When Mrs. Josephine Shaw Lowell proposed in 1900 to the National Federation of Day Nurseries that day nursery services had to be expanded in order to prevent the breakup of families and the over-institutionalization of children in orphanages, she struck the thematic note that justified the founding of most day nurseries in the early decades of this century. In the early twenties, when day care centers came increasingly under the influence of social workers, the intent of preserving the family was less important than protecting a child from an undesirable home and family situation. Most present policies are a mixture of this old protectionism and a newer, more aggressive attitude which sees day care as supportive and complementary to the family.

The new ingredient in the debate is the influence of early childhood education and development. As day care has more and more come under its influence, shedding, to a considerable extent, the image of a custodial institution, it has become highly attractive to a broad range of families—far more than would ever have been attracted by the turn-of-the-century day nursery or the child welfare establishment of three, four, and five decades ago. This normalization of day care has presented, largely to lower-middle and middle-income families, a new option in child-rearing along with an enlarged potential for increasing family income by allowing more women to work. How well this new usage can fit old welfare-oriented definitions is a matter of speculation. Can a service granted begrudgingly to the poor and desperate meet the needs and expectations of the not-so-poor and hopeful?

So long as the federal government maintains its present policies, this will be extremely difficult. The unstated family policy of the government *vis à vis* day care right now is: as a dependent welfare family we do not take your family life seriously; hence we offer you day care in order to make you less dependent; when you become self-supporting, an independent lower-income family, we will take your family life seriously and discourage you from using day care. Fortunately this policy is at variance with the attitudes of many people who run and staff day care services, most of whom are supportive and sympathetic to the families who use centers and family day care homes, accepting the families' own definitions of their aspirations and economic condition.

At this point in time, then, a decision to include lower-income families in the eligibility standards for government-subsidized day care would not likely have a tremendous impact on the family, except perhaps in a beneficial way, since many mothers in such families are already working and good day care services would be an improvement over many of their present child care arrangements. It is after this need has been met when questions of day care's effects upon the family will begin to have an impact, for it is at this point, when supply begins to create new demands, that large numbers of women who have not worked will begin to consider the possibilities. With the advent of large numbers will come questions of quality, compulsion, and control of far greater significance than those same issues pose right now. Day care is at a turning-point in defining exactly what it is and whom it should serve. Before we can examine its potential impact on the family, we must first take a broader view of the relationship between day care and the family as it presently exists, and between the family and society.

There are many kinds of day care. And there are many kinds of families. We have previously examined, in some detail, various kinds of day care, supported by a variety of public and private institutions as well as many individuals. There is day care that is educationally and developmentally oriented, there is day care that is oriented to providing good and safe babysitting, there is day care that is primarily custodial and provides little activity for the children or interaction with skilled and attentive adults. In short, there is good day care and bad day care, day care oriented toward groups, and day care aimed at improving the informal babysitting arrangements made currently. This variety of services and spectrum of quality is often overlooked by critics who show a persistent tendency to treat day care as all of a kind and all bad. Witness William Shannon's comments in an article attacking the concept behind the Comprehensive Child Development Act.

> Are child-development centers desirable for any children other than the most damaged and deprived? The unpopular truth is that any community facility—call it a day-care center or a child-development center—is at best an inadequate, unsatisfactory substitute, and at worst a dangerous, destructive substitute for a child's own mother.[1]

The simple truth of the matter is that there are day care centers which are an equivalent substitute—for their specific, limited purposes—for the most attentive and loving of mothers. To focus on poor-quality day care as a reason for not improving or expanding it creates a self-fulfilling prophecy. To deny that day care centers can never be any good and will always and everywhere be inadequate is to fly in the face of observable fact.

There is as well a wide variety of American families. There is, in a real sense, no such thing as "the American Family"; nor is there, the accusations against Dr. Spock notwithstanding, an American system of child-rearing; nor, in fact, is there common agreement about the kind of child the American child should be. One has only to observe child-rearing in France or Germany or Russia or China[2] to appreciate American diversity and heterogeneity in family styles, in child-rearing practices, and in the range of relationships allowed between American parents and their children. Whether this variety is based on personal choice, class, race, ethnic group, religion, or region, differences do exist, and they ought to be acknowledged in any discussion of day care and the family.

And even beyond these child-rearing differences there is a broad range of family size, behavior, and organization. After all, not every American Family is made up of Mama, Papa, and 2.7 children, although our art, literature, and television situation comedies usually bring the patriarchal nuclear family most readily to mind as the archetypical form. Many nuclear families are not patriarchal at all. The mother may work, the father sharing in more than a minimum of child care and domestic tasks. Other differences also exist. Many nuclear families have only one parent, and unless the family is on welfare or rich, this parent must meet not only the nurturance needs of his or her children but also be the sole breadwinner. Many cooperative efforts among families, be they something so simple as a babysitting exchange or something more complicated, like a co-operative nursery school or cooperative meal-planning and cooking, have moved many families out of the nuclear, isolation trap. The incidence of communal living remains very small, but it, too, serves as an important alternative model, suggesting to many people that the nuclear household need not be the only way to organize family life. Acknowledging this considerable variety of structures and styles brings us along the first steps toward demythologizing the American family and understanding why day care, or almost any form of cooperative, community-shared child care, has great appeal to so many families.

The relationship between day care and the family is not then a one-to-one matching of two givens, like one molecule of sodium and one molecule of chloride that put together produce common table salt. It is a rather more complicated chemical reaction. A variety of day care services that are, after all, totally voluntary, combined with a variety of family styles and child care needs, need not result in the demise of the family but in greater flexibility, choice, and opportunity for a greater number of families. Furthermore, day care could represent for many families participation in a child-centered community that removes the parents from the isolation, frustration, and sheer difficulty of going it alone in their child-rearing tasks. Good day care, in a center or in a family day care home, from a certain point of view and a certain level of commitment, could be considered a reconstitution of the extended family—the larger Family to which so many nuclearized, mobile, and isolated little families need to belong.

From this point of view, day care is not the unknown future but a return to common sense, a recognition that, just as individuals do not exist alone, neither do families; that children do not belong just to their parents but to other adults and a community larger than the nuclear family.

THE NUCLEAR FAMILY: HAS IT BEEN AND WILL IT ALWAYS BE WITH US?

The whole family structure and the way it is organized has come under pressing, even unrelenting, examination over the past several years. Is the family good for the men, women, and children who live in it, that is, about 90 percent of the population? One does not have to agree with R. D. Laing's terror stories of family life and his ultimate assessment of the whole institution—the "initial act of brutality against the average child is mother's first kiss"—one does not have to agree with his views to recognize, nonetheless, that the nuclear family is being rocked by grave questions concerning, first of all, its necessity and, then, its performance. How adequately does it meet the tasks left to it: childbearing, child-rearing, value transmission, and emotional sustenance of its members?

Population experts, in warning that the family has succeeded only too well in its childbearing functions, caution, cajole, and threaten us into a condition of restrained fecundity. Child-rearing has become a complex task at which it seems part of the population fails and the other part acts as paraprofessionals for experts. Value transmission has become a highly problematical task for all parents, with schools and television countermanding what remains of our pluralistic religious, cultural, and ethical values. And finally the emotional solace and psychological strength which the family must provide for each member has made a psychic pressure cooker of too many households.

Are these conditions the sign of a profound and fatal malaise or are they the sign of adaptive behavior to new conditions? Perhaps the hothouse atmosphere of the nuclear family, privatized and cut off from meaningful community, existing, as Richard Sennett has written, in a state of arrested adolescence, is dying; perhaps the family is turning its back on an outmoded form and groping for new ones. Possibly current questions and upheavals are not so much a sign of family disintegration as its return to the community, and world of work described by Philippe Ariès.[3]

The mythology of the American family makes it difficult to imagine how families can be any different from the patriarchal, nuclear family so familiar to us. Despite the evidence of family differences and difficulties all around us, most of us, as President Nixon indicated he did in his veto message, seem to prefer to think of the family as a fixed point, an unflinching absolute in a shaky world. But we know, if not from our own experience, from anthropologists and historians, that family structure and relationships have varied considerably in time and place, and the relationship of the family unit to the larger community has extended or contracted far beyond our present experience of the family.

Even the role of children in the family has changed. For example, Philippe Ariès, in *Centuries of Childhood*, convincingly argues that there was no notion of childhood among thirteenth-century Frenchmen. Once they ceased to be infants and to require constant care, those beings whom we call children were portrayed, treated, and spoken to like miniature adults. From the thirteenth through the seventeenth centuries Ariès found that a definite period of childhood evolved, a period in which certain styles of dress and distinctive pastimes came to characterize the lives of children, separating them from adult dress and adult behavior. New attention was given to their upbringing, their moral and physical development.[4]

This new concern about children was not without its influence on the family, which became taken up with attitudes of domesticity, privacy, and isolation more typical of the modern than the medieval family. Perhaps the most notable evidence of this change was the gradual isolation of the household from the larger community, with special rooms set aside for cooking, sleeping, and entertaining, all of them opening onto a common corridor rather than into one another as they had previously. "The rearrangement of the house and the reform of manners left more room for private life; and this was taken up by a family reduced to parents and children, a family from which servants, clients, and friends were excluded."[5] The exclusion of the community from the family and the withdrawal of the family within its own precincts concerned with its own affairs would have far-reaching consequences for society, families, and children.

It is a process that many historians have traced in colonial

America. In his study of family life in seventeenth-century Plymouth Colony, John Demos contrasts the broad-ranging community influence, activities, and responsibilities of the colonial family with the rather narrow and circumscribed activities of the family today. In those days family and community were virtually synonymous. "Broadly speaking, the history of the family in America has been a history of contraction and withdrawal; its central theme is the gradual surrender to other institutions of functions that once lay very much within the realm of family responsibility."[6] Contemporary American families are no longer centers of economic production; the family farm has, in fact, almost disappeared; nor does the family now directly give schooling or vocational training to its members; nor do most American families provide care for the aged, the orphaned, the delinquent, or the destitute. As a "little commonwealth," the families of Plymouth Colony were the community and, themselves, provided the services which sustained and supported individual members.

The demise of this closely knit structure may have been an inevitable consequence of the geographic expanse and economic potentialities of the new country. "Where land was abundant and labor at a premium it took little more to create a household than to maintain one."[7] In this process which freed families and individuals from the restraining hand of the past, allowing them mobility and a freer choice of work and residence, both the repression and support of "the little commonwealth" slowly disappeared. With vast areas of land open to new settlements fathers could not for long hold the right to inheritance over the heads of their sons; no longer could sons expect a financial head start in life nor could they draw on the accumulated experience of fathers who had sown and harvested for twenty or thirty years. So did "family governance" come to be replaced by selectmen and "towne government," and where families no longer took responsibility for the poor or elderly, the workhouse and the poorhouse came into being. The traditions and lore of child-rearing passed on from grandparents to parents were gradually replaced (especially in middle-class families) by the written advice of child care manuals—predecessors of Dr. Spock.

This too simple telescoping of two hundred and fifty years of history should not obscure the complex processes involved in the way the family changed to meet new and different social and economic circumstances. During the nineteenth century this process was considerably accelerated by industrialization and urbanization. The structure of the American family that has been regarded as normative coalesced in this period among the middle class: the wife and mother, a rearer and protector of children and domestic virtue, the father a link through his work and interests to the outside world. For all of this a bucolic setting was preferred, but if that was impossible, the home, even in the city, became a refuge from the evil, ugliness and insecurity without.[8] Certainly one of the major causes of withdrawal in nineteenth-century America was the disorder created by newcomers to the cities and the sense of insecurity created by the influx of foreign immigrants. Their strange customs, attitudes, and behaviors inspired a monumental effort at assimilation and Americanization. A host of new institutions were created—the urban school system, settlement houses, health departments, charitable and welfare organizations, and, as we saw in the second chapter, day care centers. New groups of professionals and bureaucrats evolved to service these institutions in their tasks of education and enforcement.[9] Among the many tasks undertaken and, to varying degrees, carried out, was the attempt to remake the immigrant family over into an American one.

The social message that went with these efforts at assimilation encouraged the view that the American middle-class family was an ideal to which everyone ought to aspire. The guerrilla warfare waged by "friendly visitors" or social workers against the custom of taking in boarders is a case in point, and a fine example of the feeling that only family members ought to reside within the family home. Although a sensible and obvious way for a married woman with children to earn money, the presence of boarders was felt to diminish the sanctity of the family circle and soil the domestic hearth. There was, furthermore, the unspoken fear the male boarders posed a special threat to the sexual purity of the household. Working at home, especially by women, was also frowned upon. There was certainly much that was economically exploitative and unfair about doing piecework at home for clothing factories, but it provided many women with the means to make a living while keeping an eye, albeit a fatigued one, on their children. But there were many home-centered industries, like cigar- and cigarette-rolling, done among Bohemian families that were well-paying and relatively clean. There were many small stores, saloons, newspaper stands, peddler's carts that were family enterprises, run by parents and children, which, of course, did not meet American expectations about how families should behave, especially in regard to children and then toward women.

Without doubt, by the second and third generations many immigrant families had adopted the prevailing American family life-style. In times of economic prosperity, they came to live according to that ideal; the ability of the mother to remain home because the family could be supported on one salary has been among some groups and in some generations a sure sign of status.

But it is also true that while they may have aspired to that ideal, many other families have chosen other patterns of family behavior. One has only to live in a big city in an ethnically mixed neighborhood to appreciate how distinctive family differences continue to exist, even in families who have long been Americanized and who may even have the economic means to meet the American ideal of family life in the rural suburbs.

The point is not to suggest an extreme diversity of family structure, of wildly contrasting features, but to illuminate my point that the family has been, like all social institutions, subject to economic and social pressures which have altered it in various ways. The American family is not now what it was in the seventeenth century, and will not be, in one hundred years, what it is now. The dominant form of that family is certainly to be described as a conjugal, nuclear family often supported solely by the husband's salary, with a significant minority having two members working. We must likewise recognize that even within this dominant structure there are religious, class, and regional differences that continue to exercise considerable influence over how families behave, how they raise their children, how they see themselves in relation to the larger community. On the basis of this analysis, one of the questions we ought to ask about day care's effects on many kinds of families is: What different kinds of day care do we need in order to supply the varying child care needs of these families? There are, of course, many families who have no need or desire for day care at all, and the present voluntary nature of day care respects their wishes to keep children at home until school age, when compulsory school laws do require them to send children to school. For too long, however, this norm and image of the family has dominated our vision of what the family's child care needs are. And in the days when day care services were strictly oriented toward child welfare services, they were even more narrowly restricted than they are now. In strictly economic terms, the need for day care is greatest among one-parent families and families where both parents must work in order to make a decent family wage. Present day care services do not begin to meet these needs. Furthermore, there are families where both parents work and want to, who could pay for good day care and would, if it were available. Day care has the potential, then, not for totalitarian control of parents and children but for allowing more families to make broader choices about their lives. Do we ever consider that our present system, where most mothers must remain home with young children or make use of often inadequate care, is itself narrow and restrictive, that it limits and controls families? But it does. Day care now offers the possibility that a variety of family styles could flourish in our society.

Day care now offers the possibility that the family might reassert itself into the larger community and society, both by allowing women to play a more active role and by making the good care of children the concern of both parents and society. We cannot recreate the "little commonwealth," but it is a model that deserves our attention.

Yet another issue needs to be examined, one which links some of the present dissatisfactions about the family with the possibility that day care could actually protect and enhance family life. To a significant degree, the family's authority over its children and the integrity of the parent-child relationship has already yielded for better or worse to the penetrating influence of community and larger society. The causes and consequences of this phenomenon might place the prospect of broader day care service in a more realistic perspective.

FAMILY VALUES AND CHILDREN
IN AN INDIVIDUALISTIC SOCIETY

When President Nixon refused to bring, as he said, "the vast moral authority of the federal government to the side of communal approaches over against the family-centered approach" of raising children, he managed to ignore almost one hundred years of American philanthropic, legal, and social policy. Community standards of child care, education, employment, and parent behavior toward children have evolved over the last century to the point where society has a great deal to say about the way Americans raise their children. We have, by reason of social expectations and laws, long practiced a form of child-rearing whose standards have been set, not by parents and grandparents, not by the neighborhood or local community, but by the society at large. Ironically these community standards exist in a society that, by and large, acts to protect, improve and enhance individuals rather than family units, that accounts its citizens not as family members but as independent persons. The consequences of this in a democratic society were lucidly described by de Tocqueville in the 1840's, when he contrasted the political behavior of governments toward families in aristocratic and democratic societies.

> In countries which are aristocratically constituted with all the gradations of rank, the government never makes a direct appeal to the mass of the governed; as men are united together, it is enough to lead the foremost; the rest will follow. This is applicable to the family as well to all aristocracies that have a head. Among aristocratic nations social institutions recognize, in truth, no one in the family but the father; children are received by society at his hands; society governs him, he governs them. Thus the parent not only has a natural right but acquires a political right to command them; he is the author and the support of his family, but he is also its constituted ruler.
>
> In democracies, where the government picks out every individual singly from the mass to make him subservient to the general laws of the community, no such intermediate person is required; a father is there, in the eye of the law, only a member of the community, older and richer than his sons.[10]

Ultimately these laws, social mores, and individualistic values, as we shall see, have had the unintended and unconscious effect of weakening and diluting parental authority and influence, especially over minor children, substituting for it an unthought-out set of economic and social values, which have weakened families rather than strengthened them.

The attempt to Americanize the immigrant represents the seminal effort of our society to shape, or at least, offer the family a new set of cultural values, one which was community-centered rather than family-centered. A basic ingredient of Americanization, in fact, was the remaking of the immigrant family. Local governments, benevolent societies, volunteer groups, church bodies, through the agencies of schools, health departments, charitable organizations, settlement houses, etcetera, all took an active role in shaping families to meet the needs of an increasingly complex, urban and industrial society. Compulsory school laws, child labor laws, health codes, rising standards of infant and child care created new regulations and expectations about child-rearing.

Under an agricultural economy the young were economically productive long before they were permitted to be so in an industrial economy. Young people, even children, worked in the fields, cared for gardens, tended and fed animals; in an urban society, where children no longer worked under the benevolent hand and influence of parents, but in unhealthy factories, on the street, in dangerous mines, measures were taken to exclude them from working below a certain age. Child labor laws had a dual effect in defining the family's economic capabilities and limitations. By excluding children from many kinds of work it created for adults, particularly fathers, the sole right and duty as the breadwinner to be economically productive. By prohibiting child labor and instituting compulsory school laws, children, too, acquired a new set of rights and duties. A step forward for children, but a potent combination for changing the economic structure of the family. For longer and longer periods the young could not contribute economically to the family. Being economically unproductive made it difficult for them to establish their independence from the family at the same time as they could contribute very little to it economically. The increasingly protracted period of adolescence and its attendant difficulties which have come in recent years to characterize the lives of massive numbers of young people has its origins in these economic limitations. Longer and longer periods of schooling which may well fill many of these years have come to require greater and greater amounts of parental support. In our own time it is not unusual to find one or two persons—father and possibly mother—supporting their children through twenty-one or twenty-two years of age and even beyond.

Compulsory schooling laws too changed the relative power of society and family in the education and formation of children. Where parents were once almost totally responsible for what and how children learned they are now only partially, if at all, responsible. The haphazardness of total parent control was minimized by compulsory school laws and standardized curriculums—a necessity perhaps in an industrial society that depended upon a modicum of literacy, discipline, and socialization. Recent surveys indicate that family background and interest is a crucial factor in how well children do at school but many unsuccessful attempts to increase parental influence in the schools demonstrate how adverse school bureaucracies are to having parents reassert their importance in the education of their children.

The limitations of parental control exemplified by such legal measures as child labor laws and compulsory education laws were accompanied, in the early years of this century, by rising standards of child care in such areas as health, nutrition, and discipline. Advances in hygiene and medical knowledge led to a decline in the infant mortality rate. New legal and social expectations of how children were to be raised placed the child at the center of a growing network of laws, professions, knowledge, and skills for which the betterment, even in some exaggerated forms, the perfection of the child, was the primary goal and concern. The task of social workers, public health nurses, and inspectors consisted in bringing these views to the homes of the poor, and in creating housing and health codes that would insure these standards be met by the society at large. Meeting those standards was the task of decades and even now poor housing, a high infant mortality rate, poor general health, inadequate medical and educational services are typical of many urban ghettos and rural slums.

While it is now a common task of raising children to take an infant to a pediatrician every two or three months and after the age of 2 for a yearly checkup, it was not at all common at the turn of the century. While it is now a commonplace to remedy early in life all manner of defects and deficiencies with glasses, orthodontia, casts, braces, therapy etcetera, few such elaborate treatments were known at the turn of the century. In recent years new findings about emotional and cognitive development have opened new areas of concern about children. Simply put, seventy, eighty or one hundred years ago, social pressures and legal ordinance had less control over what was required of parents in terms of their child-rearing than they do now. These efforts to better and improve the lives of children have grown considerably and have met with re-markable success coalescing in our own time, with greater affluence, better medical and developmental knowledge, and improved tech-nology, to make children more healthy, better educated, and more likely to reach adulthood than the children of seventy or eighty years ago.

From a legal point of view the power of the state to intervene in parent-child relationships, particularly as a "protector" of children, has also grown. ". . . In its efforts to protect children, the state has become more directly and thus actively involved in the parent-child relationship. The old idea that a child is somehow the 'private prop-erty' of its parents, with the impression of exclusivity of control—the right to enjoy an object to the exclusion of others—has thus diminished."[11] A vast majority of parents do not view the situation in this light since legal intrusions are relatively rare, the result of court actions taken in cases of neglect, abuse, foster care or adop-tion. These court actions, furthermore, seem to fall preponderantly upon the poor and legally undefended who because they are con-sidered atypical or abnormal seem to represent exceptions rather than rules of state intervention in family life. But as Sanford Katz, who has examined the legal situation, indicates that is not quite true.

> When one observes the expanding power of government into the family sphere, one must begin to readjust one's legal concept of family relationship, especially that of parent and child. It is not ac-curate to portray the parent-child relationship as one of the most jealously guarded in society—a frequently stated myth. Indeed, the greatest inroad the government has made in the family setting has been the parent-child relationship. From a legal perspective, that relationship is probably the least secure in the family constel-lation.[12]

He concludes, "there is a tendency to view governmental intrusions in these matters as benevolent, thus minimizing what might, in another setting or social stratum, be considered invasions into the privacy of the home.[13]

Katz's survey demonstrates so well that the apparently benevolent intrusions of society and government into the family can often have less than desirable results, not necessarily in terms of their effects on children, which are often good, but on parents and parental ability to meet not simply minimum legal prohibitions against beating and abusing children, of not treating them as "private property," but on the larger and broader standards of care and education which must be observed in order to meet the ideal of producing the optimal or near-optimal child. Is it a task that parents can reasonably be expected to perform? Is it a standard that parents can be reasonably expected to meet?

We live, after all, in a society with rapidly changing economic structures and shifting social values in which there has been a decline in the religious and psychological controls over family cohesion and stability, in which the definition of good child-rearing—value transmission, behavior control, and social attitudes—has met heavy competition from sources outside the family.

Does the economy weaken or strengthen the family? In money terms it supports some families very well; it supports other families decently if there are two wage earners; other families it supports very poorly, or not at all. In terms of life quality, wages, job assignments, transfers, work hours, and working conditions, employers are not particularly concerned with families, with children's needs, or with their schooling. Admittedly this is how it has always been, and more humane personnel policies and employment practices probably make the present working situation of many people better than it was fifty years ago. But, except as ornamentation, a man or woman's family needs and responsibilities are given little consideration in the job market. But the struggle to survive, or the need to make a living, has always been a prime determinant of family behavior and a powerful shaper of family adaptations.

Most families' lives are organized around the job situation of the breadwinner or breadwinners. The amount of money there is to spend, the hours at which meals are eaten (if they are eaten in common), the time people rise and go to bed, the amount of time a father or employed mother can spend with their children, the kinds of goods and services, housing, and schools are tied to their employment (or unemployment) situation. Quite clearly an agricultural economy allowed a considerable amount of family cohesiveness; in contrast, our technological and "almost post-industrial" society is notable for fracturing and alienating family members. The absence of the father from the home and his considerably diminished influence is a by-product of industrialization. The effect of jobs and employment on families passes largely unnoticed by most employers and economic planners. Salaries are pegged not to the number of people who must live on them, but on the skills and job classification of the breadwinner. The United States stands practically alone among Western nations in its failure to pay a family allowance to compensate for the inequities of its economic system. Most families meet this situation by tailoring expenditures and their living conditions to their income. But certain inequities built into the economic system mean that some families can never have sufficient income to attain a decent standard of living and a decent standard of child-rearing. The female-headed family is one example. Still considered secondary workers, most women, those whose husbands work, as well as those who are the sole support of their families, are systematically paid less than men doing the same job. The chronically under-employed are another example of men and women who though willing to work can never find steady employment through which to support their families. Coal miners in depressed areas of Appalachia and unskilled or semi-skilled blacks in the city are both groups that get the short end of the economic stick. That regularly employed people cannot make a family wage, that some men must work at two or three jobs to support their families, is a powerful, telling indictment against our present system of income distribution and an indicator of how little concern there actually is for the family in areas where it really matters. And one does not have to concentrate at the lower end of the income scale to support this point. Even at higher income levels, men and women may not have any more time to raise their children than the man who works two or three jobs. Frequently enough higher pay and more satisfying work requires longer hours and greater job responsibilities. And at every income level the supposed merit of the nuclear family in an industrial society—its mobility and adaptability—takes its toll. Our high level of geographic and social mobility has its effect on families, removing them from a larger community of support whether that be defined in terms of parents, neighborhoods, baseball teams, or old friends. The frequency with which so many families move, while making them free-floating and efficient units in the economy, serves to weaken the bonds which make communities possible and family life tolerable.

John Demos describes the situation in which so many families find themselves:

> The family is important not so much as the foundation for an ideal social order, but as the foil to an actual state of social disorder. It forms a bulwark against the outside world—destroy it, and anarchy reigns everywhere. It forms, too, a bulwark against anxieties of the deepest and most personal kind. For we find in the family, as nowhere else in our "open society," an indispensable type of protection against the sense of utter isolation and helplessness.[14]

What kind of retreat can the family really provide from outer social chaos? Relatively little. For families isolated from supportive communities, whether that community be geographically, psychologically, or religiously defined, have little feeling of being able to cope either with the outer or inner world. Indeed, in Demos' description one can find little purpose for the family except as a pressure vent for the individual's anxieties and struggles with the larger society. The family becomes an arena for taking things out, for relieving individual members from their sense of frustration with the economic, social, and psychological happenings outside the family.

The fact that the family continues to exist despite such pressures may be a tribute to its marvelous flexibility but it could not long survive if it did not allow people a way out when and if the pressures become intolerable. And divorce is, for most people, the way out, with desertion for those who cannot observe legal niceties. Divorce is not only a concomitant necessity to our highly romantic notions of love, unrealistic expectations about marriage and life in a nuclear family, but it serves as well to relieve individuals from the intolerable situations created in families by their economic and social situations. Like economic circumstances, divorce is both result and cause of changes in family life and has particularly affected the families' child-rearing capabilities. We have considerably revised and upgraded our standards of personal happiness; the idea that an unhappy couple should remain together for the sake of raising their children has come to seem as masochistic a notion as it once was considered selfish and irresponsible for an unhappy couple not to remain together, at least until after their children were grown. While marital fidelity and family stability may be an ideal in our society it is now legally permissible and socially acceptable for husband and wife to separate, divorce and remarry without particular reference to the effect on their children, except, of course, for what the parents are capable of observing and remedying themselves. Part of the trade-off then for our notions of marriage, family life, and economic organization is a high divorce rate, a loosening of family ties and rearing children in one-parent families.

Finally there are attitudes and values which penetrate the family and affect children quite without reference to parental desires. Television is paramount among these influences; whatever the merits or demerits of the "global village," television perhaps more than any other medium, like comic books, or other institutions, like the schools, has influenced and intruded upon the child-rearing task of parents. The exact nature and effect of this intrusion has not yet been clearly analyzed but a number of facts are commonly agreed upon. The first and most striking is the number of hours that the average child watches television. It is calculated that by the age of 18 an American child will have spent twenty thousand hours in front of the tube, according to Ben Bagdikian "more time than he has spent in classrooms, churches, and all other educational and cultural activities."[15] Not only then does television consume a great amount of time, it does so at the expense of parents and children doing other things together. In fact, watching television may be the only thing many parents and children do do together. The second fact is that the social, moral, and economic values underlying most of television have at best a dubious effect on children; at worst, they are positively detrimental to the proper socialization of children.

In this area there remains a great amount of conjecture, but violence on television has been shown to encourage violent behavior in a significant minority of children. Worse than the violent behavior itself is the systematic desensitization to violence, pain, and suffering that characterizes the attitude of so many children *and adults*. Furthermore, the bumbling father, the dreary housewife, the foolish older people that are the stock-in-trade of so many situation comedies and commercials help form attitudes that do a disservice to a child's understanding of other people's roles and ages. Even so simple a matter as what families eat is settled by which cereal company sponsors the children's favorite programs. A somewhat frivolous example perhaps but indicative that something so simple as a family's eating habits are formed outside of parental control by cereal manufacturers whose chief interest is not, after all, proper nutrition but making money. Television has radically intruded upon family-centered child-rearing, becoming, in Bagdikian's phrase, the "electronic teacher-playmate-babysitter-parent."

The fear that day care has family-weakening implications must be seen in this context which suggests that a large measure of our social and economic life, too, has its family-weakening, or, at least, family-changing implications. A high level of personal and geographic mobility, the pursuit of personal happiness, the pressures of a consumer society, a continually rising standard of living, the influence of television, among many facets of American society, create almost insurmountable pressures against the requisites we claim to have established for sound child-rearing: family cohesion and stability, intensive and exclusive care of children by mothers.

In an attempt to preserve the family most Americans are certainly not willing to return to the constraints that eighteenth- and nineteenth-century families lived with. We are not willing to return to a situation in which the family defined society as it did in seventeenth-century New England; to return to a time when people lived miserably in unhappy marriages; when the confines of a child's view were limited to what his parents knew, or what they were willing to have the child know; when our economy was inefficient and there were many more poor people than there are now. But we cannot have changed our economic and social lives without expecting that the family too would change. Having created a flexible, mobile, sometimes overheated family, we must recognize that its needs will be different from the family life that characterized our past.

The present situation of the family might be characterized as one in which parents have total responsibility for children while having almost no control over the larger social forces which impinge on the lives of their children; parents have a rather extensive set of duties toward their children but they receive little moral or psychological support from the larger society in carrying out those duties. While as a society we expect a good deal from those who are parents, we do not create an ambience in which parental responsibilities are easy to meet or in which children's needs are taken into consideration. As compensation for this lack in our society we console ourselves with the thought that with child-dominated homes and permissiveness, at least we are kind to children. But rather than a thought-out system of child-rearing, aren't these signs of parental withdrawal? Or, as Urie Bronfrenbrenner has written, of psychological abandonment, before a nearly hopeless and unrewarding task which results in parents and children resenting rather than respecting one another? We have collectively forgotten how to make "human beings human."

> We are experiencing a breakdown in the process of making human beings human. By isolating our children from the rest of society, we abandon them to a world devoid of adults and ruled by the destructive impulses and compelling pressures both of the age-segregated peer group and the aggressive and exploitive television screen. By setting our priorities elsewhere and putting children and families last, by claiming one set of values while pursuing another, we leave our children bereft of standards and support and our own lives impoverished and corrupt.[16]

These sentences from the 1970 White House Conference on Children suggest how far we really are from family-centered child-rearing. We cling to that catchword—family-centered—because it permits us to ignore the responsibilities and reordering of priorities that would go along with a social and economic system that would make the raising of children, the "making of human beings human" an important task. We are well into community-centered child-rearing without, unfortunately, having devised many successful means to accomplish it. We are horrified by the unruly young and call for greater family supervision when on every front we have diluted parental authority and capabilities.

In a time when the family is being so radically transformed by policies, both purposeful and intended, and unconscious and uncontrolled, the question is not whether day care will destroy the family but how to construct and foster a system of day care that will support, encourage, and strengthen the family in its child-rearing task. The chief danger of day care to the family is not that day care exists but that it will be organized in such a way as to foster the kind of division, intrusion, and separation that have already attenuated the ties between parents and children. A day care system, neighborhood-based, community-oriented, and parent-controlled, could go a long way toward giving families the Family they need to belong to. As an autonomous unit the family cannot long survive the pressures it now experiences; as one of many units in which there is a shared concern for children the family could meet its own need and enlarge our capacities for raising children and making human beings human.

COMMUNITY-CENTERED CHILD-REARING

Obviously day care is not the only answer to the problems and challenges that the family now faces. But modestly considered, day care is one among a number of alternatives for asserting the importance of child-rearing and the family's role in it. Many families need day care; many families could do a better job of raising their children if they had day care. But different families need different kinds of day care and they need it for varied reasons. Day care ought to be broadly defined and flexibly implemented as a way for parents to share child-rearing with the community.

Our present system does not function in this way. The result of past policies tied to a narrow patchwork outlook, it perpetuates the notion of day care as a full-time substitute for decent family life. Hence the all-or-nothing, 8 A.M. to 6 P.M. day care center or family day care home for welfare mothers. The welfare mother who stays home with her children does not have access to these resources. And she may not want them. That does not mean she does not want some kind of community support in her child-rearing. She might prefer a neighborhood resource center where she could borrow books and toys, where she could take her children for routine medical checkups, where she could meet other mothers, where she could get some support and advice about everyday child care problems. The working-class mother who has to work might prefer care in a family day care home by another mother or even a relative, one she had chosen herself, but one who had access to training courses in child development, at-home activities, and adult-child relationships. The middle-class mother who chooses to work might feel that group care in a center was better for her child who, at home, was relatively isolated from contact with other adults and other children. All of these combinations of different families with different day care needs are interchangeable. The middle-class mother who stays home needs support and advice too; a neighborhood child care center could serve her as well as the welfare mother. The purpose of day care ought to be to meet child care needs that really exist and not create ones that welfare planners, child psychologists, and politicians think ought to exist.

How do we work toward a system good for children, useful to parents, and supportive of the family?

1. The emphasis in day care should be on care, more care not less; different kinds of care, not one kind. Too often discussions and arguments about day care and its future expansion focus narrowly on group care in centers. This happens for a number of reasons: day care centers are visible and public; they have moved from custodial ideas of child care to developmental and educational ones; in contrast the other alternatives, especially family day care, seem disorganized and custodial, or they simply go unnoticed.

Certainly day care centers offering full-time care ought to be one form of day care, but such centers should be resources for establishing and supporting many other kinds of day care services. A day care center might, for example, use its resources and materials primarily for educational activities on a half-day basis and coordinate it with a family day care program allowing children to spend half a day in a center and half a day in a home. In this way a center could provide a preschool education for twice as many children as it could if running a full-day program, and yet meet the needs of many families for full-time day care.

Day care centers might also serve as neighborhood resource centers coordinating the development of play groups for children not using the center, forming babysitting services or pools for families that need only limited and temporary care for their children acting as a training center not only for its own staff but for men ar women who might be interested in caring for children in their own homes. It could act as an educational center for parents who remain home with their children but who need advice and assistance about raising their children. Nor should a center overlook the basic human need for mothers and children to be in contact with other people.

2. Day care should not be confined to professionalized, institutionalized forms of child care. Many kinds of day care would avoid the compulsory and expert-dominated institutions, like schools, which diminish rather than enhance parental care and responsibility, and which discourage rather than invite community involvement. In fact, if there is one model a day care system should avoid imitating, it is that of the school. Good child care should not be dependent on professionalization or credentials but on demonstrated ability to provide good care for other people's children. A system of internships, apprenticeships, on-site evaluations, and in-service training should characterize the education of day care workers.

Structurally considered, the self-organization, self-initiative, and self-service of child care groups would be an important counterbalance to separation of adults and children, and to dependence on experts and institutions. Most playgroups, child care co-ops, babysitting pools, organized park and playground activities, after-school children's groups, child-swapping (you take mine on Tuesday, I'll take yours on Thursday) begin and function because parents see a need and organize to meet it. They should have community support for this—whether it be resources for coordination, direction, information, or financial help. A group of mothers who organize and run a three-day-a-week child care co-op for twenty children ought to get the thousand dollars they need for equipment and supplies. Such an ad hoc system helps to bypass the bureaucratic inflexibility so typical of our other social institutions. In this regard, family day care, because it is based on personal selection and choice, ought to become a more important and better financed element in the day care picture.

Family day care, where a child is cared for with a small number of other children in a home environment, might well be a more convenient and appealing service for some parents. Such care allows for an intimacy and informality that many parents might prefer, especially for infants and younger children. As well, family day care permits greater flexibility in scheduling, catering to families who may need only part-time or odd-hour care for their children. Such home care for example might be more appropriate for nighttime care than a large center.

Unfortunately family day care in most areas of the country is totally disorganized and underdeveloped, embodying some of the worst features of out-of-home child care. Certainly in its present state it cannot supply any great amount of *quality* child care.

More training, planning and funding must go into family day care; more attention must be paid to training women and men who decide to care for children in their homes. They ought to have assistance and support in learning how to deal with children and parents. Their working conditions and fringe benefits should be regularized so as to make the work attractive to competent and skilled people. In addition to its flexibility and intimacy, family day care has the added benefit of making so many more people conscious of children's needs and of how to meet them, of multiplying the number of adults whose interest in children and child-rearing extends beyond their own children.

3. Day care ought to be more than a service for working parents. We must certainly recognize the necessity of that but go beyond it. Every working parent should have quality child care available to them, but that is not enough. Nonworking and unemployed parents should have some community resource to which they can turn for child care advice, assistance, support, and companionship.

A broad notion of quality day care for all children would provide some form of health, educational, or nutritional services, whether their parents worked or not. For some children it might mean supervised playground activities for three hours after school; for some children it might mean a playgroup three mornings a week; for some children it might mean developmental problems and learning disabilities could be diagnosed earlier and treated with optimal results. But even more important, a child's sense of social responsibility would be developed earlier and with more lasting effects than in a child raised solely in its own home with a minimal number of siblings. Finally, broadly defined day care services would release mothers and children from intensive dependence on one another, and open to children from both adequate and inadequate families a larger world of other children and other adults. Many women freed from total child-rearing would benefit from new opportunities in the world of work, but others might find outlets for their skills and energies in areas not confined to our present, narrow definitions of work.

In a thought-provoking essay Adrienne Rich has linked in fact the possibility of important changes in the larger society with the release of maternal concerns from the narrow confines of the nuclear family.

> . . . It remains true that within the family the maternal principle has survived in its least damaged form, though drained off from society and channeled into the narrowest possible vessel. Much of the fear that men, and anti-feminist women, express at the possible disappearance of the family may be dread that if women decline to become mothers physically we are robbing our culture of all motherly possibilities. . . . I believe that the women's movement is saying that we have come to an edge of history when men —in so far as they are embodiments of the patriarchal idea—have become dangerous to children and other living things, themselves included; and that we can no longer afford to keep the female principle—the mother in all women and the woman in many men —straitened within the tight little postindustrial family, or within any male-induced notion of where the female principle is valid and where it is not.[17]

From this viewpoint the possible modification of the nuclear family in our own society is not the demise of the maternal principle but its reextension into a largely nonmaternal society.

Nor is there any reason that men, husbands and fathers, should persist in the aggressive, ambitious, and driven roles that are the hallmark of the successful man in our society, all for the supposed end of providing the very best for their families. No matter what the barriers they face in attaining such success, most men take their achievement in protecting, supporting, and enhancing their wives and children as the single most important symbol of their masculinity and personhood. A redefinition of the woman's role and the child-rearing task could allow more men to share that protective and supportive role with their wives, permit them more time and energy to participate in child-rearing, and liberate them from the narrow definitions of masculinity.

4. Day care should confirm the importance of child-rearing and the parents' role in it; day care should not be defined as a substitute

for family but a support and supplement for it. This is a platitudinous observation, but not one, after all, that is agreed upon by all those who support some form of day care. As we saw in Chapter 1, there are those who from the patchwork viewpoint see day care as a substitute for deficient families, as well as some from the utopian viewpoint who see day care as a substitute for the superfluous, outmoded, and dangerous family. The family may well be deficient, dangerous, and even outmoded, but we have no good substitute for it, not even day care.

Obviously in and of itself, day care cannot force changes in conditions that stem from enormously complicated economic, social, and cultural problems. There have to be changes elsewhere in society. And perhaps one of the more important ones would be an employment policy that encouraged and allowed parents of young children to work shorter hours than they do now, with day care services providing part-time care for their children. Innovative work schedules like the shorter work week, the four-day ten-hour-a-day week, two people sharing one job, skilled and professional part-time work, would all contribute to maintaining parental responsibility while allowing mothers to join adult society.

Within the day care system itself, child care, especially in centers, must to the greatest extent possible be controlled by the parents whose children are enrolled in them. This will mean that parents hold the majority of seats on the board responsible for running the day care center. Parents should be expected and asked to contribute some time or skills to the day care center, partly as a means of involving them as working participants, partly as a means of familiarizing them with the operation of the center. Parents ought to know what happens on a day-to-day basis; they should know what is happening to their children. The day care staff and director must look upon the parents' presence, suggestions, and authority as an absolute and necessary ingredient for a good day care center.

Although acknowledging the great potential of day care for supporting the family, for allowing the family to move out of its presently narrow confines, we must finally ask ourselves whether in our kind of society, day care might not be used to push us in the direction of our worst tendencies? Would day care encourage the total age-segregation of our society, cutting off children and adults from sustained and meaningful contact with each other's worlds? In integrating women into a male-dominated world, would it make one's job the final arbiter of status and identity? Instead of bringing father and men more purposefully into the child-rearing task, might it not remove both mother and father?

Can day care be made to bear up under the weighty tasks of being the focus for parent-controlled and community-centered child-rearing? Perhaps this fragile, under-financed, and ill-supported institution can never function as an instrument for asserting the importance of the family and its child-rearing tasks. It is true, on the other hand, that so long as families, parents, and women accept the conditions of governmental bodies and bureaucracies for using and creating day care services, day care will never be very good and it will never be anything more than a tool for controlling the poor.

As a society we are not powerless to fend off some of the worst aspects of day care, nor are we incapable of creating many of its good aspects. But are we willing to do it?

Conclusion

This book was not conceived with the hope of arriving at a neat or comprehensive set of recommendations. Its purpose has been to provide a historical perspective on day care, to describe some of the ways day care currently operates, to point out the range of administrative, institutional, and educational problems day care faces, and to place the whole question in the context of larger political and social issues. All this may have raised two questions where there was only one before—and that is all to the good. The first and most fundamental conclusion that I hope the reader takes from this book—a conclusion that would be obvious were it not for the number of simple slogans about day care that continue to flourish—is that day care is a complex matter.

Leaving aside, then, the search for definitive answers and easy solutions, there are, nevertheless, a number of premises which will be our best guides to those answers.

1. *Day care is a political question.* The phrase can have two meanings—and I intend both of them. It means political in the narrower sense—proposing legislation, forming coalitions, lobbying, voting, funding, and sparring with bureaucracies. Second, it means political in the larger sense—the process by which a society shapes its values and balances its interests, decides how it shall live, *what it is.*

Against this notion, that day care is a political question both in the narrower and larger senses, the opposing view is that day care is a *professional* question. That is, that the determining factor in its development should be the kind of expertise possessed especially by a group of professionals. Such an approach may manifest itself in a desire to bracket all the larger political and social issues and focus only on the psychological or pedagogical issues within day care. Or it may be expressed as a naive "idealism" which anticipates the future of day care as hinging only on the expansion of good child development theories and practices. Or, rather, in the superior attitude that it is immoral or vulgar to inject politics into how and when and for whom we organize care for little children.

This is shortsighted. Day care poses political arguments about alternative ways of raising children, of being parents, of forming families. It touches upon our deepest, most basic values. The arguments it raises cannot be resolved by anything other than vigorous and sustained public debate and political give-and-take.

2. *Day care is a necessity.* Day care has until now been regarded as a limited and largely marginal child welfare service. Expanded in times of emergency, like wars or depressions, it has been quickly done away with once these crises pass. This improvisatorial attitude is no longer appropriate, if it ever was. Since World War II the number of working mothers of young children has grown, even though there has been a minimal amount of quality day care available. Those numbers will continue to grow whether or not there is good day care. Changing expectations about women's roles combined with the economic needs of many families will continue to swell the numbers of mothers who work.

Children and their families are the primary victims of an economic system that requires or encourages mothers to work without offering compensating child-care services; but ultimately the whole society suffers the consequences rising from a lack of quality child care for young children. One does not have to be an enthusiast of every vision projected in the name of women's liberation to recognize that a major shift in the opportunities open to women is now underway—and to approve of the fact. If some proposals for women's liberation seem to treat the care of children as an afterthought, some opponents of all day care seem to give as cursory attention to the situation of women and the need of many of them to combine motherhood with work in new ways. No one can say that women's liberation requires this or that particular kind—or amount—of day care. It can be said that some new patterns of child care, including day care, are and will continue to be a necessity.

3. *Day care should be "normalized."* Throughout its history, day care has been linked with welfare, and social deviancy. In our society, services thus linked are almost inevitably substandard. For day care, this link should be broken. Day care must not be seen as a device for solving the welfare problem, let alone as a means of forcing welfare mothers of young children to take jobs. This does not mean day care cannot be an important support for welfare mothers who want it, or that it cannot offer help to children whose home life is inadequate or disruptive. But it should also be available to working-class and middle-class mothers—on a sliding-scale fee basis, if necessary—and to families in general whose decision to avail themselves of day care would be seen as simply another one of those choices we all make about how and where to live, and not as an indication of any problem status.

To be "normalized" does not necessarily imply anything about the extent of day care—that, for instance, the average preschool child would be in a day care center. It simply means that to the extent that day care is available, it is available, in roughly similar varieties or forms, to all classes and types of families. Problems of disparity in quality will continue to exist, as they always will as long as there are disparities in wealth and political power. But the danger of day care "ghettos" or purely custodial institutions will be minimized if day care, in the eyes of planners, staffs, evaluators, and users, is perceived as a normal part of the social scene and not as a "benevolent" service oriented toward categories of families seen as especially in need of help.

4. *Day care and the future of the family are linked.* To organize day care without acknowledging that relationship invites a mindless and bureaucratic solution to child-care needs and promotes an expert-dominated system of day care. Day care will have an impact on the family. What is more, public day care ought to be formally committed to the strengthening of the family—at least until that time when private experiments demonstrate that they have a better invention for "making human beings human." This commitment means that parents must have a primary role in any day care program; there must be sustained and purposeful interaction between day care services and the parents using them. No doubt, maintaining such interaction is frequently difficult and from the professional's

point of view troublesome, but it should be considered no more an "optional" item than the physical safety of the children.

5. *Day care should be expanded but it should be expanded gradually.* This is not suggested out of a begrudging attitude toward day care but because of its importance and value. The fact is that there are severe limits to available trained personnel and the speed with which new day care staff can be trained. To expand day care too rapidly with only a thought for immediate and intensive expansion, and without attention to quality and real human needs, will mean creating a new institution at a rate that may freeze it into unfortunate and very possibly permanent patterns. Day care should be expanded at a pace that allows sufficient time for training day care workers and for evaluating the effects of a variety of day care programs on the children and families that use them.

6. *Day care must be more than custodial; it must be developmental and educational.* This point is obvious except to those who see day care primarily as a means of reducing welfare rolls. To expand a system that has at its core an attitude of providing baby-sitters for working mothers is dangerous for children and unfair to the great numbers of mothers who must work.

7. *Day care should not be limited to group care in centers.* Because day care centers are visible, and other programs such as family day care are often underdeveloped, there is a danger that day care will be only conceived of as day care *centers*, with other forms totally ignored or treated as poor substitutes. The nature of day care training, the very notion of a career in day care, the assumptions about parent and paraprofessional roles in day care will then all derive from the center model. Emphasis on centers alone may also freeze day care into rigid patterns, reinforce our tendency to always depend on institutional solutions, and satisfy bureaucratic "edifice complexes." Day care centers are important, but they are not the only way to provide child-care services. Much more money and organizational effort should go into family day care, and into experimenting with day care services which could support informal and private child-care arrangements.

8. *Day care should be only one of many possible changes which could encourage the emergence of new child-rearing patterns, new roles for women, and genuine family and child centeredness.* Day care should not merely be an instrument for tailoring our lives to the

present economic system. It should be accompanied by pressure for more flexibility in the economic system so that child-rearing can be shared between mothers and fathers, so that careers can be paced according to stages in family life, and so that children and families become major concerns of the world beyond the household.

Notes

CHAPTER I
Who Wants Day Care and Why

1. Representative Bella Abzug (Dem., N.Y.), for example, has called for 24-hour child-care centers to be funded at the rate of ten billion dollars annually by the end of the 1970's. *The New York Times*, February 23, 1971.
2. Boston: Little, Brown and Company, 1971.
3. See Chapter 2.
4. U.S. Congress, Senate Committee on Finance, *Material Related to Child Care Legislation: Description of S. 2003*, 92nd Congress, 1st session, 1971, pp. 39–47.
5. U.S. Congress, Senate Subcommittee on Children and Youth, *Comprehensive Child Development Act of 1971: Hearings on S. 1512*, 92nd Congress, 1st session, 1971, pp. 3–55; and U.S. Congress, House H.R. 6748: *A Bill to Provide a Comprehensive Child Development Act*, 92nd Congress, 1st session.
6. *Hearings on S. 1512*, p. 3.
7. U.S., President, Message, "Veto of Economic Opportunity Amendments of 1971," *Weekly Compilation of Presidential Documents*, December 13, 1971, pp. 1634–36.
8. For examples of this work see: Fred M. Hechinger, ed., *Pre-School Education Today* and Maya Pines, *Revolution in Learning: The Years from Birth to Six*.
9. Bettye M. Caldwell, "A Timid Giant Grows Bolder," *Saturday Review*, February 20, 1971, p. 49; John Bowlby, *Maternal Care and Mental Health*, and Margaret Mead, *et al.*, *Deprivation of Maternal Care: A Reassessment of Its Effects* (New York: Schocken Books, 1967).
10. A recent study of preschool education by the United States Office of Education suggests that this picture may have changed somewhat. Among children age 3 and 4, the percentage of black children enrolled in preschool programs (14.4 and 30.9) was slightly higher than the percentage of white children (12.6 and 27.1). *The New York Times*, October 5, 1971.
11. *Material Related*, pp. 11–12.
12. U.S., Office of Economic Opportunity, *Day Care: Resources for Decisions*, 1971, pp. 91–94.
13. *Hearings on S. 1512*, pp. 366–71.
14. *Day Care: Resources for Decisions*, p. 136.
15. For example, the Amalgamated Clothing Workers Union at its Chicago day care center found that the center's policy of "no corporeal punishment for misconduct . . . often

raises conflict with the parents, who are more accustomed to responding to misconduct or conflict with a more severe or physical means of punishment." *Hearings on S. 1512*, p. 484.

16. *Material Related*, p. 14; see also Jule Sugarman's testimony, *Hearings on S. 1512*, p. 167.

17. Pines, p. 272.

18. Alvin Toffler, *Future Shock* (New York: Random House, 1970), pp. 215-16.

19. *The New York Times*, October 29, 1970; Illinois Bell *Employees' House Organ*, n.d.

20. To be exact, a statement of the NOW Task Force on Child Care, "Why Feminists Want Child Care," declares: "NOW believes that the care and welfare of children is incumbent on society *and* parents. We reject the idea that mothers have a special child care role that is not to be shared equally by fathers. Men need the humanizing experiences of nurturance and guidance of another human organism." The concrete proposals in the statement, however, deal only with day care and not at all with enlarging the present child-rearing roles of fathers.

21. Shulamith Firestone, *The Dialectic of Sex*, pp. 206, 238-40.

22. Eva Figes, *Patriarchal Attitudes* p. 179.

23. Linda Gordon, "Functions of the Family," *Voices from Women's Liberation*, pp. 186-87.

24. These phrases are from Linda Gordon's pamphlet "Families" (Cambridge, Mass.: Bread & Roses Publications, 1970), pp. 23-24. The ending to the pamphlet is essentially the same as that of the article cited above with a few changes in wording.

25. National Organization of Women, "Why Feminists Want Children."

26. Vicki Breitbart, "Day Care, Who Cares?," p. 7.

27. "Day Care," a five-page mime-ographed pamphlet from the Women's Center of New York, 36 West 22nd Street, New York, N.Y.

28. *Ibid.*

29. Urie Bronfenbrenner, *Two Worlds of Childhood*, pp. 152-66; *The New York Times*, March 28, 1971, an interview with Bronfenbrenner; and "Children and Parents: Together in the World," Report of Forum 15: 1970 White House Conference on Children.

30. Caldwell, pp. 65-66.

CHAPTER 2
A History of Day Care: From the Beginning to World War II

1. Association of Day Nurseries of New York City, *Report*, 1910.

2. Ilse Forest, *Preschool Education: A Historical and Critical Study*, pp. 52-56.

3. Albert Fried and Ronald Sanders, eds., *Socialist Thought: A Documentary History* (Garden City, N.Y.: Doubleday Anchor, 1964), p. 159.

4. Ethel S. Beer, *Working Mothers and the Day Nursery*, p. 36.

5. *Constitution and By-Laws of the Infant School Society* (Boston, 1828), n.p.

6. *Constitution, By-Laws and Regulations of the Nursery for the Children of Poor Women in the City of New York*, 1854, n.p.

7. Forest, pp. 170-72.

8. Robert H. Bremner, *From the Depths: The Discovery of Poverty in the United States*, pp. 7-9.

9. Philip H. Bagenal, *The American Irish and Their Influence on Irish Politics* (Boston: Roberts Bros., 1882), pp. 70-72.

10. Charles Loring Brace, *The Dangerous Classes of New York and Twenty Years' Work Among Them*, p. 28.

11. See David J. Rothman, *The Dis-*

covery of the Asylum.

12. See Anthony Platt, *The Child Savers: The Invention of Delinquency,* and Miss Sophie E. Minton, "Family Life versus Institution Life," *Report* of Committee on History of Child Saving, 20th National Conference of Charities and Correction, 1893, pp. 37–53.

13. "Origins of Day Nursery Work," typescript in the Child Welfare League of America Library, with a chronology to 1919; typescript dated 1940.

14. National Federation of Day Nurseries, *Report* of Conference, 1905, p. 19.

15. *Ibid.,* pp. 16–17.

16. William L. O'Neill, *Everyone Was Brave: The Rise and Fall of Feminism in America* (Chicago: Quadrangle Books, 1969), p. 34.

17. Platt, p. 78.

18. H. Solomon, "Helen Day Nursery of Chicago," *Charities,* 18:438–39, July 20, 1907, and *The Survey,* 25: 465–67, December 17, 1910.

19. Wayside Day Nursery, *Annual Report,* 1887.

20. St. Agnes Day Nursery, *Annual Report,* 1898.

21. Armitage Day Nursery, *Annual Report,* 1895.

22. *Proceedings of the Day Nursery Conference,* New York, 1892.

23. The Virginia Nursery, *Report,* 1896; Riverside Day Nursery, *Report,* 1894; St. Agnes Day Nursery, *Report,* 1897.

24. M. Hall, "Administration of a Day Nursery," *Charities,* 8:544–46, June 14, 1902, p. 544.

25. Riverside Day Nursery, *Report,* 1893. Leila Day Nursery, *Report,* 1903, 1904.

26. Wayside Day Nursery, *Report,* 1884; St. Agnes Day Nursery, *Report,* 1888; Sunnyside Day Nursery, *Report,* 1884.

27. Leila Day Nursery, *Report,*

1894, New Haven, Connecticut.

28. Sunnyside Day Nursery, *Report,* 1895.

29. Little Sisters' Infant School, *Annual Report,* 1884, San Francisco.

30. Beer, pp. 43–44.

31. Conference of Day Nurseries, New York, *Report,* 1892.

32. Edward T. Devine, *The Principles of Relief,* pp. 339–40.

33. It should be noted that the most prominent of these gradually merged their efforts. *Charities* became *Charities and Common* which in turn became *The Survey,* the title under which all these magazines are indexed in libraries. It is the single best periodical source for day care information and discussion in this period; see also Bremner, pp. 155–57.

34. National Federation of Day Nurseries, *Report* of Conference, 1905; see also The Cleveland Day Nursery and Free Kindergarten Association, *Annual Report;* and Association of Day Nurseries, New York City, *Annual Report,* 1910–1936. These publications will all be found in the New York Public Library under "Day Nurseries." The publications of the National Federation and the New York Day Nursery Association are particularly valuable and informative. The Cleveland Day Nursery Association reports are incomplete, containing reports only for 1891; 1905; 1914–1915; 1917–1918.

35. National Federation of Day Nurseries, *Report* of Conference, 1912, pp. 14–17; 1914, pp. 15–16.

36. Association of Day Nurseries, New York City, *Report,* 1913.

37. *Proceedings* of the Day Nursery Conference, New York City, 1892, p. 4.

38. Association of Day Nurseries, New York City, *Report,* 1911, p. 8.

39. *Ibid.,* 1917.

40. *Ibid.,* 1918.

41. For these articles see National Federation of Day Nurseries, *Bulletin,* I:6; I:8; I:9; V:7; and I:12.

42. *Ibid.*, 1:8.

43. *Ibid.*, III:3.

44. *Ibid.*, I:5; III:2.

45. Marjory Hall, "For What Does the Day Nursery Stand?", *Charities*, 12:764–67, July 23, 1904.

46. National Federation of Day Nurseries, *Report* of Conference, 1912, pp. 28–30; *Ibid.*, 1914.

47. See "Origins of Day Nursery Work," and Cleveland Day Nursery and Kindergarten Association, *Report*, 1917.

48. Beer, pp. 39–40.

49. Beer, p. 15; Lois Barclay Murphy, "Individualization of Child Care and Its Relation to Environment," in *Early Child Care: The New Perspectives*, ed. Laura L. Dittman (New York: Atherton Press, n.d.), p. 84.

50. Grace Caldwell, "Standards of Admission to Day Nurseries," National Conference of Social Work, *Proceedings*, 1919, pp. 42–43.

51. *Ibid.*, p. 43.

52. *Ibid.*, p. 44.

53. *Case Work Programs in Day Nurseries:* A Symposium, Five Papers Presented at the Twentieth Biennial Conference of the National Federation of Day Nurseries, New York, April, 1937, p. 7.

54. *Ibid.*, p. 1.

55. *Ibid.*, pp. 3–4.

56. Beer, p. 121.

57. John Higham, *Strangers in the Land: Patterns of American Nativism, 1860–1925* (New York: Atheneum, 1970), pp. 300–30.

58. Association of Day Nurseries, New York City, *Report*, 1924; F. Colbourne, "How Good Are Day Nurseries," *The Survey*, 54:441–43, July 15, 1925.

59. Kips Bay Day Nursery, *Report*, 1928.

60. Anna B. Mayer and Alfred J. Kahn, *Day Care as a Social Instrument*, pp. 24–25. Bound mimeographed copies are to be found in the New York Public Library, the Child Welfare League of America Library, and the Columbia University School of Social Work Library.

61. Katherine Close, "Day Care Up to Now," *The Survey*, 79:194–97, July, 1943, p. 195.

62. *Ibid.*

63. Mayer and Kahn, pp. 24–25.

64. Close, p. 196; also see, "Kaiser's Children, Care Centers in Shipyards," *The Survey*, 80:351, December, 1944.

65. Katherine Close, "After Lanham Funds, What?", *The Survey*, 81:131–35, May, 1945, p. 131.

66. Close, 1945, p. 131.

67. For typical samples of these opinions see: Agnes E. Meyer, *Journey Through Chaos* and E. O. Lundberg, *Unto the Least of These: Social Services for Children*, pp. 287–96.

CHAPTER 3
A History of Day Care:
From World War II to 1970

1. *Status of Day Care Programs for Children*, Federal Security Agency, Social Security Administration, Children's Bureau (Washington, D.C.: October 31, 1950), Xerox of typescript in Child Welfare League of America Library.

2. *Ibid.*

3. U.S. Department of Health, Education and Welfare and Department of Labor, *Child Care Arrangements of Working Mothers in the United States*, by Seth Low and Pearl G. Spindler, Children's Bureau Publication number 461–1968, table M–54, p. 58.

4. Florence A. Ruderman, *Child Care and Working Mothers*, p. 4, Robert W. Smuts, *Women and Work in America*, with an introduction by Eli Ginzberg, pp. viii–ix.

5. *Ibid.*, pp. 63–64.

6. *Ibid.*, p. 146.
7. See Ruderman, and Spindler and Low.
8. Maya Pines, *Revolution in Learning*, chapter 8.
9. Ruderman, p. 15, fn. 12.
10. *Ibid.*, p. 14.
11. *Ibid.*, pp. 8–9.
12. *Ibid.*, pp. 211–13.
13. *Ibid.*, pp. 329–31.
14. Betty Friedan, *The Feminine Mystique.*
15. *Ibid.*, p. 113.
16. *Ibid.*, p. 118.
17. John Bowlby, *Maternal Care and Mental Health* (New York: Schocken Books, 1966). Included in the same volume is a valuable and interesting collection of comments on *Deprivation of Maternal Care: A Reassessment of Its Effects.* Among the contributors are Margaret Mead, Robert G. Harlow, and Mary D. Ainsworth.
18. Bowlby, p. 11.
19. Milton Willner, "Day Care: A Reassessment," and Bettye M. Caldwell and Julius B. Richmond, "Programmed Day Care for the Very Young Child—A Preliminary Report," in *Child Welfare*, XLIV, No. 3, pp. 125–33; pp. 134–42.
20. U.S. Department of Health, Education and Welfare, *Proceedings of the National Conference on Day-Care Services*, May 13–15, 1965, Children's Bureau Publication number 438–1966; U.S. Department of Labor, *Report of a Consultation on Working Women and Day Care Needs*, June 1, 1967.
21. Willner, p. 127.
22. *Ibid.*, p. 126.
23. Caldwell and Richmond, pp. 135–136.
24. *Ibid.*, p. 135.
25. *Day-Care Services*, p. 63.
26. *Ibid.*, pp. 19–26; 35–40; 41–48.
27. *Working Women and Day Care*, p. 14.

28. Low and Spindler.
29. Gilbert Y. Steiner, *The State of Welfare*, p. 58.
30. See Chapter 1.
31. U.S. Department of Health, Education and Welfare, Social and Rehabilitation Service, "Memorandum: Child (Day) Care Costs," August 25, 1971.
32. In Fred M. Hechinger, *Pre-School Education Today;* also in *Merrill Palmer Quarterly* of Behavior and Development, 10:3, July, 1964.
33. H. M. Skeels *et al.*, "A Study of Environmental Stimulation: an orphanage preschool project," *Iowa Studies in Child Welfare*, 15:4. Also see H. M. Skeels, "Adult Status of Children with Contrasting Early Life Experiences," *Monograph Social Research and Child Development*, XXXI: 3.
34. *The New York Times*, March 10, 1971.
35. B. Caldwell and J. Richmond, "The Children's Center in Syracuse, New York," in *Early Child Care: The New Perspectives*, ed. Laura L. Dittman (New York: Atherton Press, n.d.), p. 341.
36. Cynthia Fuchs Epstein, *Woman's Place: Options and Limits in Professional Careers*, pp. 108–12; and M. M. Poloma and T. N. Garland, "The Married Professional Woman: A Study in the Tolerance of Domestication," *Journal of Marriage and the Family*, 33:3, pp. 531–39.
37. See Eli Ginzberg, *et al.*, *Life Styles of Educated Women.*

CHAPTER 4
How Day Care Works

1. A good pictorial presentation of such designs is Paul Abramson, "Schools for Early Childhood." The same group has published an equally interesting booklet called "Found

Spaces and Equipment for Children's Centers," 1972. It is available for $2.00 per copy from EFL, 477 Madison Avenue, New York, N.Y. 10022.

2. For example, New York State has legislatively provided for construction costs through its Youth Facilities Act; to date, the bond issue that would raise the money has never been released. The Comprehensive Child Development Act of 1971 (vetoed) provided funds for construction. In some areas mortgage loan programs provide money for renovations with bank loans guaranteed by local government. In fact, most day care centers must depend on a hit-or-miss system of charity, in-kind services, fund-raising schemes, etcetera, to meet renovation or construction costs.

3. There has been a federal survey of state licensing requirements. U.S. Department of Health, Education and Welfare, Office of Child Development, *Abstracts of State Day Care Licensing Requirements, Part 2: Day Care Centers*, DHEW Publication No. (OCD) 72–12, 1971. Part I is a survey of state regulations concerning family and group day care homes. A summary survey is also available, "A Survey of State Day Care Licensing Requirements," *Child Care Bulletin*, No. 4 (Washington, D.C.: The Day Care and Child Development Council of America, Inc., 1971). City and county governments often have regulations governing day care in addition to those of the state. There is no national survey of these.

4. U.S. Congress, Senate Subcommittee on Employment, Manpower, and Poverty, and the Subcommittee on Children and Youth of the Committee on Labor and Public Welfare: *Hearings on S.1512*, 92nd Congress, 1st session, 1971, p. 368.

5. U.S. Office of Economic Opportunity, *Day Care: Resources for Decisions*, ed. Edith H. Grotberg (Washington, D.C. 1971), p. ix. A comprehensive bibliography of such research follows several articles in this collection.

6. *Ibid.*, p. 253.

7. *Ibid.*, p. 119.

8. *Ibid.*, p. 122.

9. *Ibid.*, p. 163.

10. *Ibid.*, p. 239.

11. *Ibid.*, p. 147.

12. U.S., President, Message, "Veto of Economic Opportunity Amendments of 1971," *Weekly Compilation of Presidential Documents*, December 13, 1971, pp. 1634–36.

13. *Hearings on S.1512*, pp. 308–09.

14. There is, in fact, a day care union, at last in New York City. It is Local 1707 of the Community and Social Agency Employes.

15. Dorothy Beers Boguslawski, *Guide for Establishing and Operating Day Care Centers for Young Children* (New York: Child Welfare League of America, Inc., 1970), p. 57.

16. See Chapter 2.

17. *A Study in Child Care*, 1970–71, Richard R. Ruopp, Case Study Coordinator (Cambridge: Abt. Associates, 1971), Vol. II–A.

18. Figures are from a leaflet distributed by the Pre-School Association of the West Side, Inc., 530 West End Avenue, New York, N.Y. 10024.

19. New York and Chicago are prime examples of cities that have consolidated a previously far-flung bureaucracy. When questioned on ways of speeding up the licensing process, state licensing officials, predictably enough, suggested hiring more state licensing officials. See "A Survey of State Day Care Licensing Requirements," p. 24.

20. Such complexities are many, and readers who would like to pursue the legal, philosophical, and some of the other practical difficulties of licensing and regulation from a sympathetic point of view should see Norris E. Class, "Licensing of Child

Care Facilities by State Welfare Departments: A Conceptual Statement" (Washington, D.C.: Children's Bureau, Publication number 462–1968); and Gwen G. Morgan, "Regulations of Early Childhood Programs" (Washington, D.C.: The Day Care and Child Development Council of America, Inc., 1972).

CHAPTER 5
What Day Care Looks Like

1. Joseph Featherstone, "Kentucky Fried Children: The Day Care Problem," *The New Republic*, September 12, 1970.
2. *Chicago Today*, March 3, 1970, p. 36.
3. *A Study in Child Care*, Vol. II-A.
4. Paul Abramson, pp. 26–29.
5. *A Study in Child Care*, p. 5.
6. *Ibid.*, p. 8.
7. *Ibid.*, p. 13.
8. *Ibid.*, p. 7–8.
9. Abramson, p. 27.
10. *Wall Street Journal*, November 27, 1972. This survey by the *Wall Street Journal* suggests that many franchisers are having difficulties delivering their services to the people who have purchased franchises.
11. *Administrative Management*, May, 1972, pp. 62–66; *Progressive Architecture*, February, 1971, pp. 102–05.
12. *H&H*, August, 1971, pp. 55–59.
13. U.S. Department of Labor, "Day Care Services: Industry's Involvement," Bulletin 296, 1971.
14. *A Study in Child Care*.
15. See Chapter 4.
16. Mary Dublin Keyserling, *Windows on Day Care*.
17. *A Study in Child Care*.
18. *Ibid.*, p. 5.
19. See Chapter 2.
20. Maya Pines, *Revolution in*

Learning, pp. 187–89.
21. For a good example of her opinions, see Bettye M. Caldwell, "A Timid Giant Grows Bolder," *Saturday Review*, February 20, 1971; and "The Effects of Infant Care," in *Review of Child Development Research*, Vol. I, pp. 9–87.
22. J. Ronald Lally, "The Family Development Research Program: A Program for Prenatal, Infant and Early Childhood Enrichment," p. 3.
23. *Ibid.*, p. 2.
24. *Windows on Day Care*, p. 130.
25. Pines, *Revolution in Learning*, p. 187–90.
26. *Windows on Day Care*, pp. 135–36.
27. Milton Willner, "Unsupervised Family Day Care in New York City," p. 60.
28. *A Study in Child Care*, Vol. II-B.

CHAPTER 7
Politics and Policies

1. The transcript of the hearings will be found in: U.S. Congress, House Select Subcommittee on Education of the Committee on Education and Labor, *Comprehensive Preschool Education and Child Day-Care Act of 1969: Hearings on H.R. 13520*, 91st Congress, 1st and 2nd sessions, 1969 and 1970.
U.S. Congress, Senate Subcommittee on Employment, Manpower, and Poverty and the Subcommittee on Children and Youth of the Committee on Labor and Public Welfare, *Comprehensive Child Development Act of 1971: Hearings on S.1512*, 92nd Congress, 1st session, 1971.
The House bill for 1971 was: U.S. Congress, House, *H.R. 6748*, 92nd Congress, 1st session, 1971.
The Comprehensive Child Development Act was eventually attached to the Economic Opportunity Amend-

ments of 1971 and was sent to a Senate-House Conference in mid-November. The final version of the bill and the one which President Nixon vetoed will be found: U.S. Congress, House, *Economic Opportunity Amendments of 1971: Conference Report,* 92nd Congress, 1st session, 1971, Report No. 92–682.

2. U.S. Congress, Senate, Senator Walter Mondale speaking for the *Comprehensive Child Development Act,* 92nd Congress, 1st session, April 6, 1971, *Congressional Record,* 117:49.

3. *The New York Times,* August 6, 1969.

4. See William Raspberry's discussion in: *Wall Street Journal,* December 1, 1969. A typographical error makes the number of children 150,000 when the number should read 450,000.

5. U.S. Congress, House, 92nd Congress, 1st session, December 1, 1971, *Congressional Record,* 117:11602–11604. These pages refer to a long and interesting analysis with interviews and some legislative history, originally published in the *National Journal* by John K. Iglehart entitled, "Welfare Report/Congress Presses Major Child Care Program Despite White House Veto Threat." For other stories on the subject see: *The New York Times,* November 20, 1971; *Washington Post,* November 1, 1971.

6. *Chicago Tribune,* October 4, 1971.

7. *Hearings on S.1512,* p. 14.

8. *Conference Report.*

9. U.S., President, Message, "Veto of Economic Opportunity Amendments of 1971," *Weekly Compilation of Presidential Documents,* December 13, 1971, pp. 1634–36. For excerpts from the veto message, see *The New York Times,* December 10, 1971.

10. See for example: *The New Republic,* December 25, 1971; Carl T. Rowan, *Chicago Daily News,* December 14, 1971.

11. James J. Kilpatrick, *Chicago Daily News,* October 22, 1971.

12. *Hearings on S.1512,* p. 790.

13. *Chicago Sun-Times,* January 6, 1972.

14. See Chapter 3.

15. See Chapter 3.

16. The 1968 Westinghouse-Ohio survey suggested this. About its conclusions Christopher Jencks *et al.* write: "The largest single follow-up of preschool alumni was the 1968 Westinghouse-Ohio survey of Head Start graduates. This study concluded that neither year-round nor summer Head Start programs had a significant long-term effect on children's cognitive growth. When we reanalyzed this data, we found a few year-round centers in which the Head Start children's advantage over non-Head Start children persisted through first grade. Beyond first grade, however, the picture was gloomy. Overall, the evidence strongly suggested that Head Start's effects on children's cognitive growth had been quite transitory.

"This is not surprising. Unlike politicians and parents, Head Start teachers and directors have not been primarily concerned with raising children's test scores. They have favored 'supportive, unstructured socialization programs rather than structured informational programs.' They have assumed that a child would get plenty of disciplined instruction when he reached first grade and that he would not do any better in first grade if he started such work a year or two early. The evidence suggests that the teachers and administrators were right." Christopher Jencks, *et al., Inequality: A Reassessment of the Effect of Family and Schooling in America,* p. 86.

17. *Inequality,* p. 255.

18. *Ibid.,* p. 256–57; in concluding his whole study, Jencks argues that inequality will only be eradicated by

a more equitable distribution of income; money, not schools, will create a more just and equitable distribution of national resources. The burden of inequality is put where it justifiably belongs—on our economic structures. The book concludes:

> In America, as elsewhere, the general trend over the past 200 years has been toward equality. In the economic realm, however, the contribution of public policy to this drift has been slight. As long as egalitarians assume that public policy cannot contribute to economic equality directly but must proceed by ingenious manipulations of marginal institutions like the schools, progress will remain *glacial*. If we want to move beyond this tradition, we will have to establish political control over the economic institutions that shape our society. (p. 265) (Italics mine)

If the rate of change made through intervention in the schools be "glacial," it is hard to imagine passing through less than three ice ages to make our economic institutions a resource of greater equality.

19. See Chapter 3.

20. U.S. Office of Economic Opportunity, *Day Care: Resources for Decisions*, ed. Edith H. Grotberg (Washington, D.C., 1971), p. 20.

21. See Jerome Kagan's remarks in Sheila Cole, "The Search for the Truth about Day Care," *The New York Times Magazine*, December 12, 1971, pp. 91 and 94; Kagan's article in *Resources for Decisions* is also illustrative, especially pp. 146–47; for Urie Bronfenbrenner see *Children and Parents: Together in the World*, 1970 White House Conference on Children: Report of Forum 15; and an interview in *The New York Times*, March 28, 1971.

22. *National Review*, December 31, 1971.

23. Breitbart, Radical Education Project.

24. *National Review*, December 31, 1971; Senator Buckley was not hesitant to use white-coated bureaucrats when they agreed with him; see his use of Meer's article in U.S. Congress, Senate, *Congressional Record*, 92nd Congress, 1st session, December 2, 1971, 117, 186, part II: S20274.

25. *Hearings on S.1512*, pp. 21–22.

26. Mary Diggles, "Letters to Editor," *Chicago Daily News*, December 28, 1972.

27. U.S. Office of Economic Opportunity, *Day Care Survey: 1970*, Westinghouse Learning Corporation and Westat Research, Inc., April, 1971, p. 204; U.S. Office of Economic Opportunity, *A Study in Child Care, 1970–71*, Vol. III: *Cost and Quality Issues for Operators*, Abt Associates Inc., April, 1971; U.S. Congress, Senate Committee on Finance, *Child Care: Data and Materials*, June 16, 1971, pp. 130–31.

28. The latter is William Shannon's suggestion, "A Radical, Direct, Simple, Utopian Alternative to Day-Care Centers" *The New York Times Magazine*, April 30, 1972.

29. Gilbert Y. Steiner, *The State of Welfare*, chapter 2, especially pp. 68–74.

30. Blanche Bernstein and Priscilla Giacchino, "Costs of Day Care: Implications for Public Policy," in *City Almanac*, August, 1971, 6:2, pp. 13–14. (The *City Almanac* is published by the Center for New York City Affairs of the New School for Social Research, 72 Fifth Avenue, New York, N.Y. 10011.)

31. *Hearings on S.1512*, pp. 436 and 722; as well see the testimony of Jule Sugarman and John Niemeyer, pp. 154–75.

32. George F. Gilder, "The Case
Against Universal Day Care," *The
New Leader*, April 3, 1972, p. 12.

CHAPTER 8
Larger Questions: Day Care, the
Family, and Society

1. William Shannon, *The New
York Times Magazine*, April 30, 1972,
p. 82.
2. In the case of France and Ger-
many this is a matter of personal
observation. See Françoise Dolto,
"French and American Children as
Seen by a French Child Analyst," in
Childhood in Contemporary Cultures,
ed. Margaret Mead and Martha Wolf-
enstein (Chicago: The University of
Chicago Press, 1963), pp. 408–23; Ruth
Sidel, *Women and Child Care in
China: A Firsthand Report;* Urie
Bronfenbrenner, *Two Worlds of
Childhood: U.S. and U.S.S.R.*
3. Richard Sennett, *The Uses of
Disorder: Personal Identity and City
Life*, pp. 3–26; Philippe Ariès, *Cen-
turies of Childhood: A Social History
of Family Life*, tr. Robert Baldick.
4. *Ibid.*, p. 133.
5. *Ibid.*, p. 400.
6. John Demos, *A Little Commonwealth: Family Life in Plymouth
Colony*, p. 183.

7. Bernard Bailyn, *Education in
the Forming of American Society*,
p. 8.
8. Richard Sennett, *Families Against
the City: Middle-Class Homes of Industrial Chicago;* Kirk Jeffrey, "The
Family as Utopian Retreat from the
City: The Nineteenth-Century Contribution," *Soundings*, LV:1, pp. 21–
41.
9. Roy Lubove, *The Professional
Altruist: The Emergence of Social
Work as a Career, 1880–1930* (Cambridge, Mass.: Harvard University
Press, 1965).
10. Alexis de Tocqueville, *Democ-
racy in America* (New York: Random
House-Vintage Books), Vol. II, pp.
203–04.
11. Sanford N. Katz, *When Parents
Fail: The Law's Response to Family
Breakdown*, p. 4.
12. *Ibid.*, p. 5.
13. *Ibid.*
14. Demos, p. 185.
15. Ben Bagdikian, *The Information
Machines* (New York: Harper and
Row, Colophon Books, 1970), p. 183.
16. Urie Bronfenbrenner, *et al.*,
"Children and Parents: Together in
the World," Report of Forum 15:
1970 White House Conference on
Children, p. 4.
17. Adrienne Rich, *The New York
Review of Books*, November 30, 1972,
pp. 39–40.

Bibliography

BIBLIOGRAPHICAL RESOURCES

Day Care: An Annotated Bibliography, Urbana, Illinois: Educational Resources Information Center (ERIC), June, 1971.*

Directory of Resources on Early Childhood Education. ERIC, 1971. Reprint of Day Care and Child Development Council of America, 1971.

Early Childhood Facilities/1: An Annotated Bibliography on Early Childhood. Architectural Research Laboratory of the University of Michigan, 1970. Available from Educational Facilities Laboratories, Inc.

Resources for Day Care: A List of Publications. Washington, D.C.: Day Care and Child Development Council of America.

Day Care: Resources for Decisions. Ed. Edith H. Grotberg. Office of Economic Opportunity. Washington, D.C.: U.S. Government Printing Office, 1971. The articles in this volume are followed by extensive bibliographies.

U.S. Department of Health, Education and Welfare. Children's Bureau. *Good References on Day Care—Federal Panel on Early Childhood.* Publication no. 0–332–303. Washington, D.C., 1969.

HISTORY

All the day-nursery annual reports mentioned in the notes of Chapter 2 will be found in the New York Public Library, where there is a rather extensive collection for nurseries in New York City and miscellaneous reports from other areas. In general these reports date from 1895 through 1920 and are a valuable resource for providing an image and idea of

* Addresses will be found in the directory following the bibliography.

these early day nurseries. In addition, the following articles, books and manuscripts are valuable source materials.

Association of Day Nurseries of New York City. *Report.* 1910–1936.
Beer, Ethel. "The Day Nursery and Crime Prevention." *Probation,* December 1940.
—— *Working Mothers and the Day Nursery.* New York: Whiteside, Inc., 1957.
Brace, Charles Loring. *The Dangerous Classes of New York and Twenty Years' Work Among Them.* New York: Wynkoop and Hallenbeck, 1872.
Bremner, Robert H. *From the Depths: The Discovery of Poverty in the United States.* New York: New York University Press, 1967.
Caldwell, Grace. "Standards of Admission to Day Nurseries." *National Conference of Social Work,* 1919:42–45.
Case Work Programs in Day Nurseries: A Symposium. Five Papers Presented at the Twentieth Biennial Conference of the National Federation of Day Nurseries. New York, April, 1937.
"A City Improves Day Care for Its Children." *The Child.* 11:8 (February 1947).
Clark, Elizabeth Woodruff. "A Challenge to Case Work." *The Family.* 22: 291–95 (January 1942).
Close, Katherine. "After Lanham Funds, What?" *Survey,* 81:131–35 (May 1945).
—— "Day Care Up to Now." *Survey,* 79:194–97 (July 1943).
—— "While Mothers Work." *Survey Midmonthly,* July 1942.
Colbourne, F. "Day Nursery and the Community." *Survey,* 45:129–30 (October 30, 1920).
—— "How Good Are Day Nurseries?" *Survey,* 54:441–43 (July 15, 1925).
—— "Too Near to Be Seen." *Survey,* 51:395–96 (January 15, 1924).
Conference of Day Nurseries. *Proceedings,* New York, 1892.
"Danger in Day Nurseries." *Charities,* 8:2 (January 4, 1902).
Devine, Edward T. "Day Nursery." *Charities Review,* 10:263–65 (August 1900).
—— *The Principles of Relief.* New York: The Macmillan Co., 1910.
Dodge, A. M. "Neighborhood Work and Day Nurseries." *Conference Charities and Correction,* 1912:113–18.
—— "Development of the Day Nursery Idea." *Outlook,* 56:60–67 (May 1, 1897).
Everett, L. B. "High School Nurseries." *Survey,* 57:804 (March 15, 1927).
Flather, R. L. "Day Care of Children of Working Mothers: The Problems in a 'Boom' War-Industry Town." Child Welfare League of America, *Bulletin,* October 1943.
Forest, Ilse. *Preschool Education: A Historical and Critical Study.* New York: The Macmillan Co., 1927.

"Function of the Day Nursery." *Charities*, 8:542–43 (June 14, 1902).

Gillam, M. A. "New Interpretation of the Task of Day Nurseries." *National Conference of Social Work*, 1921:109–11.

"Governmental Day Nurseries." *Public Administration Review*, 2:3, p. 271.

Hall, Marjorie. "Administration of a Day Nursery." *Charities*, 8:544–46 (June 14, 1902).

—— "For What Does the Day Nursery Stand?" *Charities*, 12:764 (July 23, 1904).

Hedger, Caroline. "Standards of Hygiene and Equipment of Day Nurseries." *National Conference of Social Work*, 1919:45–48.

"Kaiser's Children; Care Centers in Shipyards." *Survey*, 80:351 (December, 1944).

Kenny, Luna E. *Foster Day Care*. Philadelphia: Philadelphia Association of Day Nurseries, 1933.

—— "A Ten Year Experiment in Foster Day Care." Child Welfare League of America *Bulletin*, 5 (1939).

Lundberg, E. O. *Unto the Least of These: Social Services for Children*. New York: D. Appleton-Century Co., 1947.

Meyer, Agnes E. *Journey Through Chaos*. New York: Harcourt, Brace and Co., 1943.

Minton, Sophie E. "Family Life Versus Institution Life." *Report* of Committee on History of Child Saving, 20th National Conference of Charities and Correction, 1893.

"Mushroom Day Nurseries Checked." *Survey*, 41:229–30 (November 23, 1918).

"National Conference on Day Nurseries." *Charities*, 14:775–78 (May 27, 1905).

National Federation of Day Nurseries. *Bulletin*. March, 1925–October, 1933.

—— *Report of Conference*. 1905–1925.

"Origins of Day Nursery Work." Library, Child Welfare League of America. (Typescript, dated 1940).

Phillips, M. C. "Russia's Drive Toward Health; Work of the Department for the Protection of Motherhood and Childhood." *Survey*, 64:388–93 (August 1, 1930).

Platt, Anthony M. *The Child Savers: The Invention of Delinquency*. Chicago: University of Chicago Press, 1969.

Rothman, David J. *The Discovery of the Asylum*. Boston: Little, Brown and Company, 1971.

"Scope of Day Nursery Work." *Charities*, 8:546–47 (June 14, 1902).

Solomon, H. "Helen Day Nursery of Chicago." *Charities*, 18:438–39 (July 20, 1907).

—— "Mothers and Children's Building." *Survey*, 25:465–67 (December 17, 1910).

Stolz, L. M. "Nursery Comes to the Shipyard." *The New York Times Magazine,* November 7, 1943.

U.S. Federal Security Agency, Children's Bureau. "Status of Day Care Programs for Children." Washington, D.C., October 31, 1950. (Xerox of typescript in library, Child Welfare League of America.)

"War Area Day Care Bill." *Social Service Review.* 17:369 (September, 1943).

HEARINGS AND LEGISLATION

U.S. Congress. House. *H.R. 6748: A Bill to Provide a Comprehensive Child Development Act.* 92nd Cong., 1st sess., 1971.

U.S. Congress. House. *Economic Opportunity Amendments of 1971: Conference Report.* 92nd Cong., 1st sess., 1971. Report No. 92-682.

U.S. Congress. House. Select Subcommittee on Education, Committee on Education and Labor. *Comprehensive Preschool and Child Day-Care Act of 1969: Hearings on H.R. 13520.* 91st Cong., 1st and 2nd sess., 1969 and 1970.

U.S. Congress. Senate. Committee on Finance. *Material Related to Child Care Legislation: Description of S.2003.* 92nd Cong., 1st sess., 1971.

U.S. Congress. Senate. Committee on Finance. *Child Care: Data and Materials.* Committee Print, 92nd Cong., 1st sess., June 16, 1971.

U.S. Congress. Senate. Committee on Finance. *Child Care Legislation.* Committee Print, 92nd Cong. 1st sess., July 23, 1971.

U.S. Congress. Senate. Committee on Finance. *Additional Material Related to Child Care Legislation.* Committee Print, 92nd Cong., 1st sess., September 21, 1971.

U.S. Congress. Senate. Subcommittee on Children and Youth, Committee on Labor and Public Welfare. *Comprehensive Child Development Act of 1971: Hearings on S.1512.* 92nd Cong., 1st sess., 1971.

U.S. President. Message, "Veto of Economic Opportunity Amendments of 1971," *Weekly Compilation of Presidential Documents,* December 13, 1971.

CURRENT REPORTS, RESEARCH AND INTERPRETATIONS

Adair, Thelma, and Esther Eckstein. *Parents and the Day Care Center.* New York: Federation of Protestant Welfare Agencies, Inc., 1961.

Abramson, Paul. *Schools for Early Childhood.* New York: Educational Facilities Laboratories, Inc., 1970.

Bank Street College of Education. Day Care Consultation Service. "Some Notes on Recruiting and Hiring Staff for Your Day Care Center." New York, 1970. (Mimeographed.)

——— "Suggestions for Equipment for a Day Care Classroom and

Ideas for Equipping Day Care Programs with Materials Available at Minimal Costs." New York, 1971.

Barclay, D. "Child Care Co-ops." *The New York Times Magazine*, January 13, 1952.

Bernstein, Blanche, and Priscilla Giacchino. "Costs of Day Care: Implications for Public Policy." *City Almanac*, 6:2 (August 1971). New York: New School for Social Research.

Bettelheim, Bruno. *The Children of the Dream: Communal Child Rearing and American Education*. New York: The Macmillan Co., 1969.

Boguslawski, Dorothy Beers. *Guide for Establishing and Operating Day Care Centers for Young Children*. New York: Child Welfare League of America, Inc., 1970.

Bourne, Patricia Gerald, Elliott A. Medrich, Louis Steadwell, and Donald Barr. *Day Care Nightmare—A Child Centered View of Child Care*. Berkeley: Institute of Urban and Regional Development, 1971. (Mimeographed.)

Bourne, Patricia Gerald. "What Day Care Ought to Be." *The New Republic*, February 12, 1972.

Bowlby, John. *Maternal Care and Mental Health*. Margaret Mead, *et al. Deprivation of Maternal Care: A Reassessment of Its Effects*. New York: Schocken Books, 1967.

Breitbart, Vicki. "Day Care, Who Cares?" Detroit: Radical Education Project, n.d. (Mimeographed).

Bronfenbrenner, Urie, *et al.* "Children and Parents: Together in the World." Report of Forum 15: 1970 White House Conference on Children. (Mimeographed.)

—— *Two Worlds of Childhood: U.S. and U.S.S.R.* New York: Russell Sage Foundation, 1970.

Caldwell, Bettye M. "The Effects of Infant Care." *Review of Child Development Research*, Vol. I. New York: Russell Sage Foundation, 1964.

—— "A Timid Giant Grows Bolder." *Saturday Review*, February 20, 1971.

—— "What Is the Optimal Learning Environment for the Young Child?" *American Journal of Orthopsychiatry*, 37:1 (January 19, 1967).

Caldwell, Bettye M., and Julius H. Richmond. "Programmed Day Care for the Very Young Child—A Preliminary Report." *Child Welfare*, 44:3.

The Changing Dimensions of Day Care: Highlights from Child Welfare. New York: Child Welfare League of America, Inc., 1970.

The Children Are Waiting. Report of the Early Childhood Development Task Force. New York, July 20, 1970.

Cohen, Monroe D., ed. *Helps for Day Care Workers*. Reprints from *Childhood Education*. Washington, D.C.: Association for Childhood Education International, 1971.

Cole, Sheila. "The Search for the Truth about Day Care." *The New York Times Magazine*, December 12, 1971.

Collins, A. H., and E. L. Watson. "Exploring the Neighborhood Family Day Care System." *Social Casework*, 50:527–33.

Day Care—An Expanding Resource for Children. New York: Child Welfare League of America, Inc., 1967.

"Day Care Centers: A New Marketing Tool for Apartment Builders." *H&H*, August 1971.

Day Care: A Preventive Service. New York: Child Welfare League of America, Inc., 1968.

"Education as Business." *Progressive Architecture*, February 1971.

Evans, E. Belle, Beth Shub and Marlene Weinstein. *Day Care: How to Plan, Develop, and Operate a Day Care Center.* Boston: Beacon Press, 1971.

Evans, E. Belle, and George E. Sais. *Day Care for Infants: A Case for Infant Day Care and a Practical Guide.* Boston: Beacon Press, 1972.

"Facts About Starting a Day-Care Center." *Good Housekeeping*, September 1970.

Featherstone, Joseph. "Kentucky-Fried Children." *The New Republic*, September 5, 1970.

Found Spaces and Equipment for Children's Centers. Educational Facilities Laboratories, Inc. New York, 1972.

Gilder, George F. "The Case Against Universal Day Care." *The New Leader*, April 3, 1972.

Hechinger, Fred M., ed. *Pre-School Education Today.* New York: Doubleday and Co., Inc., 1971.

Illinois. State Department of Children and Family Services. *Day Care for Children in Illinois: 1970 Report.* Springfield, Illinois, 1971.

Jacoby, Susan. "Who Raises Russia's Children?" *Saturday Review*, August 21, 1971.

Jencks, Christopher, *et al. Inequality: A Reassessment of the Effect of Family and Schooling in America.* New York: Basic Books, Inc., 1972.

Keyserling, Mary Dublin. *Windows on Day Care.* New York: National Council of Jewish Women, 1972.

Lally, J. Ronald. "Syracuse University Children's Center: A Day Care Center for Young Children." Narrative description, February 22, 1970. Syracuse, New York: Department of Family and Child Development, Syracuse University. (Mimeographed).

—— "The Family Development Research Program: A Program for Prenatal, Infant and Early Childhood Enrichment." Syracuse: College for Human Development, Syracuse University, February 22, 1971. (Mimeographed).

—— *Progress Report, 1970–71.* "Development of a Day Care Center for Young Children." Syracuse, New York: College for Human Development, Syracuse University, February 22, 1971.

Lilleskov, Roy K., Martha Lou Gilbert, Thelma Mihalov, Clara Karksdale. "Planning an Infant Care Unit with Community Participation." New York: Child Development Center of the Jewish Board of Guardians. Paper presented at the Annual Meeting of the American Orthopsychiatric Association, San Francisco, March 23–26, 1970.

Massachusetts Early Education Project. *Child Care in Massachusetts: The Public Responsibility.* Washington, D.C.: The Day Care and Child Development Council of America, Inc., 1972.

Mayer, Anna B., with the collaboration of Alfred J. Kahn. *Day Care as a Social Instrument.* Columbia University, School of Social Work, January 1965. (Mimeographed.)

Maxwell, Tom. "Corporate Day Care Takes Its First Steps." *Administrative Management,* May 1972.

Meade, Marion. "The Politics of Day Care." *Commonweal,* April 10, 1971.

"Mothers at Work, Children Alone." *The New York Times Magazine,* February 5, 1961.

Morgan, Gwen G. *Regulations of Early Childhood Programs.* Washington, D.C.: The Day Care and Child Development Council of America, Inc., 1972.

Pines, Maya. *Revolution in Learning: The Years from Birth to Six.* New York: Har/Row Books, 1970.

——— "Slum Children Must Make Up for Lost Time." *The New York Times Magazine,* October 15, 1967.

——— "Someone to Mind the Baby." *The New York Times Magazine,* January 7, 1968.

Prescott, Elizabeth, Cynthia Milich and Elizabeth Jones. *Day Care.* Vol. I, *The Politics of Day Care;* Vol. II, *Day Care as a Child-Rearing Environment.* Washington, D.C.: The National Association for the Education of Young Children, 1972.

Provence, Sally, M.D. *Guide for the Care of Infants in Groups.* New York: Child Welfare League of America, Inc., 1967.

Rothman, Sheila. "Other People's Children," *The Public Interest.* Winter, 1973.

Sale, June S., and Yolanda L. Torres. *"I'm Not Just a Babysitter,"* A Descriptive Report of the Community Family Day Care Project. Reprinted by The Day Care and Child Development Council of America, Inc., 1972.

Shannon, William. "A Radical, Direct, Simple, Utopian Alternative to Day-Care Centers." *The New York Times Magazine,* April 30, 1972.

Sidel, Ruth. *Women and Child Care in China: A Firsthand Report.* New York: Hill and Wang, 1972.

Skeels, H. M. "Adult Status of Children with Contrasting Early Life Experiences." *Monograph Social Research and Child Development,* 31:3.

Skeels, H. M., et al. "A Study of Environmental Stimulation: An Orphanage Preschool Project." *Iowa Studies in Child Welfare,* 15:4.

Spock, Benjamin. "Communes and Nurseries: Are They as Good for Children as They Are Helpful to Mothers?" *Redbook*, 135:28.

Stanley, Julian C., ed. *Preschool Programs for the Disadvantaged: Five Experimental Approaches to Early Childhood Education*. Baltimore: The Johns Hopkins University Press, 1972.

Steiner, Gilbert Y. *The State of Welfare*. Washington, D.C.: The Brookings Institution, 1971.

A Study in Child Care, 1970–71. Case Study Coordinator, Richard R. Ruopp. Vol. I, *Findings;* Vol. II-A, *Center Case Studies;* Vol. II-B, *System Case Studies;* Vol. III, *Cost and Quality Issues for Operators*. Cambridge, Mass.: Abt Associates, Inc., 1971.

"A Survey of State Day Care Licensing Requirements." *Child Care Bulletin*, No. 4. Washington, D.C.: The Day Care and Child Development Council of America, Inc., 1971.

Swift, Joan W. "Effects of Early Group Experience: The Nursery School and Day Nursery." In *Review of Child Development Research*. Vol. I. New York: Russell Sage Foundation, 1964.

U.S. Department of Health, Education and Welfare. *Abstracts of State Day Care Licensing Requirements:* Vol. 1, *Family Day Care Homes and Group Day Care Homes;* Vol. 2, *Day Care Centers*. DHEW Publication No. (OCD) 72–12. Washington, D.C., 1971.

—— *Children in Day Care*. Children's Bureau Publication No. 444–1967, by Laura Dittman. Washington, D.C., 1967.

—— *Designing the Child Development Center*. Office of Child Development. Project Head Start. Publication No. 0–369–699. Washington, D.C., 1969.

—— *Federal Interagency Day Care Requirements Pursuant to Sec. 522(d) of the Economic Opportunity Act*. Federal Panel on Early Childhood. Washington, D.C., 1968.

—— *Findings of the 1969 AFDC Study*. Washington, D.C., 1970. (Including statistics on the child care arrangements of AFDC mothers.)

—— *Licensing of Child Care Facilities by State Welfare Departments: A Conceptual Statement*. Children's Bureau Publication No. 462–1968, by Norris E. Class. Washington, D.C., 1968.

—— *Proceedings of the National Conference on Day Care Services, May 13–15, 1965*. Children's Bureau Publication No. 438–1966. Washington, D.C., 1966.

—— "Memorandum: Child (Day) Care Costs." Social and Rehabilitation Service. Washington, D.C., August 25, 1971. (Mimeographed.)

—— *A Pilot Study of Day Care Centers and Their Clientele*. Children's Bureau Publication No. 428–1965, by Elizabeth Prescott. Washington, D.C., 1965.

U.S. Department of Labor. *Day Care Services: Industry's Involvement*. Bulletin 296. Washington, D.C., 1971.

—— "Day Care Facts." Prepared by Beatrice Rosenberg. Washington, D.C., 1970. (Mimeographed.)

—— *Federal Funds for Day Care Projects*. Washington, D.C., February 1969.

U.S. Office of Economic Opportunity. *Day Care: Resources for Decisions*. Washington, D.C., 1971.

—— *Day Care Survey: 1970*. Westinghouse Learning Corporation and Westat Research, Inc., Washington, D.C., 1971.

Weaver, Kitty D. *Lenin's Grandchildren: Preschool Education in the Soviet Union*. New York: Simon and Schuster, 1971.

Willner, Milton. "Day Care: A Reassessment." *Child Welfare*, XLIV, No. 3.

—— "Unsupervised Family Day Care in New York City." *The Changing Dimensions of Day Care: Highlights from Child Welfare*. New York: Child Welfare League of America, 1970.

CHILDREN, FAMILIES AND WORKING MOTHERS

Ariès, Philippe. *Centuries of Childhood: A Social History of Family Life*. Tr. by Robert Baldick. New York: Vintage Books, 1962.

Bailyn, Bernard. *Education in the Forming of American Society*. New York: Vintage Books, 1960.

Demos, John. *A Little Commonwealth: Family Life in Plymouth Colony*. New York: Oxford University Press, 1970.

Epstein, Cynthia Fuchs. *Woman's Place: Options and Limits in Professional Careers*. Berkeley: University of California Press, 1971.

Figes, Eva. *Patriarchal Attitudes*. Greenwich, Conn.: Fawcett Publications, Inc., 1970.

Firestone, Shulamith. *The Dialectics of Sex*. New York: Bantam Books, 1971.

Friedan, Betty. *The Feminine Mystique*. New York: Dell Publishing Co., 1970.

Ginzberg, Eli, *et al. Life Styles of Educated Women*. New York: Columbia University Press, 1966.

Gordon, Linda. "Functions of the Family." In *Voices from Women's Liberation*. Ed. by Leslie B. Tanner. New York: New American Library-Signet, 1971.

Howe, Louise Kapp, ed. *The Future of the Family*. New York: Simon and Schuster. 1972.

Jeffrey, Kirk. "The Family as Utopian Retreat from the City: The Nineteenth-Century Contribution." *Soundings*, 55:1.

Katz, Sanford N. *When Parents Fail: The Law's Response to Family Breakdown*. Boston: Beacon Press, 1971.

Miller, Joyce D. "Unions and Day Care Centers for the Children of Working Mothers." *Child Welfare*, 50:1.

National Organization of Women. "Why Feminists Want Child Care," n.d. (Mimeographed.)

Poloma, M. M., and T. M. Garland. "The Married Professional Woman: A Study in the Tolerance of Domestication." *Journal of Marriage and the Family*, 33:3.

Ruderman, Florence A. *Child Care and Working Mothers*. New York: Child Welfare League of America, Inc., 1968.

Sennett, Richard. *The Uses of Disorder: Personal Identity and City Life*. New York: Alfred A. Knopf, 1970.

——— *Families Against the City: Middle-Class Homes of Industrial Chicago*. Cambridge, Mass.: Harvard University Press, 1970.

Smuts, Robert W. *Women and Work in America*. New York: Schocken Books, 1971.

U.S. Department of Health, Education and Welfare. *Child Care Arrangements of Working Mothers in the United States*, by Seth Low and Pearl G. Spindler. Children's Bureau Publication No. 461–1968. Washington, D.C., 1968.

U.S. Department of Labor. *Report of a Consultation on Working Women and Day Care Needs*. Washington, D.C., June 1, 1967.

RESOURCES FOR DAY CARE INFORMATION AND PUBLICATIONS

Child Welfare League of America
44 East 23rd Street
New York, N.Y. 10010

Day Care and Child Development Council of America
1426 H. Street N.W.
Washington, D.C.

ERIC/ECE (Educational Resources Information Center, Early Childhood Education)
University of Illinois at Urbana-Champaign
805 West Pennsylvania Avenue
Urbana, Illinois 61801

Superintendent of Documents
Government Printing Office
Washington, D.C.

Index

ABOUT THE AUTHOR

Margaret O'Brien Steinfels was born in 1941 and grew up in Chicago. She graduated from Loyola University, studied art and film history at Columbia University, and has a Master's Degree in American History from New York University, where she studied the experience of Irish immigrant families in New York during the nineteenth century. She has written film criticism, articles, and book reviews for Commonweal, Today, *and* Jubilee, *and was a columnist for the* National Catholic Reporter. *She contributed essays to* The Working Mother, *edited by Sidney Callahan, and* The Family, Communes and Utopian Societies, *edited by Sallie TeSelle. She is married and has two children.*